COGNITIVE THEORY
Volume 1

COGNITIVE THEORY
Volume 1

edited by

Frank Restle
Richard M. Shiffrin
N. John Castellan
Harold R. Lindman
David B. Pisoni

 LAWRENCE ERLBAUM ASSOCIATES, PUBLISHERS

1975   Hillsdale, New Jersey

DISTRIBUTED BY THE HALSTED PRESS DIVISION OF

JOHN WILEY & SONS
New York   Toronto   London   Sydney

Lawrence Erlbaum Associates, Inc., Publishers
62 Maria Drive
Hillsdale, New Jersey 07642

Distributed solely by Halsted Press Division
John Wiley & Sons, Inc., New York

Library of Congress Cataloging in Publication Data

Main entry under title:

Cognitive theory.

    Includes bibliographical references and indexes.
    1. Cognition.   2. Speech perception.
3. Judgment.   4. Memory.   I. Restle, Frank.
BF311.C553   153.4   74-14293
ISBN 0-470-71732-7

Printed in the United States of America

CONTENTS

v

PREFACE

This book contains the content of the Indiana Conference of 1974. This Conference has met for each of the last seven years. At one time it was known as the "Midwestern Mathematical Psychology Meeting," but as interest drifted toward more experimental and theoretical, but less purely mathematical work, the title became the "Indiana Theoretical and Cognitive Psychology Meetings." Finally, this year the Conference was called the "Indiana Cognitive/Mathematical Psychology Conference."

The Conference has always been fairly small, rarely having over 100 people in an audience, but has one of the most sophisticated and interested audiences in the world. Speakers have come to expect penetrating questions and discussion. While we have not tried to include transcripts of these discussions in the book, the authors of chapters have been able to incorporate relevant ideas from the discussions into their chapters.

The contributors to this Conference were requested to emphasize the relatively broad theoretical significance of their work, to incorporate the work of others, and if they were willing, to speculate about future developments. Each of the chapters of this book has these characteristics of breadth and theory, rather than the mere report of new experiments. A number of the authors are relatively young, and that reflects the long-standing policy of the Conference to try to bring forth new ideas that might otherwise remain hidden for several years.

We, the editors, took the main responsibility for choosing the speakers, and acted as hosts for the Conference. Our role as editors has been most enjoyable, primarily because of the quality of the participants. We should like to express our appreciation to the Mathematical Social Science Board at the Center for Advanced Study in the Social Sciences for support of portions of the Conference in 1973 and 1974. We also wish to thank Ramona Swaine, Jam Waltz, and Karlene Ball for their secretarial and editorial aid and for helping to coordinate the efforts of all involved in assembling the book. Finally we would like to thank Lawrence Erlbaum for all his assistance.

COGNITIVE THEORY

Volume 1

PART I
CONTEMPORARY ISSUES IN SPEECH PERCEPTION

David B. Pisoni

The study of speech perception is a rich and complex interdisciplinary field involving workers from psychology, linguistics, and speech science. Central to much of the current research in this area is the assumption that speech perception includes specialized processes and mechanisms that are not employed in the perception of other auditory stimuli. We can cite at least four reasons why this assumption seems to be true. First, the acoustic properties of speech sounds are much more complex than the stimuli typically used to study the functioning of the peripheral auditory system. As a consequence, the acoustic parameters important for distinguishing different classes of speech sounds (i.e., phonemes) are usually found in complex changes in the fine structure or spectrum of the signal. In addition, most investigators who study speech perception are ultimately concerned with the way in which acoustic–phonetic information maps into the more general linguistic system the observer.

A second reason involves the unique characteristics of speech sounds as acoustic stimuli in the environment. Speech sounds are distinct from other acoustic stimuli because they are produced by a sound source that has well-known acoustic constraints for the listener. Research over the last few years has shown very close correspondences between changes in vocal tract shape and characteristics of the acoustic output. Indeed, a quick persual of the literature reveals that many of the descriptive categories used in speech perception and acoustic phonetics have been carried over from the traditional articulatory categories developed by phoneticians. As we shall see, a good deal of recent theoretical work has been directed toward the hypothesized link between speech perception and production.

The third reason why speech perception may be different from the perception of other auditory stimuli is that both speech perception and production appear to be mediated by processes that are lateralized in one cerebral hemisphere—usually the left. This suggests that distinct physiological mechanisms may underlie both speech perception and production. It also points to the possible existence of specialized neural structures for speech perception. Although research on the potential role of feature detectors in speech perception is only in the earliest stages, a sizable body of empirical data has already been obtained on some of the characteristics of these detectors.

The fourth reason deals with two related problems for speech perception theory: invariance and segmentation. One of the earliest observations that emerged about speech sounds was the lack of invariance between units in the acoustic signal and units of linguistic analysis. Examination of sound spectrograms showed that, in general, there were no segments in the speech signal that corresponded uniquely to segments in the message. The earliest perceptual experiments with synthetic speech stimuli at Haskins Laboratories showed that a single segment of the acoustic signal carried information about several successive segments. Thus, phonemes were not concatenated successively like the letters of the alphabet or beads on a string, but were represented by merged and overlapping parts of the acoustic signal. These initial findings have led investigators to suspect that there is something peculiar about speech and the processes involved in its perception—there is an intricate and complex restructuring of the linguistic message in terms of the acoustic signal.

We should point out that much of the theoretical work in speech perception has not been very well developed by the standards applied to other areas of experimental psychology, and the link between data and theory has often been quite weak. This situation probably arose because of the relatively few researchers in the field and the enormous difficulty in conducting experiments that almost inevitably require the use of synthetically produced speech stimuli. Fortunately, this state of affairs is changing quite rapidly. Judging by the increased number of publications that deal with speech perception in the major psychological journals, the area is now a well-integrated and accepted domain of study in modern experimental psychology. More and more cognitive psychologists have turned their interests to speech perception primarily because this is the earliest and most accessible stage of linguistic processing. Furthermore, in recent years it has become far easier to obtain very high quality synthetically produced speech stimuli for experimental purposes.

The focus of the four chapters in this part is on contemporary issues in speech perception. Each chapter deals with a somewhat different area of research in order to present a comprehensive picture of the types of questions that are currently under investigation and some of the problems to be considered in the immediate future. Although each chapter contains some background and review material, the emphasis for the most part in these contributions is on very recent empirical work or theoretical formulations.

The chapter by Michael Studdert-Kennedy is the most general and deals with the nature and function of phonetic categories. The main point here is that the sound categories (i.e., phonetic structure) of language are not arbitrary but bear a necessary relation to both the vocal apparatus which produces these sounds and the phonological structure onto which they are mapped. Studdert-Kennedy deals with a number of important issues in speech perception including categorical perception, auditory short-term memory, and various types of perceptual units. He concludes the chapter by considering how a young child might develop the knowledge of phonetic categories. In the course of this, a new version of the motor theory of speech perception is proposed which deals with the acquisition and development of speech perception.

The second chapter is by William E. Cooper, who presents a very comprehensive picture of recent work using selective adaptation procedures to study the possible existence of feature detectors in speech perception. The main focus of this chapter is first on describing the methodology used in the early adaptation experiments and then on detailing the particular locus of the adaptation effects. In the first part of the chapter, Cooper deals with perceptual adaptation in an attempt to map out some of the stages of processing involved in decoding speech sounds. Much of this research is quite recent and should be new to most readers although it has been circulating through the underground speech perception community since early 1974. The second part of the chapter is concerned with perceptuomotor adaptation, which has provided a novel way of examining the question of whether speech perception and production interact during early stages of perceptual processing. The work reported by Cooper in this section is perhaps the first time that direct evidence has been found in support of such an interaction between perception and production.

In the third chapter, Charles C. Wood presents a model for redundancy gains in speech discrimination. The emphasis in this chapter is on the organization of auditory and phonetic stages of processing in speech perception. Wood deals with the issue of serial versus parallel processing of auditory and phonetic information and their possible interaction. This chapter represents an important advance in speech perception work because of its quantitative treatment of this problem. Moreover, it brings research in speech perception somewhat closer to other more traditional areas of research in human information processing.

The final chapter, by David B. Pisoni, deals with dichotic listening. Work in this area has increased quite dramatically within the last few years primarily because it provides a simple way to study the speech perception system under stress. In this chapter, Pisoni is concerned with the types of interactions that occur between dichotic speech inputs. The right ear advantage is touched upon briefly at various times. In the first section, two types of dichotic interactions are considered: the feature sharing advantage and the lag effect. Both types of interactions appear to occur at different levels of perceptual processing. Results of several recent dichotic recognition masking experiments which focused on these interactions are presented. A rough model of the stages of processing in speech perception is proposed for these results. The model involves several stages where dichotic inputs can interact. Pisoni argues that the feature-sharing advantage in dichotic listening results after phonetic analysis when redundant phonetic features are maintained in a feature buffer. On the other hand, the lag effect is assumed to occur when the auditory features in both dichotic inputs interact before phonetic analysis. The model also can account for the various types of phonetic feature errors that occur in dichotic listening experiments.

1

THE NATURE AND FUNCTION OF PHONETIC CATEGORIES

Michael Studdert-Kennedy
Haskins Laboratories

Speech perception differs from general auditory perception in both stimulus and percept. Acoustically, the sounds of speech constitute a distinctive class, drawn from the set of sounds that can be produced by the human vocal mechanism. Perceptually, they form a set of "natural categories," similar to those described by Rosch (1973). The point is well made in a study by House, Stevens, Sandel, and Arnold (1962). They constructed several ensembles of sounds along an acoustic continuum from clearly nonspeech to clearly speech, and asked subjects to associate the sounds with buttons on a response panel. The time taken to learn these associations was least for the speech ensemble, and did not decrease with the acoustic approximation of the ensembles to speech. Among the reasons for this was presumably that subjects already possessed for speech, but not for nonspeech, a well-learned code into which they could transform the acoustic signals for storage and recall.

The term used by linguists to describe this code is "phonetic," a term derived from the Greek word for "sound." However, although phonetic events clearly have auditory correlates, no one has yet succeeded in describing them. On the contrary, phonetic description is almost invariably couched in articulatory terms, and the "phonetic transcription" of an utterance is generally agreed to be a sequence of shorthand instructions, not for hearing, but for speaking. The peculiarity of speech perception, then, is that it entails the rapid, automatic transformation of a distinctive sensory input into a distinctive nonsensory code.

Furthermore, the input bears a necessary, rather than an arbitrary, relation to the code. This is not true of the visual counterparts of phonetic entities. The forms of the alphabet are arbitrary, and we are not concerned that the same visual symbol, ω stands for [w] in the English alphabet, for [o] in the Greek. Alphabets, of course, are secondary, while the speech signal is primary, its acoustic pattern at once the natural realization of phonological system and the necessary source of phonetic percept. Among the goals of current research are to define the phonetic percept and to explore the mechanisms by which it is derived from the acoustic signal.

THE FUNCTION OF PHONETIC CATEGORIES

Every language has a dual hierarchical structure. At its base are a few dozen phonetic segments—or even fewer phonetic features—from which higher-order syntactic and semantic structures are formed. From a linguistic point of view, the function of segmental phonetic categories is to serve as the finite set of commutable elements of which language will make infinite use. However, if this were their only function, there would be no grounds for the universal linguistic division of segmental phonetic categories into consonants and vowels. But, in fact, every language makes a double demand on its elements: to convey a segmental message and to convey a suprasegmental, or prosodic, message. From this opposition there emerges the syllable. All languages are syllabic, and all languages constrain syllabic structure in terms of consonants and vowels, assigning the bulk of the segmental phonetic load to consonants, the prosodic load to vowels.

To fulfill linguistic function, a general perceptual process is invoked, namely, division into "stages." Among the functions of "perceptual stages"—whether defined in time or in neural locus—seem to be to isolate one process from another, and to store energy or information for later use. We may see this most clearly at the periphery. Every sensory system integrates energy: if the system were infinitely damped, threshold for activation would never be reached. Accumulation of energy over some finite period permits the mechanical response of the ear, for example, to develop. On the other hand, the period of integration must be finite to prevent physical destruction of the system: mechanical energy is therefore transduced into bioelectricity. Analogous cycles of integration and transformation presumably recur, as energy progresses through the system. Activity in afferent fibers gives rise to more central neural activity and, ultimately (jumping levels of discourse), to a preperceptual "image" (Massaro, 1972). The "image," in turn, must have some finite duration, long enough to institute further processing, short enough to prevent "babble."

Returning with this metaphor to language, we note that speech is arrayed in time, and that both syntax and meaning demand some minimum quantity of information before linguistic structure can emerge. The perceptual function of phonetic categories is then, on the one hand, to forestall auditory babble, on the other, to store information derived from the signal until such time as it can be granted a linguistic interpretation. In other words, the perceptual function of phonetic categories is that of a buffer between signal and message.

However, there are two forms of linguistic information to be conveyed, each with its characteristic temporal density: rapidly changing segmental features, and more slowly changing prosodic features. Accordingly, two forms of storage are required. For the vowels, to which both segmental and prosodic functions are assigned, both a relatively long-term auditory store and a rapidly accessed phonetic store. For the consonants, only the latter. The operation of both these stores has been repeatedly demonstrated in a variety of experimental paradigms.

CATEGORICAL PERCEPTION

The distinction between auditory and phonetic processes in speech perception is an old one (see, for example, Fry, 1956). But only recently have students discovered its theoretical worth. Among the leaders in this were Fujisaki and Kawashima (1969, 1970), who applied the distinction to the analysis of what has been termed "categorical perception." Let us begin with a description of the phenomenon.

Study of sound spectrograms reveals that portions of the acoustic patterns for related phonetic segments often lie along an apparent acoustic continuum. For example, center frequencies of the first two or three formants[1] of the front vowels, [i, ɪ, ɛ, æ], form a monotonic series; syllable-initial voiced–voiceless pairs, [b, p], [d, t], [k, g], differ systematically in voice onset time; voiced stops, [b, d, g], before a particular vowel, differ primarily in the extent and direction of their formant transitions.

To establish the perceptual function of such variations speech synthesis is used. Figure 1 is a sketch of a schematic spectrogram of a synthetic series in which changes of slope in second formant transition effect perceptual changes from [b] through [d] to [g]. Asked to identify the dozen or so sounds along such a continuum, listeners divide them into distinct categories. For example, a listener might consistently identify stimuli —6

[1] A formant is a resonance of the vocal tract, or its acoustic correlate: a concentration of energy in a limited band of the frequency spectrum. The relative positions of formants on the frequency scale are important acoustic cues in the perception of speech.

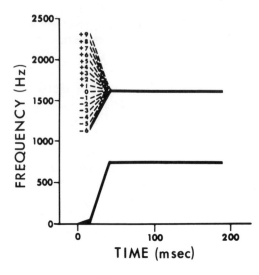

FIG. 1. Schematic spectrogram for a series of synthetic stop-vowel syllables varying only in second formant transition. Second formant steady state, first formant transition and steady state remain constant. As second formant transition changes from −6 to +9, perception of initial consonant shifts from [b] through [d] to [g].

through −3 of Fig. 1 as [b], stimuli −1 through +3 as [d] and stimuli +5 through +9 as [g]. In other words, he does not, as might be expected on psychophysical grounds, hear a series of stimuli gradually changing from one phonetic class to another, but rather a series of stimuli, each of which (with the exception of one or two boundary stimuli) belongs unambiguously to a single class. The important point to note is that, although steps along the continuum are well above nonspeech auditory discrimination threshold, listeners disregard acoustic differences within categories.

To determine whether listeners can, in fact, hear the acoustic differences belied by their identifications, discrimination tests are carried out, usually in *ABX* format. Here, on a given trial, the listener hears three stimuli, separated by a second or so of silence: the first (*A*) is drawn from a point on the continuum two or three steps removed from the second (*B*), and the third (*X*) is a repetition of either *A* or *B*. The listener's task is to say whether the third stimulus is the same as the first or the second. The typical outcome for a stop-consonant continuum, is that listeners hear few more auditory differences than phonetic categories: they discriminate very well between stimuli drawn from different phonetic categories, very poorly (somewhat better than chance) between stimuli drawn from the same category. The resulting function displays peaks at phonetic boundaries, troughs within phonetic categories. In fact, discriminative performance can be predicted with fair accuracy from identifications: the probability that acoustically different syllables are correctly discriminated is a positive function of the probability that they are differently identified (Liberman, Harris,

Kinney, & Lane, 1961). It is this close relation between identification and discrimination that has been termed "categorical perception," or perception by assignment to category. Figure 2 (left side) illustrates the phenomenon. Note that, although prediction from identification to discrimination is good, it is not perfect: listeners can sometimes discriminate between different acoustic tokens of the same phonetic type. Note, further, that neither identification nor discrimination functions display quantal leaps across category boundaries. This is not a result of data averaging, since the effect is given

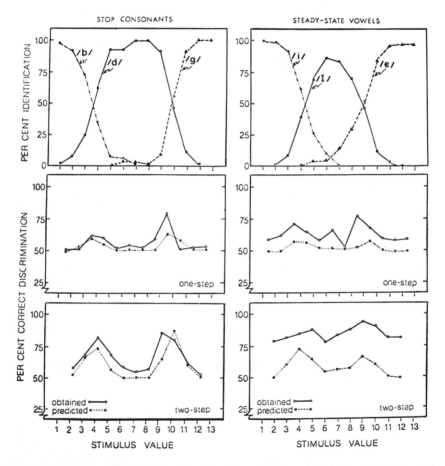

FIG. 2.   Average identification functions for synthetic series of stop consonants and vowels (top). Average one-step (middle) and two-step (bottom) predicted and obtained ABX discrimination functions for the same series. (After Pisoni, 1971, with permission of the author.)

by individual subjects. Evidently auditory information about consonants is slight, but not entirely lacking.

We may now contrast categorical perception of stop consonants with "continuous perception" of vowels. Figure 2 (right side) illustrates the effect. There are two points to note. First, the vowel identification function is not as clear cut as the consonant. Vowels, particularly those close to a phonetic boundary, are subject to context effects: for example, a token close to the [i–ɪ] boundary will tend to be heard, by contrast, as [i], if preceded by a clear [ɪ], as [ɪ], if preceded by a clear [i]. The second point to note is that vowel discrimination is high across the entire continuum. Phonetic class is not totally irrelevant (there is a peak in the discrimination function at the category boundary), but both within and between categories listeners discriminate many more differences than they identify. Their perception is then said to be "continuous."

Continuous perception is typical not only of vowels, but also of many nonspeech psychophysical continua along which we can discriminate more steps than we can identify (Miller, 1956). This fact has been taken as evidence both that categorical perception is peculiar to speech, and that stop consonants and vowels engage fundamentally different perceptual processes (Liberman, Cooper, Shankweiler, & Studdert-Kennedy, 1967; Studdert-Kennedy, Liberman, Harris, & Cooper, 1970). In fact, an early account of the phenomenon invoked a motor theory of speech perception (Liberman *et al.,* 1967), arguing that, while the vowels were *heard* much as any other acoustic pattern, the consonants were perceived by reference to the discrete articulatory gestures from which they arose.

As we shall see shortly, there is a germ of truth in this account. However, recent work has carried us beyond it. For one thing, we now know that categorical perception is not confined to speech (Cutting & Rosner, in press; Locke & Kellar, 1973; Miller, Pastore, Wier, Kelly, & Dooling, 1974). For another, we have a deeper and more general account of the phenomenon.

AUDITORY AND PHONETIC PROCESSES IN CATEGORICAL PERCEPTION

A long series of experiments over the past few years has shown that listeners' difficulty in discriminating among members of a category is largely due to the low energy transience of the acoustic signal on the basis of which phonetic categories are assigned. Lane (1965) pointed to the greater duration and intensity of the vowels and showed that they were more categorically perceived if they were *degraded* by being presented in noise. Stevens (1968) remarked the brief, transient nature of stop consonant acoustic cues, and showed, as did Sachs (1969), that vowels were more categorically perceived if their duration and acoustic stability were reduced by placing them in CVC syllables.

The roles of phonetic and auditory memory, implicit in the work just cited, were first made explicit by Fujisaki and Kawashima (1969, 1970) in a model of the decision process during ABX discrimination. If a listener assigns A and B to different phonetic categories (i.e., if A and B lie on opposite sides of a phonetic boundary), his only task is to determine whether X belongs to the same category as A or as $B:$ his performance is then good and a discrimination peak appears in the function for both consonants and vowels. However, if a listener assigns A and B to the same phonetic category, he is forced to compare X with his auditory memory of A and $B:$ his performance is then slightly reduced for vowels, for which auditory memory is presumed to be relatively strong, but sharply reduced for consonants, for which auditory memory is presumed to be weak. Evidence for the operation of such a two-step process within phonetic categories in man, but not in monkey, has recently been reported by Sinnott (1974).

However, the strongest support for Fujisaki and Kawashima has come from the work of Pisoni (1971, 1973, in press). In the first of several experiments (Pisoni, 1973), he varied the A to X delay interval from 0 to 2 sec in an AX same–different task for vowel and stop consonant continua. Between-category performance (presumably based on phonetic store) was high and independent of delay interval for both consonants and vowels; within-category performance (presumably based on auditory store) was low and independent of delay interval for consonants, but for vowels was high and declined systematically as delay interval increased. In subsequent experiments, Pisoni (in press) demonstrated that the degree of categorical (or continuous) perception of vowels can be manipulated by the memory demands of the discrimination paradigm and by the amount of interference from neighboring stimuli.

The conclusion of these and other studies is pointed up by the work of Raphael (1972). He studied voiced–voiceless VC continua, manipulating initial vowel duration as acoustic cue to voicing of the final stop. Here, where perceptual object was consonantal, but acoustic cue vocalic, perception was continuous. In short, consonants and vowels are distinguished in the experiments we have been considering, not by their phonetic class or the processes of assignment to that class, but by their acoustic characteristics and by the duration of their auditory stores.

We may now see where the truth lay in the early account of Liberman et al. (1967). Stop consonants are indeed perceived differently than vowels. For while the vowel, carrier of stress, rhythm, and prosody, leaves a rapidly fading "echo," the consonant leaves none. The initial sound of

[da], for example, is difficult, if not impossible, to hear: the sound escapes us and we perceive the event, almost instantly, as phonetic.

PRECATEGORICAL ACOUSTIC STORAGE (PAS)

Experiments in short-term memory converge on the same conclusion. As is well known, Crowder and Morton (1969) developed the concept of a precategorical acoustic store (PAS), analogous to the iconic store of visual theory. Evidence for the store first came from studies of immediate, ordered recall of span-length digit lists. Typically, error probability increases from beginning to end of list with some slight drop on terminal items. The terminal drop is significantly increased (recency effect), if the list is presented by ear rather than by eye (modality effect). Crowder and Morton (1969) argue that these two effects reflect the operation of distinct visual and auditory stores for precategorical (prelinguistic) information, and of an auditory store that persists longer than the visual. Support comes from demonstrations that the recency effect is significantly reduced, or abolished, if subjects are required to recall the list by speaking rather than by writing (Crowder, 1971a), or if an auditory list is followed by a redundant spoken suffix (such as the word "zero"), as a signal for the subject to begin recall (suffix effect). That the suffix interferes with auditory, rather than linguistic store is argued by the facts that the effect: (1) does not occur if the suffix is a sound spectrally distinct from speech, such as a tone or burst of noise; (2) is unaffected if the spoken suffix is played backward; (3) is unaffected by degree of semantic similarity between suffix and list; (4) is reduced if suffix and list are spoken in different voices; (5) is reduced if suffix and list are presented to opposite ears.

Of particular interest in the present context is that all three effects (modality, recency, suffix) are observed for CV lists of which members differ in vowel alone or in both vowel and consonant (spoken letter names), but not for voiced stop consonant CV or VC lists of which members differ only in the consonant. Crowder (1971a) concludes that "vowels receive some form of representation in PAS while voiced stop consonants receive none" (p. 595). Liberman, Mattingly, and Turvey (1972) argue further that phonetic classification "strips away all auditory information" from stop consonants.

However, this last claim is unlikely to be true. First, there is no good reason why the process of categorization should affect vowels and consonants differently. Second, we have a variety of evidence that listeners retain at least some auditory trace of stop consonants (see Pisoni & Lazarus, 1974; Pisoni & Tash, 1974). Third, consonant and vowel differences in PAS can be reduced by appropriate manipulation of the signal array

(Darwin & Baddeley, 1974). These investigators demonstrated a recency effect for tokens of a stop CV, [ga], and two highly discriminable CV syllables in which the consonantal portion is of longer duration, [ʃa], [ma]. They also demonstrated that the recency effect for vowels can be eliminated if the vowels are both very short (30 msec of a 60-msec CV syllable) and close spectral neighbors. They conclude that ". . . the consonant–vowel distinction is largely irrelevant [Darwin & Baddeley, 1974, p. 48]," and that items in PAS cannot be reliably accessed if, like [ba, da, ga] or [ɪ, ɛ, æ], they are acoustically similar. The effect of acoustic similarity is, of course, to confound auditory memory. As Darwin and Baddeley (1974) cogently argue, it is to the more general concept of auditory memory that we must have recourse, if we are to understand the full range of experiments in which consonant–vowel differences have been demonstrated.

Consider now the duration of PAS and the mechanisms underlying its reflection in behavior. Crowder (1971b) points out that an 8-item list, presented at a rate of 2 per second, is usually recalled at roughly the same rate, so that time between presentation and recall is roughly equal for all items. The recency effect cannot, therefore, be attributed to differential decay across the list, but is due rather to the absence of "overwriting" or interference from succeeding items. Further, since degree of interference (i.e., probability of recall error) decreases as time between items increases, and since the suffix effect virtually disappears if the interval between the last item and suffix is increased to 2 sec, we are faced with the paradox that performance improves as time allowed for PAS decay increases. Crowder's (1971b) solution is to posit an active "readout" or rehearsal process at the articulatory level. Time for a covert run through the list is "a second or two [p. 339]." If a suffix occurs during this period, PAS for the last couple of items is spoiled before they are reached; if no suffix occurs, the subject has time to check his rehearsal of later items against his auditory store, and to confirm or correct his preliminary decision.

Notice that the term "precategorical" refers to the nature of the information stored, not to the period of time during which it is stored. A preliminary articulatory, if not phonetic, decision must have been made before PAS is lost, if rehearsal is to permit cross-check with the store. If we assume, as seems reasonable, that such decisions are made at least as rapidly for stop consonants as for vowels, the exclusion of consonants from PAS must be due to rapid acoustic decay rather than to either "overwriting" or tardy articulatory decision.

In short, stop consonant perception entails the transformation, into a nonsensory code, of acoustic information so rapidly transient that its conscious recovery as an auditory image is seldom possible. Vowel perception, in its segmental aspects, entails a similar transformation, but, for its prosodic function, employs the resources of auditory memory. The results of some half-dozen experimental paradigms—categorical perception, PAS, reaction-time studies, dichotic listening, backward masking and others—lead to the same conclusion. (For a review, see Studdert-Kennedy, 1975.)

THE PROBLEM OF PHONETIC TRANSCRIPTION

If the distinction between auditory and phonetic processes seems forced on us by the evidence, it nonetheless raises questions as difficult as any that it may answer. Between "auditory" and "phonetic" there is a gap, not unlike the gap between sign and meaning. In what follows, I want, first, to show that the gap exists, second, to speculate on a mechanism for closing it. In the process, we may approach a definition of the phonetic percept.

Even a cursory survey of the literature on speech perception will reveal the ailments of the signal: its general lack of isomorphism with the linguistic message, its want of segments, its gross contextual variability. These, in fact, are the stumbling blocks in the path of automatic speech recognition devices, and one may be tempted to believe that, were they removed, the problems of speech perception would be solved, at least in principle.

However, there is a more fundamental problem which the student of automatic speech recognition evades by imposing his linguistic knowledge on the machine. He already knows that he wants to segment the acoustic signal and to resolve its variability; he knows how many segments should emerge from his recognition routine; above all, he knows the phonetic names of the segments that emerge. To grasp the extent of his assumptions, imagine the approach to the acoustic signal of a cryptoanalyst. [This is, in fact, very much the approach of Fant (1968).] Imagine, further, that, by systematic acoustic and distributional analysis, we have discovered that the signal consists of a small number of commutable elements, which, we may hypothesize, correspond precisely to linguistic elements. How now are we to identify these elements? By number, as the factor analyst? By poetic name, as the personality theorist? Whatever our choice, we shall at best have hoisted ourselves into the position of an epigraphist confronted with Minoan Linear B (Chadwick, 1958). We shall have before us a sequence of discrete signs, forming clear and interesting patterns. But their meaning will be opaque.

Our condition will, in fact, be very much that of the human infant, equipped, as some have supposed him to be, with banks of neural filters and acoustic property detectors, tuned to speech (cf. Cutting & Eimas, 1974; Eimas, 1974; Eimas, Siqueland, Jusczyk, & Vigorito, 1971; Marler, 1975; Stevens, 1973; Stevens & Klatt, 1974). Whether these hypothesized property detectors yield outputs that correspond one-to-one with phonetic features or (as seems more likely, given the known contextual variability of speech) demand further processing to establish signal-to-message iso-morphism, the auditory analysis can be no more than an auditory analysis. How does the infant leap the gap from auditory array to phonetic percept?

THE NATURE OF PHONETIC CATEGORIES

Here the work of Marler (1970, 1975; Marler & Mundinger, 1971) may lend insight. He has proposed a general model of the evolution of vocal learning, based on studies of the ontogenesis of male "song" in certain sparrows. Briefly, the hypothesis is that development of motor song-pattern is guided by sensory feedback matched to modifiable, innate auditory templates (cf. Mattingly, 1972). Marler describes three classes of birds. The first (for example, the dove or the chicken) needs to hear neither an external model nor its own voice for song to emerge: crowing and cooing develop normally if the birds are reared in isolation and even if they are deafened shortly after birth. The second (for example, the song sparrow) needs no external model, but does need to hear its own voice: if reared in isolation, song develops normally, unless the bird is deafened in early life, in which case song is highly abnormal and insect-like.

An example of the third class of bird is the white-crowned sparrow, which needs both an external model and the sound of its own voice. Reared in isolation, the white-crown develops an abnormal song with ". . . certain natural characteristics, particularly the sustained pure tones which are one basic element in the natural song [Marler & Mundinger, 1971, p. 429]." If the bird is deafened in early life, even this rudimentary song does not develop. There emerges instead a highly abnormal song ". . . rather like that of a deafened song sparrow . . . perhaps the basic output of the syringeal apparatus with a flow of air through it [p. 429]." However, reared in isolation but exposed to recordings of normal male song during a critical period (10–50 days after birth), the male (and the female, if injected with male hormone) develops normal song some 50 or more days after exposure. Exposure to the songs of other species will not serve, and deafening either before or after exposure to conspecific song prevents normal development (Konishi, 1965, cited by Marler, 1975).

Marler (1975) proposes that the rudimentary song of the undeafened, isolated white-crown reflects the existence of an auditory template, ". . . lying in the auditory pathway, embodying information about the structure of vocal sounds." The template matches certain features of normal song, and serves to guide development of the rudimentary song, as well as to ". . . focus . . . attention on an appropriate class of external models." Exposure to these models modifies and enriches the template, which then serves to guide normal development, through subsong and plastic song, as the bird gradually discovers the motor controls needed to match its output with the modified template. [Several studies have reported evidence for the "tuning" by experience of visual detecting systems in the cat (Blakemore & Cooper, 1970; Hirsch & Spinelli, 1970; Pettigrew & Freeman, 1973) and man (Annis & Frost, in press), and of auditory detecting systems in rhesus monkey (Miller, Sutton, Pfingst, Ryan, & Beaton, 1972).]

Marler (1975) draws the analogy with language learning. He suggests that sensory control of ontogenetic motor development may have been the evolutionary change that made possible an elaborate communicative system as pivot of avian and human social organization. He argues that "new sensory mechanisms for processing speech sounds, applied first, in infancy, to analyzing sounds of others, and somewhat later in life to analysis of the child's own sounds, was a significant step toward achieving the strategy of speech development of *Homo sapiens*." On the motor side, he points out, vocal development must have become dependent on auditory feedback: there must have developed "neural circuitry necessary to modify patterns of motor outflow so that sounds generated can be matched to preestablished auditory templates."

Certainly, human and avian parallels are striking. Deafened at birth, the human infant does not learn to speak: babbling begins normally, but dies away around the sixth month (Marvilya, 1972). Whether this is because the infant has been deprived of the sound of its own voice, of an external model or of both, we do not know. But there does seem to be an ill-defined critical period during which exposure to speech is a necessary condition of normal development (Lenneberg, 1967; but see Fromkin, Krashen, Curtiss, Rigler, & Rigler, 1974). And the work of Eimas and his colleagues (Cutting & Eimas, 1975; Eimas *et al.*, 1971; Eimas, 1974) has demonstrated the sensitivity of the infant to functionally important acoustic features of the speech signal. At least one of these features, the short voice-onset time-lag associated with stop consonants in many languages (Lisker & Abramson, 1964), is known to be among the first to appear in infant babble (Port & Preston, 1972). Finally, Sussman (1971) and Sussman and MacNeilage (1975) have reported evidence for a speech-related auditory sensorimotor mechanism that may serve to modify patterns of motor outflow, so as to match sounds generated by the vocal mechanism against some standard. In short, Marler's account is consistent with a good deal of our limited knowledge of speech development. Its virtue is to emphasize sensorimotor interaction and to accord the infant a mechanism for discovering auditory–articulatory correspondences.

Paradoxically, if we are to draw on this account of motor development for insight into perceptual development, we must place more emphasis on the relatively rich articulatory patterns revealed in early infant babble. The infant is not born without articulatory potential. In fact, the work of Lieberman and his colleagues would suggest quite specific capacities (Lieberman, 1968, 1972, 1973; Lieberman & Crelin, 1971; Lieberman, Crelin, & Klatt, 1972; Lieberman, Harris, Wolff, & Russell, 1972). They have developed systematic evidence for evolution of the human vocal tract from a form with a relatively high larynx, opening almost directly into the oral cavity, capable of producing a limited set of schwa-like vowel sounds, to a form with a lowered larynx, a large pharyngeal cavity and a right-angle bend in the supralaryngeal vocal tract, capable of producing the full array of human vowels. Lieberman (1973) argues that this development, taken with many other factors, including the capacity to encode and decode syllables, paved the way for the development of language. Associated with changes in morphology must have come neurological changes to permit increasingly fine motor control of breathing and articulation, including in all likelihood, cerebral lateralization (cf. Geschwind & Levitsky, 1968; Lenneberg, 1967; Nottebohm, 1971, 1972). The outcome of these developments would have been a range of articulatory possibilities as determinate in their form as the patterns of manual praxis that gave rise to toolmaking. The inchoate forms of these patterns might then emerge in infant babble under the control of rudimentary articulatory templates.

In short, I hypothesize that the infant is born with both auditory and articulatory templates. Each embodies capacities that may be modified by, and deployed in, the particular language to which the infant is exposed. Presumably, these templates evolved more or less *pari passu* and are matched, in some sense, as key to lock. But they differ in their degree of specificity. For effective function in language acquisition the auditory template must be tuned to specific acoustic properties of speech. The articulatory template, on the other hand, is more abstract, a range of gestural control, potentially isomorphic with the segmented feature matrix of the language by which it is modified (cf. Chomsky & Halle, 1968, p. 294).

Among the grounds for this statement are the results of several studies of adult speech production. Lindblom and Sundberg (1971), for example, found that if subjects were thwarted in their habitual articulatory gestures by the presence of a bite block between their front teeth, they were nonetheless able to approximate normal vowel quality, even within the first pitch period of the utterance. Bell-Berti (1973) has shown that the pattern of electromyographic potentials associated with pharyngeal enlargement during medial voiced stop consonant closure varies from individual to individual and from time to time within an individual. Finally, Ladefoged, DeClerk, Lindau, and Papçun (1972) have demonstrated that different speakers of the same dialect may use different patterns of tongue height and tongue root advancement to achieve phonetically identical vowels. Since individuals obviously differ in the precise dimensions of their vocal tracts, it would be surprising if they accomplished a particular gesture and a particular acoustic pattern by precisely the same pattern of muscular action. In short, it seems likely that both infant and adult articulatory templates are control systems for a range of functionally equivalent vocal-tract shapes rather than for specific patterns of muscular action. In fact, it is precisely to exploration of its own vocal tract and to discovery of its own patterns of muscular action that the infant's motor learning must be directed.

It should be emphasized that neither template can fulfill its communicative function in the absence of the other. Modified and enriched by experience, the auditory template may provide a "description" of the acoustic properties of the signal, but the description can be no different in principle than that provided by any other form of spectral analysis: alone, the output of auditory analysis is void. Similarly, babble without auditory feedback has no meaning. The infant discovers phonetic "meaning" (and linguistic function) by discovering auditory–articulatory correspondences, that is, by discovering the commands required by its own vocal tract to match the output of its auditory template. Since the articulatory template is relatively abstract, the infant will begin to discover these correspondences before it has acquired the detailed motor skills of articulation: perceptual skill will precede motor skill. In rare instances of peripheral articulatory pathology, the infant (like the female white-crowned sparrow who learns the song without singing) may even discover language without speaking (cf. MacNeilage, Rootes, & Chase, 1967).

I hypothesize, then, that the infant is born with two distinct capacities, and that its task to establish their links. Auditory feedback from its own vocalizations serves to modify the articulatory template, to guide motor development, and to establish the links. The process endows the communicatively empty outputs of auditory analysis and articulatory gesture with communicative significance. In due course, the system serves to segment the acoustic signal and perhaps, as analysis-by-synthesis models propose, to resolve acoustic variability. But its prior and more fundamental function is to establish the "natural categories" of speech. To perceive these categories is to trace the sound patterns of speech to their articulatory source, to recover the commands from which they arose. The phonetic percept is then the correlate of these commands.

CONCLUSION

Much research would be needed to explore the detailed speculations of the last section. Experimental paradigms adequate to test even the postulated relation between perception and articulation are not easily come by. In fact, the recent work of Cooper (Chapter 2, this volume), demonstrating shifts in a speaker's stop consonant voice onset timing, as a function of perceptual adaptation, provides the first direct evidence in support of the hypothesis.

Nonetheless, if this general approach to the nature and function of phonetic categories is correct, it may not be without implication for cognitive theory (cf. Liberman *et al.,* 1972). Studies of verbal short-term memory, for example, put to peculiar use a function of which the form and limits are determined by the demands of spoken language. The function appears to entail covert activation of commands for a well-learned set of motor responses. It is by no means clear how the form of this code is related to that of long-term lexical memory. For example, the elements coded in short-term memory for a list of nonsense syllables can hardly be a simple subset of elements coded in the long-term lexicon, since the items to be remembered have never been entered in the lexicon. Furthermore, even when a list of familiar words is used, the absence of syntactic context must preclude full activation of the syntactic and semantic components of any particular lexical item. Short-term recall of word lists may therefore activate not so much particular items in the long-term lexicon, as a general phonetic, or motoric, control function, analogous to that evoked for the copying of a sequence of unrelated manual gestures. This is certainly not without interest, as studies of PAS have shown. However, it does raise a question as to the level of the language process upon which certain short-term memory studies may be expected to throw light. More generally, it suggests that theorists of verbal memory may profit from bearing in mind that the processes they model are integral to linguistic communication and must ultimately be fitted into a theory of normal language function.

ACKNOWLEDGMENTS

Preparation of this chapter was supported in part by a grant to Haskins Laboratories from the National Institute of Child Health and Human Development, Bethesda, Maryland.

I thank Alvin Liberman, Ignatius Mattingly, and Donald Shankweiler for their valuable comments and criticism, David Pisoni for fruitful conversation and for drawing my attention to the work of Eleanor Rosch.

REFERENCES

Annis, R. C., & Frost, B. Human visual ecology and orientation anisotropies in acuity. *Science,* in press.

Bell-Berti, F. The velopharyngeal mechanism: An electromyographic study. Unpublished doctoral dissertation, City University of New York, 1973.

Blakemore, C., & Cooper, G. F. Development of the brain depends on visual environment. *Science,* 1970, **168,** 477–478.

Chadwick, J. *The decipherment of Linear B.* Cambridge, England: Cambridge Univ. Press, 1958.

Chomsky, N. & Halle, M. *The sound pattern of English.* New York: Harper and Row, 1968.

Crowder, R. G. The sound of vowels and consonants in immediate memory. *Journal of Verbal Learning & Verbal Behavior,* 1971, **10,** 587–596.   (a)

Crowder, R. G. Waiting for the stimulus suffix: Decay, delay, rhythm and readout in immediate memory. *Quarterly Journal of Experimental Psychology,* 1971, **23,** 324–340.   (b)

Crowder, R. G., & Morton, J. Precategorical acoustic storage (PAS). *Perception & Psychophysics,* 1969, **5,** 365–373.

Cutting, J. E., & Eimas, P. D. Phonetic feature analyzers in the processing of speech by infants. In J. F. Kavanagh & J. E. Cutting (Eds.), *The role of speech in language.* Cambridge, Massachusetts: M.I.T. Press. 1975.

Cutting, J. E., & Rosner, B. S. Categories and boundaries in speech and music. *Perception & Psychophysics,* in press.

Darwin, C. J., & Baddeley, A. D. Acoustic memory and the perception of speech. *Cognitive Psychology,* 1974, **6,** 41–60.

Eimas, P. D. Speech perception in early infancy. In L. B. Cohen & P. Salapatek (Eds.), *Infant perception.* New York: Academic Press, 1974.

Eimas, P. D., Siqueland, E. R., Jusczyk, P., & Vigorito, J. M. Speech perception in infants. *Science,* 1971, **171,** 303–306.

Fant, C. G. M. Analysis and synthesis of speech processes. In B. Malmberg (Ed.), *Manual of phonetics.* Amsterdam: North-Holland Publ., 1968.

Fromkin, V. A., Krashen, S., Curtiss, S., Rigler, D., & Rigler, M. The development of language in Genie: A case of language acquisition beyond the "Critical Period." *Brain & Language,* 1974, **1,** 81–107.

Fry, D. B. Perception and recognition in speech. In M. Halle, H. G. Lunt, H. Mc-Clean, & C. H. Van Schoonefeld (Eds.), *For Roman Jakobson.* The Hague: Mouton, 1956. Pp. 169–173.

Fujisaki, H., & Kawashima, T. On the modes and mechanisms of speech perception. *Annual Report of the Engineering Research Institute, University of Tokyo,* 1969, **28,** 67–73.

Fujisaki, H., & Kawashima, T. Some experiments on speech perception and a model for the perceptual mechanism. *Annual Report of the Engineering Research Institute, University of Tokyo,* 1970, **29,** 207–214.

Geschwind, N., & Levitsky, W. Human brain: Left–right asymmetries in temporal speech region. *Science,* 1968, **161,** 186–187.

Hirsch, H. V. B., & Spinelli, D. N. Visual experience modifies distribution of horizontally and vertically oriented receptive fields in cat. *Science,* 1970, **168,** 869–871.

House, A. S., Stevens, K. N., Sandel, T. T., & Arnold, J. B. On the learning of speech-like vocabularies. *Journal of Verbal Learning & Verbal Behavior,* 1962, **1,** 133–143.

Konishi, M. The role of auditory feedback in the control of vocalization in the white-crowned sparrow. *Zeitschrift für Tierpsychologie,* 1965, **22,** 770–783.

Ladefoged, P., DeClerk, J., Lindau, M., & Papcun, G. An auditory–motor theory of speech production. *UCLA Working Papers in Phonetics,* 1972, **22,** 48–75.

Lane, H. L. The motor theory of speech perception: A critical review. *Psychological Review,* 1965, **72,** 275–309.

Lenneberg, E. H. *The biological foundations of language.* New York: Wiley, 1967.

Liberman, A. M., Cooper, F. S. Shankweiler, D. S., & Studdert-Kennedy, M. Perception of the speech code. *Psychological Review,* 1967, **74,** 431–461.

Liberman, A. M., Harris, K. S., Kinney, J., & Lane, H. The discrimination of relative onset time of the components of certain speech and nonspeech patterns. *Journal of Experimental Psychology,* 1961, **61,** 379–388.

Liberman, A. M., Mattingly, I. G., & Turvey, M. T. Language codes and memory codes. In A. W. Melton & E. Martin (Eds.), *Coding processes in human memory.* New York: Wiley, 1972.

Lieberman, P. Primate vocalization and human linguistic ability. *Journal of the Acoustical Society of America,* 1968, **44,** 1574–1584.

Lieberman, P. *The speech of primates.* The Hague: Mouton, 1972.

Lieberman, P. On the evolution of language: A unified view. *Cognition,* 1973, **2,** 59–94.

Lieberman, P., & Crelin, E. S. On the speech of Neanderthal man. *Linguistic Inquiry,* 1971, **2,** 203–222.

Lieberman, P., Crelin, E. S., & Klatt, D. H. Phonetic ability and related anatomy of the newborn, adult human, Neanderthal man and the chimpanzee. *American Anthropologist,* 1972, **74,** 287–307.

Lieberman, P., Harris, K. S., Wolff, P., & Russell, L. H. Newborn infant cry and non-human primate vocalizations. *Journal of Speech & Hearing Research,* 1972, **14,** 718–727.

Lindblom, B. E. F., & Sundberg, J. Neurophysiological representation of speech sounds. Paper presented at the XVth World Congress on Logopedics and Phoniatrics, Buenos Aires, Argentina, August, 1971.

Lisker, L., & Abramson, A. S. A cross-language study of voicing in initial stops: acoustical measurements. *Word,* 1964, **20,** 384–422.

Locke, S., & Kellar, L. Categorical perception in a nonlinguistic mode. *Cortex,* 1973, **9,** 355–369.

MacNeilage, P. F., Rootes, T. P., & Chase, R. A. Speech production and perception in a patient with severe impairment of somesthetic perception and motor control. *Journal of Speech & Hearing Research,* 1967, **10,** 449–467.

Marler, P. Birdsong and speech development: Could there be parallels? *American Scientist,* 1970, **58,** 669–673.

Marler, P. On the origin of speech from animal sounds. In J. F. Kavanagh & J E. Cutting (Eds.), *The role of speech in language.* Cambridge, Massachusetts: M.I.T. Press, 1975.

Marler, P., & Mundinger, P. Vocal learning in birds. In H. Moltz (Ed.), *Ontogeny of vertebrate behavior.* New York: Academic Press, 1971.

Marvilya, M. P. Spontaneous vocalization and babbling in hearing-impaired infants. In C. G. M. Fant (Ed.), *Speech communication ability and profound deafness.* Washington, D.C.: A. G. Bell Association for the Deaf, 1972.

Massaro, D. W. Preperceptual images, processing time, and perceptual units in auditory perception. *Psychological Review,* 1972, **79,** 124–145.

Mattingly, I. G. Speech cues and sign stimuli. *American Scientist,* 1972, **60,** 327–337.

Miller, G. A. The magical number seven plus or minus two, or, some limits on our capacity for processing information *Psychological Review,* 1956, **63,** 81–96.

Miller, J. D., Pastore, R. E., Wier, C. C., Kelly, W. J., & Dooling, R. J. Discrimination and labeling of noise-buzz sequences with varying noise-lead times. *Journal of the Acoustical Society of America,* 1974, **55,** 390.

Miller, J. M., Sutton, D., Pfingst, B., Ryan, A., & Beaton, R. Single cell activity in the auditory cortex of rhesus monkeys: Behavioral dependency. *Science,* 1972, **177,** 449–451.

Nottebohm, F. Neural lateralization of vocal control in a passerine bird. I. Song. *Journal of Experimental Zoology*, 1971, **177**, 229–262.

Nottebohm, F. Neural lateralization of vocal control in a passerine bird. II. Subsong, calls and theory of vocal learning. *Journal of Experimental Zoology*, 1972, **179**, 35–50.

Pettigrew, J. D., & Freeman, R. D. Visual experience without lines: Effect on development cortical neurons. *Science*, 1973, **182**, 599–600.

Pisoni, D. B. On the nature of categorical perception of speech sounds. Unpublished doctoral dissertation, University of Michigan, 1971. (Also *Supplement to Status Report of Speech Research*, **SR-27**, Haskins Laboratories, New Haven, Connecticut, November, 1971, p. 101.)

Pisoni, D. B. Auditory and phonetic memory codes in the discrimination of consonants and vowels. *Perception & Psychophysics*, 1973, **13**, 253–260.

Pisoni, D. B. Auditory short-term memory and vowel perception. *Memory & Cognition*, in press.

Pisoni, D. B., & Lazarus, J. H. Categorical and noncategorical modes of speech perception along the voicing continuum. *Journal of the Acoustical Society of America*, 1974, **55**, 328–333.

Pisoni, D. B., & Tash, J. Reaction times to comparisons within and across phonetic categories. *Perception & Psychophysics*, 1974, **15**, 285–290.

Port, D. K., & Preston, M. S. Early apical stop production: A voice onset time analysis. *Haskins Laboratories Status Report on Speech Research*, 1972, **SR29/30**, 125–149.

Raphael, L. J. Preceding vowel duration as a cue to the perception of the voicing characteristic of word-final consonants in American English. *Journal of the Acoustical Society of America*, 1972, **51**, 1296–1303.

Rosch, E. H. Natural categories. *Cognitive Psychology*, 1973, **4**, 328–350.

Sachs, R. H. Vowel identification and discrimination in isolation vs. word context. *Quarterly Progress Report 93*, Research Laboratory of Electronics, M.I.T., Cambridge, Massachusetts, 1969. Pp. 220–229.

Sinnott, J. M. A comparison of speech sound discrimination in humans and monkeys. Unpublished doctoral dissertation, University of Michigan, 1974.

Stevens, K. N. On the relations between speech movements and speech perception. *Zeitschrift für Phonetik Sprachwissenschaft und Kommunikationforschung*, 1968, **21**, 102–106.

Stevens, K. N. The potential role of property detectors in the perception of consonants. Paper presented at the Symposium on Auditory Analysis and Perception of Speech, Leningrad, USSR, August, 1973.

Stevens, K. N., & Klatt, D. H. The role of format transitions in the voiced–voiceless distinction for stops. *Journal of the Acoustical Society of America*, 1974, **55**, 653–659.

Studdert-Kennedy, M. Speech perception. In N. J. Lass (Ed.), *Contemporary issues in experimental phonetics*. Springfield, Illinois: Thomas, 1975.

Studdert-Kennedy, M., Liberman, A. M., Harris, K. S., & Cooper, F. S. Motor theory of speech perception: a reply to Lane's critical review. *Psychological Review*, 1970, **77**, 234–249.

Sussman, H. The laterality effect in lingual-auditory tracking. *Journal of the Acoustical Society of America*, 1971, **49**, 1874–1880.

Sussman, H. M., & MacNeilage, P. F. Studies of hemispheric specialization for speech production. *Brain & Language*, 1975, **2**, in press.

2

SELECTIVE ADAPTATION TO SPEECH

William E. Cooper
Massachusetts Institute of Technology

As members of the human species, we are able (on most occasions) to produce and perceive the sounds of speech with remarkable grace. Our effort to understand the nature of speech activities, however, proceeds altogether less smoothly. Although the selective adaptation research to be outlined here cannot hope to remedy this situation, new and important clues are beginning to emerge. It is believed that these clues will serve as part of the foundation for a detailed model of information flow during the speech transmission process.

The technique of selective adaptation has been used to study stages of human information processing in each of the major sensory modalities (for recent reviews, see Barlow, 1972; Engen, 1971; Jameson & Hurvich, 1972; Kenshalo, 1971; Pfaffman, Bartoshuk, & McBurney, 1971; Riggs & Wooten, 1972; Small, 1963; Ward, 1963). Since many aspects of human sensation are not otherwise accessible to study, psychophysicists have long regarded the selective adaptation method as one of their more useful experimental tools. To at least some of these traditional psychophysicists, it must come as a surprise to learn that the adaptation technique has been applied to the study of speech processing only within the past few years (cf. Eimas & Corbit, 1973). The recent research in selective adaptation to speech variables, like all adaptation research, has been concerned with answering three broad questions. The first of these is simply whether a measurable adaptation effect can be obtained for the speech variable under investigation. If so, two further questions arise: What is the neural site of the adapted part of the speech system? and, of primary concern: What operations does this component of the system normally perform?

Although we are some distance away from providing definitive answers to these questions, preliminary answers have been obtained in the case of a few major speech cues, in particular, cues to the properties of *voicing* and *place of articulation* among the stop consonants in English (cf. Abercrombie, 1967). We will consider two areas of research that deal with the processing of these cues.

The first area involves studies of *perceptual* adaptation—research designed to provide information about the organizational properties of the speech decoding mechanism (cf. Studdert-Kennedy, 1974). This line of research has been aimed at studying levels of decoding involved in both (*a*) preliminary processing of individual auditory cues during speech perception (cf. Stevens, 1972, 1973) and (*b*) processing of phonetic feature information (cf. Chomsky & Halle, 1968; Fant, 1973; Jakobson, Fant, & Halle, 1963; Ladefoged, 1971). There exists little agreement among speech theorists regarding either the particular acoustic or phonetic properties that are processed *as such* during speech perception, and it was hoped that the selective adaptation method might be useful in shedding some empirical light here. To date, progress on this front has been modest, but if anything our initial hope has been strengthened by the gains that have already been made.

After reviewing general aspects of the perceptual adaptation work, I will discuss a second major area of adaptation research to speech variables, namely *perceptuomotor* adaptation. Such work has provided a new way of looking at a very old and much-discussed problem: namely, whether the perceptual and motor aspects of speech processing are mediated by a common processor (cf. de Cordemoy, 1668; von Humboldt, 1836; Lashley, 1951; Liberman, 1957; Liberman, Cooper, Shankweiler, & Studdert-Kennedy, 1967; Stevens & Halle, 1967). We will see that recent work in perceptuomotor adaptation has provided some fairly direct evidence in support of such a mechanism. This evidence comes at a rather critical time, since a number of recent findings that bear indirectly on this issue have prompted some to cast doubt on the possibility of perceptuomotor processing for speech (cf. Bailey & Haggard, 1973; Eimas, to appear; Eimas, forthcoming; Peterson & Johnson, 1971).

PERCEPTUAL ADAPTATION TO CONSONANT CUES

A Description of the Effect

The first systematic studies of speech adaptation were conducted by Eimas and Corbit (1973).[1] These experiments provided a useful starting

---

[1] Speech adaptation studies dating back to Warren and Gregory (1958) have been concerned with the effects of *verbal transformations,* or phonemic alterations that

point for later work in speech adaptation, and will thus be reviewed here in some detail. In the Eimas and Corbit experiments, listeners were first instructed to identify two series of synthetic consonant–vowel syllables varying in their initial consonants. The syllables of one series were identifiable as either [ba] or [pʰa], and the syllables of the other were identifiable as either [da] or [tʰa].

The stimuli of each series varied along an acoustic dimension known as voice onset time (VOT),[2] defined for word-initial stop consonants as the interval between the onset of the release burst of the consonant and the onset of laryngeal pulsing. The VOT cue roughly distinguishes phonemic variations of voicing for stop consonants in a variety of natural languages (cf. Lisker & Abramson, 1970). In English, voiceless stops ([pʰ], [tʰ], [kʰ]) are normally produced such that laryngeal pulsing lags the release burst of the consonant by more than 40 msec. Voiced stops ([b], [d], [g]), on the other hand, are accompanied in English by shorter-lag VOTs, and may even be prevoiced, with voicing onset preceding the release burst. In some other languages (e.g., Spanish), phonemic distinctions are marked by short-lag versus prevoiced VOTs (cf. Lisker & Abramson, 1964).

Each of the two VOT series in the Eimas and Corbit experiments included some stop consonants with short-lag VOTs, normally perceived as voiced (i.e., as [b] or [d]), some with long-lag VOTs, perceived as voiceless (i.e., as [pʰ] or [tʰ]), and some with intermediate VOTs whose classification as either voiced or voiceless was potentially ambiguous. The initial

---

are perceived when listeners are presented with repetitions of a single syllable or word. Unlike the selective adaptation research initiated by Eimas and Corbit (1973), the verbal transformation studies typically do not utilize *test* (in addition to *adapting*) stimuli to permit quantitative assessments of the adaptation effects along single acoustic or phonetic dimensions. Because studies of verbal transformations typically employ real-speech stimuli only, it is impossible to try to assign aspects of these perceptual alteration effects to specific acoustic features of the stimulus. The primary objection raised against using synthetic speech materials (that such stimuli are not natural sounding) has been countered partially in recent selective adaptation work by the use of five-formant synthetic patterns that closely approximate real speech (Klatt, forthcoming). In our experiments, verbal transformations are often reported by listeners after adaptation to synthetic syllables, although we have not studied these transformations systematically.

[2] Another cue to voicing distinctions in initial stops, namely the presence or absence of significant formant transitions after voice onset, covaried with absolute VOT in the test series of the Eimas and Corbit experiments (Stevens & Klatt, 1974; Cooper, 1974a). Consequently, we could not be certain whether adaptation along the "VOT series" in these experiments was due to the fatiguing of analyzers that detect VOT information per se, as Eimas and Corbit suggested. The experiment by Cooper (1974a) shows that, in fact, the formant transitions cue plays some role in obtaining the adaptation effects.

experiment was designed to yield estimates of the 50% VOT crossover point between voiced and voiceless identification responses for each listener in the unadapted state. This crossover point, or *phonetic boundary locus,* was estimated by presenting listeners with randomized sequences of the test stimuli and requiring the listeners to identify these stimuli as either [ba] or [pʰa] (in the bilabial test series) or as either [da] or [tʰa] (in the alveolar test series). A least-mean-squares analysis was applied to the transformed percentage of responses to yield an estimate of the phonetic boundary locus for each test series, for each listener.

After the initial identification measures were obtained, listeners were presented with randomly selected items from the same two series to identify after periods of repetitive listening to each of four different adapting syllables. The four adapting syllables, [ba], [pʰa], [da], and [tʰa], were chosen from the extreme ends of the two VOT series. In a given adaptation session, one of these adapting syllables was played to listeners at a rate of about two repetitions per second, for a period of 1 min on each trial prior to the presentation of a test item to be identified.

Identification performance after adaptation was then compared with the performance obtained for the same test stimuli in the unadapted state. The results of the experiments for a typical listener appear in Fig. 1.

Repetitive listening to each of the four adapting syllables affected the subject's ability to identify the VOT test syllables in a highly systematic fashion. After adaptation to either of the voiced stops [b] or [d], shifts were obtained in the loci of the phonetic boundaries for both the [ba]–[pʰa] and the [da]–[tʰa] test series. The magnitude of these shifts typically ranged from about 5 to 15 msec in VOT. For each series, the shifts were in the direction toward the voiced category, signifying that listeners assigned fewer responses to this category after adaptation. Adaptation with either of the voiceless stops [pʰ] or [tʰ] produced systematic shifts in the opposite direction. After adaptation with these syllables, the phonetic boundary loci for both series shifted toward the voiceless category.

We should note three specific characteristics of these original adaptation effects. First, the displacements in the identification functions obtained after adaptation were, for the most part, restricted to stimuli in the immediate region of the phonetic boundary locus.[3] Second, the slopes of the identification functions obtained after adaptation were as steep as the slopes of functions obtained in the unadapted state. And third, the magnitude of the crossed-series adaptation shifts (e.g., [da] adaptation with [ba]–[pʰa] identification) was about 80% as large as the magnitude of the

---

[3] This characteristic of the original adaptation effects has been observed in most, but not all, of the subsequent adaptation studies (Cooper, 1974b).

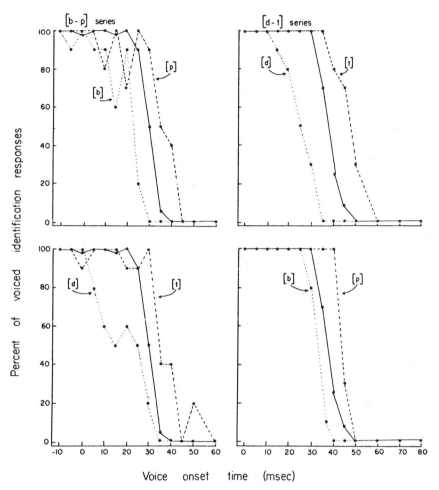

FIG. 1. Percentages of voiced identification responses ([b or d]) obtained with and without adaptation for a single subject. The functions for the [b, p] series are on the left and those for the [d, t] series are on the right. The solid lines indicate the unadapted identification functions and the dotted and dashed lines, the identification functions after adaptation. The phonetic symbols indicate the adapting stimulus. (From Eimas & Corbit, 1973.)

effects obtained for the same-series tests (e.g., [ba] adaptation with [ba]–[pʰa] identification).

Each of these three characteristics provided some initial indication about the nature of the adaptation effects. The strong presence of the crossed-series adaptation shifts was particularly important. In effect, adaptation along a test dimension varying in the feature voicing was obtained even when the adapting and test stimuli differed in place of articulation (recall from elementary phonetics that the pairs [b]–[pʰ] and [d]–[tʰ] share place of articulation but differ in voicing, whereas the pairs [b]–[d] and [pʰ]–[tʰ] share voicing but differ in place of articulation; Abercrombie, 1967). The existence of the strong crossed-series shifts provided support for the notion that the primary adaptation effect operates on a mechanism that extracts information about the voicing property of the consonant, not a mechanism that processes the consonant sound as a unit. The assumption underlying this claim is that the presence of crossed-adaptation effects indicates the sharing of a common property between the adapting stimulus and the adapted members of the test series; in the present case, this property is the feature *voicing,* represented acoustically by variations in VOT.[4]

Since VOT is not the only cue relevant to voicing distinctions in initial stop consonants (cf. Haggard, Ambler, & Callow, 1970; Stevens & Klatt, 1974; Summerfield & Haggard, 1972), it was not clear from the original adaptation results whether the effect operated on analyzers of the *voicing* property per se or on analyzers selectively sensitive to the VOT acoustic cue. Nevertheless, Eimas and Corbit (1973) strongly advocated the latter possibility in their proposed model of the adaptation effects:

> (*a*) There exist *two* detectors that are differentially sensitive to a range of VOT values with greatest sensitivity (as might be measured, in principle, by the output signal of the detector) occurring at the modal production value for a particular voicing distinction (Lisker and Abramson, 1964). (*b*) Some VOT values excite both detectors, but all other things being equal, only the output signal with the greater strength reaches higher centers of processing and integration. (*c*) The phonetic boundary will lie at the VOT value that excites both detectors equally, all other factors being equal. (*d*) After adaptation, the sensitivity of a detector is lessened; that is, the output signal is weakened or decreased. Furthermore, for purposes of simplicity, the signal strength is assumed to decrease equally for the entire range of VOT values to which the detector is sensitive. From this it follows that selective adaptation shifts the phonetic boundary by shifting the point of equilibrium along the VOT continuum [p. 108].

Important aspects of this model have since been revised and extended on the basis of additional findings. For now, let us take up a very general criticism of the proposed explanation of the adaptation effects: namely, that the effects could be accounted for by means other than an effect of sensory fatigue. Given the results of the Eimas and Corbit identification tests, it did indeed remain possible that the adaptation effects might be attributable to a response contrast factor, operating at the level of the

[4] Although this assumption is probably valid, it should not go unchallenged in future work.

listeners' decision rule. According to the response contrast interpretation, shifts in the loci of the phonetic boundaries occur simply because listeners tend to identify stimuli as being more unlike the stimulus presented repeatedly beforehand, independent of any fatigue effect on VOT detectors.

To provide initial evidence against this interpretation, Eimas and Corbit conducted a second series of experiments, using a response measure of discrimination. Discrimination functions were obtained for the [ba]–[pʰa] stimuli both before adaptation and after adaptation to either [ba] or [pʰa]. It was found that the peaks in the discrimination functions, normally located at the phonetic boundary locus (Liberman, Harris, Hoffman, & Griffith, 1957), were displaced after adaptation as predicted on the basis of the earlier identification shifts. Eimas and Corbit believed that the obtained peak shifts provided evidence against the contrast interpretation, since the contrast factor presumably operates on a decision rule strictly involving *identification*.

However, it could reasonably be argued that the discrimination results did not rule out the contrast interpretation effectively. The very presence of peaks in the discrimination functions for consonants has been accounted for by the influence of *covert* identification of the stimuli to be discriminated (Liberman *et al.*, 1957). The contrast interpretation could thus, in principle, account for the discrimination findings in the same manner as it could for the results of experiments requiring overt identification.

More recently, however, Sawusch and Pisoni (1973) and Sawusch, Pisoni, and Cutting (1974) have obtained somewhat stronger evidence against the response contrast interpretation. They showed that the location of the phonetic boundary for stimuli varying in VOT remains quite stable in a normal identification task, despite wide variations in the stimulus presentation schedule, variations large enough to produce significant anchor effects (Appley, 1971) for nonspeech tones of varying intensity and for a CV syllable of varying fundamental frequency. These results, as well as the results of Bailey (1973; discussed later in another context), indicate that the adaptation effects cannot be accounted for by either a response contrast effect or an effect of adaptation level (cf. Helson, 1964). Rather, the adaptation effects appear to reflect the fatiguing of a speech processing mechanism that operates at some stage or stages of processing prior to the response decision stage. The following work was designed to provide a more narrow definition of this proposed adaptation site.

Location of the Effect

In a second series of experiments, Eimas, Cooper, and Corbit (1973) replicated the initial work on selective adaptation and conducted additional tests to determine the general location of the effect. One experiment was designed to test for the possibility of interaural transfer of adaptation. In this experiment, the adapting stimulus [tʰa] was presented to one ear, while the [da]–[tʰa] test stimuli were presented for identification to the other, unadapted ear. A substantial interaural transfer effect was obtained and was measured to be about 95% of the binaural effect obtained for the same group of listeners.

This result suggested that the adaptation effect operates primarily on a binaurally driven mechanism; that is, a mechanism that receives its input in the form of fused information from the two ears. One might be led to suspect further that the effect operates unilaterally on the language-dominant cerebral hemisphere (Kimura, 1961; Studdert-Kennedy & Shank-weiler, 1970). However, as Ades (1974a) has pointed out, the latter conclusion is not strictly warranted, since binaurally driven units probably exist as early as the midbrain in man (Bocca & Caleary, 1963).

Although the results of the interaural transfer experiment provided support for the notion that the adaptation effect operates subsequent to binaural fusion, the results did not rule out the possibility that some other part of the effect operates on a mechanism that receives only exclusively input. Ades (1974a) designed an important experiment to test this latter possibility. Working with stimuli that varied in the feature place of articulation, as opposed to voicing (discussed later), Ades presented the adapting syllable [bæ] to one ear and the adapting syllable [dæ] to the other ear, simultaneously. He then tested subjects' identification of a [bæ]–[dæ] test series in each ear separately. Small, but statistically significant, shifts were obtained after such adaptation, indicating the presence of a monaural component of the adaptation effect. After adaptation with [bæ] to the left ear and [dæ] to the right ear, for example, the phonetic boundary locus for the [bæ]–[dæ] test series shifted toward the [bæ] category when subjects were tested in the left ear, but this boundary locus shifted toward the [dæ] category when the same subjects were tested in the right ear.

In two additional experiments, Ades provided support for the existence of another portion of the adaptation effect that operates binaurally. In one experiment, significant interaural transfer of adaptation was obtained for stimuli of the [bæ]–[dæ] test series. More to the point, adaptation along the [bæ]–[dæ] series was obtained in a binaural fusion test in which the first-formant transition of the adapting stimulus was presented to one ear, while the second- and third-format transitions were simultaneously presented to the other ear. Significant adaptation with these stimulus components was obtained in the case of simultaneous presentation, but not when the transitions (which sound like nonspeech chirps to most listeners; cf. Mattingly, Liberman, Syrdal, & Hawles, 1971) were presented to each ear in an alternating (unfused) sequence.

We are left, then, with fairly convincing evidence in support of both binaurally and monaurally driven sites of the adaptation effect. It is quite probable that both sites account for the total effect obtained during regular binaural testing. Since all other relevant experiments conducted in the meantime have involved binaural testing only, we find ourselves in the unfortunate position of being unable to assign the results of such tests to either or both of the two adaptation sites. We will review these binaural studies nonetheless in the hope that they will provide useful background for later work aimed at assigning properties to each site.

Selective Adaptation for Voicing

A first study of the properties of the adapted mechanism for voicing was conducted by Eimas *et al.* (1973). In one experiment, an attempt was made to determine whether the adaptation effect operates on detectors of general auditory information (cf. Stevens, 1972, 1973), or on detectors that are specialized for processing auditory information only to the extent that it is contained in a linguistic context. In the experiment, subjects' identification of a [da]–[t^{h}a] VOT series was tested both before and after adaptation with a shortened nonspeech version of the [da] adapting syllable. The shortened stimulus was 50 msec in duration and represented the initial segment of the full [da]. This segment contained the same VOT information as the full syllable, yet was typically heard as a nonspeech chirp or water drip. Adaptation with this stimulus produced no significant shift in the locus of the [da]–[t^{h}a] phonetic boundary, unlike the results obtained for the same listeners after adaptation with [da]. It was concluded from these data that the adaptation effect for the CV test syllables operates primarily on a speech-specific analyzing mechanism.

This conclusion turned out to be wide of the mark, however. A slight boundary shift in the direction toward the [d] category was obtained for five of the seven listeners tested in the experiment, and a replication study by Ades (unpublished) revealed similar small, but in his case, statistically significant shifts using comparable VOT stimuli. It appears, on the basis of these additional results, that part of the adaptation effect reflects the fatiguing of general auditory analyzers, sensitive to either (*a*) absolute VOT information (Lisker & Abramson, 1970), (*b*) the presence or absence of a rapid spectral change following the onset of voicing (Stevens & Klatt, 1974, discussed later), or (*c*) some weighted combination of these two factors (Summerfield & Haggard, 1972; Cooper, 1974a).

To provide a different means of testing the voicing analyzers, Cooper (1974a) conducted a study in which the VOT cue was pitted against another acoustic cue relevant to voicing distinctions among word-initial stops, namely, the presence or absence of significant formant transitions following voice onset (Stevens & Klatt, 1974). The aim of this experiment was to test for the existence of a component of the effect that could not be attributed to adaptation of a detector that is selectively sensitive to either the VOT cue or the formant transitions cue per se, but could be attributed to a more integrative property. Two adapting syllables were selected from the Stevens and Klatt series that contained the same absolute VOT information, but contained different amounts of formant transitions after voice onset. Spectrograms of these two stimuli appear in Fig. 2.

Adaptation with these two stimuli produced significantly different phonetic boundary loci for a [ba]–[pʰa] test series varying in VOT. The differential effect could not be attributed to either the VOT cue or the formant transitions cue individually. Some of the [ba]–[pʰa] stimuli whose identification was differentially affected by this procedure contained only slight or no formant transitions after voice onset, permitting us to rule out the formant transitions cue as being responsible for the differential adaptation effect. An account of the effect based strictly on VOT information was

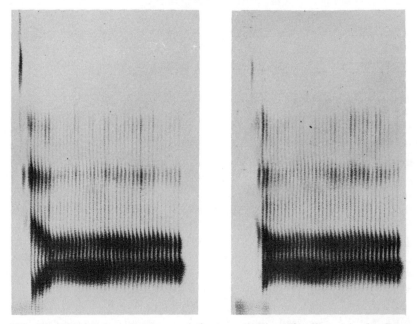

FIG. 2.   Wide-band spectrograms of the two adapting stimuli used in the Cooper (1974a) study. Both stimuli have a VOT value of +25 msec. The stimulus on the left contains 40-msec formant transitions after voice onset; the stimulus on the right contains 10-msec formant transitions after voice onset. In the latter case, the duration of the transitions is probably shorter than the threshold of detection for such a spectral change (Stevens & Klatt, 1974, Expt. 2). The adapting stimuli were constructed by Stevens and Klatt (1974).

also, of course, untenable, since the two adapting syllables contained the exact same VOT information yet produced significantly different effects. The present results appeared, rather, to be attributable to the fatiguing of an integrative, possibly phonetic, feature analyzer, whose task it is to extract voicing information from consonants, receiving as its input any of a number of hypothetical voicing cues (Haggard, Ambler, & Callow, 1970; Lisker & Abramson, 1970; Stevens & Klatt, 1974; Summerfield & Haggard, 1972).

The combined results of the past sets of experiments may seem, at first glance, to suggest the presence of two components of the adaptation effect, one operating at a stage of auditory property detection (Stevens, 1972, 1973), another operating at a stage of integrative feature extraction (cf. Cooper, 1974a). However, it is very important to consider the possibility that, based on the evidence reviewed thus far, the results supporting an integrative site of adaptation may instead reflect adaptation of relatively low-level auditory property detectors. If one assumes that two types of feature detectors exist, and that these detectors are organized serially such that the output of the lower-level auditory detectors feeds into more integrative detectors, then one could argue that any adaptation effects that alter the state of the former would be faithfully transmitted to the level of the latter, and, in turn, to the response decision stage (in the case where listeners are asked to respond by identifying syllables as belonging to one linguistic category or another). Given these particular assumptions, which, while not supported by recent work (see Wood, Chapter 3), can certainly not yet be ruled out for the speech variables in question, it becomes quite difficult to provide convincing support for the notion that a distinct integrative stage of processing serves as a site of adaptation. In order to provide such a test, the preliminary stages of auditory processing must be completely bypassed. We shall see later that this requirement has been met, fortunately, in the case of visually presented adapting stimuli, and that the preliminary results of such tests appear to support the existence of an integrative, and, in particular, phonetic site of adaptation (see Cooper, 1974a, for the distinction between phonetic and auditory types of integrators). I will therefore assume for the remainder of this discussion that the selective adaptation procedure affects both low-level auditory and phonetic stages of processing.

It is tempting to speculate that each of these two components can be uniquely associated with a monaural or binaural site of adaptation. Based on evidence from studies of dichotic listening (Pisoni, Chapter 4; Studdert-Kennedy & Shankweiler, 1970; Studdert-Kennedy, Shankweiler, & Pisoni, 1972), one would predict that the auditory component is monaurally driven, whereas the more integrative component involves a mechanism which operates subsequent to binaural fusion (but see Ades, 1974a, fusion experiment). If this prediction were confirmed, we would be in a position to isolate the auditory and phonetic components of the adaptation effect within the same test situation and thereby set the stage for studying properties of each component in greater detail, as well as their possible interaction. Whether or not this rather lofty hope can be realized awaits further investigation. In the meantime, we will move on here to consider other properties of the proposed voicing analyzers.

In a second group of experiments, Eimas *et al.* (1973) attempted to compare the magnitudes of shift obtained after adaptation with voiced versus voiceless stop consonants. It was found that adaptation with the voiceless stops produced reliably greater shifts in the phonetic boundary loci for syllables varying in VOT. The magnitude of the shifts was on the average about 13 msec after adaptation with voiceless stops and only about 7 msec after adaptation with voiced stops. This asymmetry, also noted in the more limited data of the Eimas and Corbit (1973) experiments, was found to be in agreement with independent evidence on speech production for the VOT variable. The speech production evidence indicates (*a*) that the voiced, or short-lag VOT mode, occurs more generally in natural languages than either the long-lag or prevoiced VOT modes (cf. Lisker & Abramson, 1964), and (*b*) that the short-lag VOT mode appears first in the speech of young children (Port & Preston, 1972; Preston, 1971).[5] We will see later that this intriguing voiced–voiceless asymmetry applies to data on perceptuomotor adaptation as well (cf. Cooper, 1974d).

Another property of the voicing analyzers that has recently been investigated is the extent to which voicing analysis in the stop consonants is carried out independent of vowel environment. In the original experiments of Eimas and Corbit (1973) and Eimas *et al.* (1973), the vowel of the adapting and test stimuli was always held constant. Since early measurements of speech production had shown the VOT variable to be quite insensitive to differences in vowel environment (cf. Lisker & Abramson, 1967), it was reasonable to suppose that the original adaptation effects operated on analyzers that extract voicing information from consonants irrespective of their vowel context. Nevertheless, because of the importance of this assumption to any information-flow model of the perceptual process, I considered it important to design an experiment to provide a test of the alternative possibility—that voicing information in the stops is indeed analyzed with respect to vowel environment at some stage of processing.

[5] The voiced–voiceless asymmetry obtained in the adaptation studies of Eimas and Corbit (1973) and Eimas *et al.* (1973) is in opposition to the voiced–voiceless asymmetry obtained by Goldstein and Lackner (1974) in a study of real speech verbal transformations (Warren & Gregory, 1958). The discrepancy may well be due to acoustic differences in the stimulus materials (see also Footnote 1).

The experiment (Cooper, 1974b) utilized a contingent adaptation procedure (Fidell, 1970; Harris & Gibson, 1968; Held & Shattuck, 1971; Mayhew & Anstis, 1972; cf. McCollough, 1965) to permit independent variation in both the voicing property of the consonant and the vowel environment. Two series of VOT stimuli were used as test syllables; they were identifiable as either [ba]–[pʰa] [bi]–[pʰi]. After the initial measures of identification were obtained for these stimuli, listeners were required to identify the same stimuli after adaptation to an alternating sequence to two syllables, [da] and [tʰi]. These two syllables differed from each other in both voicing and vowel context.

According to the vowel-independent hypothesis, adaptation with this alternating sequence of [da] and [tʰi] should produce no differential effect on the two series of test stimuli. However, significantly different effects were, in fact, obtained supporting the hypothesis that voicing analysis is contingent on vowel environment. A graph of the identification functions for a group of 14 listeners is presented in Fig. 3.

After adaptation with the alternating [da]–[tʰi] sequence, the phonetic boundary of the [ba]–[pʰa] series shifted toward the [b] category, whereas the phonetic boundary of the [bi]–[pʰi] series shifted toward [pʰ]. In each case, the adapting syllable having the same vowel as the test series exerted the controlling adaptation effect. The average magnitude of the contingent effect was quite small, on the order of 2–3 msec of VOT, yet the significant presence of this effect indicated that the perceptual analysis of voicing in initial stops is carried out at some stage of processing with respect to the following vowel. It remains an important next step in our research to determine whether this vowel-contingent processing occurs prior to or subsequent to binaural fusion.

Additional support for the vowel-contingent hypothesis was obtained from an analysis of the identification functions for the [ba]–[pʰa] and [bi]–[pʰi] series obtained in the unadapted condition of this experiment. The locus of the unadapted phonetic boundary for the [bi]–[pi] series was significantly greater (as measured in milliseconds of VOT) than the locus of the comparable [ba]–[pʰa] series. This result was found to be in agreement with measurements of VOT production recently obtained by Klatt (1973). In contrast to the findings of Lisker and Abramson (1967), Klatt obtained significantly greater VOT values for voiceless stops in initial position when these stops were spoken in the context of high as opposed to low vowels (e.g., [pʰay] versus [pʰi]).

The contingent-adaptation procedure applied here should become a useful tool in future speech-adaptation research. The perception of phonetic properties, for consonants, in particular, appears to be more often contingent on a variety of factors than has generally been appreciated by those who postulate the existence of detector mechanisms for extracting speech

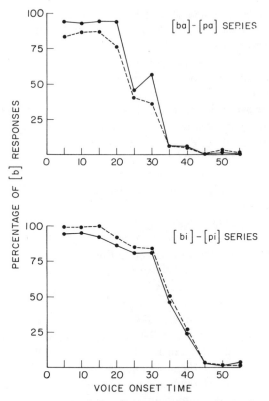

FIG. 3. The percentage of [b] identification responses for a group of 14 subjects. Solid lines denote the identification functions obtained in the unadapted state. The dotted lines denote the identification functions obtained after adaptation to the alternating [da]–[ti] sequence. (From Cooper, 1974b.)

feature information. The contingencies include relations between two or more properties of the stimulus (Lisker & Abramson, 1967; Summerfield & Haggard, 1972), and probably response-contingencies of the kind proposed by Smith (1973) as well. The ability to specify both the existence of these contingencies and the stages of processing at which they operate would help to provide a much-improved map of the flow of information during speech perception.

Selective Adaptation for Place of Articulation

The first adaptation study of place of articulation was conducted by Cooper (1974c). The place feature was of special interest because of the well-known lack of invariance accompanying a major acoustic cue for this feature—the direction and extent of the second- and third-formant transitions. These transitions vary considerably (for a given consonant) in both direction and extent as a function of both vowel context and position within the syllable (Liberman, Delattre, Cooper, & Gerstman, 1954). Because of the rather extreme lack of acoustic invariance in this case, it was by no means certain a priori that the selective adaptation procedure would affect the perception of stimuli varying in place in the same way it affected the perception of stimuli varying in the feature voicing (Eimas & Corbit, 1973; Eimas *et al.*, 1973).

The *place* dimension was also of interest because this dimension distinguishes three phonetic categories among the English stops (i.e., [b] versus [d] versus [g], and [pʰ] versus [tʰ] versus [kʰ]), whereas the feature voicing distinguishes only two (i.e., [b] versus [pʰ]; [d] versus [tʰ]; [g] versus [kʰ]). With the place feature, we could thus study the presence or absence of adaptation effects on two separate phonetic boundaries within the same test situation.

In the original *place* adaptation study (Cooper, 1974c), the test series consisted of 13 synthetic syllables ([bæ]–[dæ]–[gæ]) varying only in the second- and third-formant transitions (Pisoni, 1971). Systematic effects of adaptation were obtained after repetitive listening to each of the adapting syllables [bæ], [dæ], and [gæ]. The data for a typical listener appear in Fig. 4.[6]

After adaptation with the syllable [bæ], the listener's phonetic boundary locus between [b] and [d] (henceforth the "[b]–[d] locus") shifted toward the [b] category, whereas the [d]–[g] locus remained relatively stable. Analogously, after adaptation with [gæ], the [d]–[g] boundary locus shifted toward the [g] category, while the [b]–[d] locus remained relatively fixed. These findings indicated that the adaptation effects were fairly well localized, affecting only the phonetic boundary locus that borders the category of the adapting syllable. As in the case of the adaptation along the voicing dimension, the direction of each boundary shift was toward the phonetic category of the adapting stimulus.

Adaptation effects for [dæ], the middle category of the [bæ]–[dæ]–[gæ] formant transitions series, turned out to be of particular significance. In this case, adaptation resulted in shifts in both the [b]–[d] and the [d]–[g] phonetic boundary loci. Both of the bordering boundaries shifted in the direction toward [d]. This result was noteworthy because the [dæ] adapting syllable contained slightly falling second- and third-formant transitions, yet it affected listeners' perception of stimuli near the [b]–[d] boundary which

[6] It would be of interest to determine if the pattern of results obtained here for stimuli varying in the formant transitions also occurs for stimuli varying in the initial burst cue for *place of articulation* (cf. Halle, Hughes, & Radley, 1957).

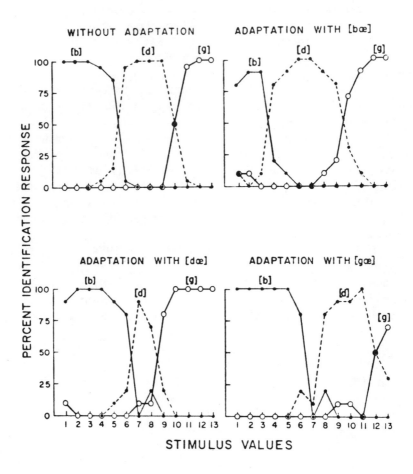

FIG. 4. Percentages of identification responses ([b], [d], or [g]) obtained for a single subject in the unadapted state and after adaptation with [bæ], [dæ], and [gæ]. (From Cooper, 1974c.)

contained second- and third-formant transitions that were both *rising* in direction, as well as stimuli near the [d]–[g] boundary with falling transitions. It was thus tentatively concluded that a component of the adaptation effect for *place,* as for *voicing,* represents the fatiguing of a mechanism that extracts phonetic feature information, information which cannot be easily traced to any single invariant acoustic property. Here, the presence of the adaptation effects for the [dæ] adapting syllable ruled out explanations based on the fatiguing of auditory detectors for either (a) the absolute starting frequency or direction of the second- and third-formant transitions, or (b) the inferred frequency locus to which these transitions "point" (Delattre, Liberman, & Cooper, 1955).

Added support for the phonetic basis of one component of the *place* adaptation effects was provided in a crossed-vowel adaptation test. In this experiment (Cooper, 1974c), the syllable [bi] was employed as an adapting stimulus, having a different vowel from the fixed vowel of the [bæ]–[dæ]–[gæ] test series. The [bi] syllable contained second- and third-formant transitions that differed significantly in starting and steady state frequencies from the corresponding transitions of the [b] members of the test series. Nevertheless, adaptation with [bi] produced a significant shift on the locus of the [b]–[d] phonetic boundary locus of the [bæ]–[dæ]–[gæ] series, similar to the effect produced by the adapting syllable [bæ]. The magnitude of the crossed-vowel effect was about 50% as great as the effect produced in the same-vowel adaptation test.

Ades (1974b) and Bailey (1973) have extended the crossed-vowel experiment to the case of [be]–[de] versus [bæ]–[dæ] (Ades) and to [ba]–[da] versus [bɛ]–[dɛ] (Bailey). In these crossed-vowel experiments, the second- and third-formant transitions of the adapting syllables differed not only in starting frequency but also in direction from the test series members of the same phonetic category. Positive transfer effects were obtained in each of these experiments, adding further support to the notion that a component of the adaptation effect for place is not tied to a single invariant property of the stimulus. It is important to note, however, that these crossed-vowel effects by no means imply that the analysis of place is carried out wholly independent of vowel context (Cooper, 1974b).

Bailey (1973) conducted an additional experiment, which indicates the presence of a low-level auditory component of the adaptation effect for place as well. In this experiment, Bailey independently varied the second- and third-formant transitions of a series of [ba]–[da] test syllables. Two sets of these syllables were constructed, one varying from [ba] to [da] by variations in the second-formant transition with the third-formant absent, the other varying from [ba] to [da] by variations in the third-formant with a fixed transition of F_2. The adapting stimuli taken from the series varying in F_3 produced no adaptation effect on the stimuli varying in F_2. This result provided some support for the presence of an auditory analyzer, which possibly serves to track individual formants alternatively or merely registers the initial and final frequencies of the formant transitions. The ability of the auditory system to process information contained within the formant transitions is currently being studied in our laboratory with synthetic syllables in which the formant transitions have constant "endpoint" frequencies but vary in their frequency accelerations.

With the place feature, as with voicing, we seem to have discovered both auditory and phonetic components of the adaptation effect. We will now review two studies concerned with the individual properties of the adapted place analyzers. Although we cannot yet assign these properties to the auditory and/or phonetic components, future work can reasonably be expected to improve on this situation.

Cooper and Blumstein (1974) conducted experiments to determine the nature of one of the more general properties of the place analyzers. The question of interest here was whether the processing of place is carried out independently of the consonants' *manner* of articulation; that is, whether the place property is extracted from stops (e.g., [b]), nasals (e.g., [m]) and fricatives (e.g., [v]) in a unitary fashion, or whether place is extracted from each of these major classes individually.

The test series of the experiments consisted of the synthetic [bæ]–[dæ]–[gæ] series constructed by Pisoni (1971). The adapting stimuli consisted of five real-speech syllables, [bæ], [pʰæ], [mæ], [væ], and [wæ], all of which contain a labial initial segment (Chomsky & Halle, 1968).

A sizable adaptation effect restricted to the [bæ]–[dæ] phonetic boundary was obtained for the [bæ]–[dæ]–[gæ] test series after adaptation with each of the real-speech syllables [bæ], [pʰæ], [mæ], and [væ]. A slight and inconsistent effect on the locus of the same boundary was obtained after adaptation with the semivowel [wæ]. The data for a single subject appear in Fig. 5.

The crossed-manner adaptation effects obtained for the adapting syllables [mæ] and [væ] suggest the presence of a single set of analyzers specialized for extracting *place* information from the consonants, irrespective of the particular manner class of consonant to which the consonants belong (stop, nasal, or fricative). In addition, the lack of consistent shifts after adaptation with [wæ] suggests that the presence of a relatively rapid spectral change at the onset of the syllable may be an important trigger feature of these analyzers. Although [wæ] contains rising second- and third-formant transitions (similar in direction to the transitions for [bæ], [mæ], and [væ]), the slopes of these transitions are not nearly as steep as for the stop, nasal, and fricative consonants, and, in addition, the duration of the transitions for [wæ] are about twice as long (see spectrograms of [bæ] and [wæ] in Fig. 6).

A related property of the place analyzers has been studied by Ades (1974b), in an experiment designed to test whether the adaptation effects for place transfer from one syllable position to another. This question was of interest because the formant transitions distinguishing place in syllable-initial consonants are acoustically quite different from those that distinguish place in syllable-final consonants, the transitions being nearly mirror images

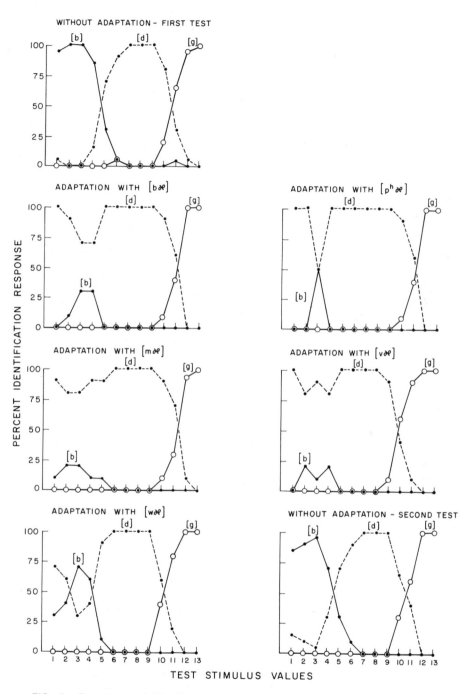

FIG. 5. Percentage of identification responses ([b], [d], or [g]) obtained for a single listener in the unadapted state and after adaptation with [bæ], [pʰæ], [mæ], [væ], and [wæ]. (From Cooper & Blumstein, 1974.)

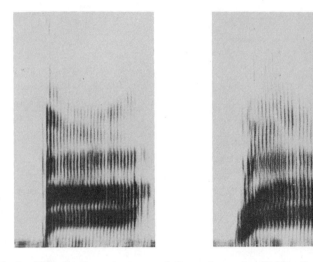

FIG. 6. Wide-band spectrograms of the real speech syllables [bæ] and [wæ] used as adapting stimuli in the Cooper and Blumstein (1974) study. The spectrogram on the left represents [bæ].

of one another (Liberman *et al.,* 1954). Two series of stimuli were constructed which varied in the second- and third-formant transitions, one series ranging from [bæ] to [dæ], the other series ranging from [æb] to [æd].

No place-specific transfer effects of adaptation were obtained across the two syllable positions. Significant effects were obtained, however, when the adapting and test stimuli contained consonants in the same syllable position.

From the combined results of Ades (1974b) and Cooper and Blumstein (1974), it appears that place analyzers exist which extract information about place independent of the major manner classes of stop, nasal, and fricative, and yet process this information for initial and final consonants separately. Furthermore, the analyzers that extract place for initial consonants appear to be activated by the presence of a rapid spectral change at the onset of the syllable. The existence of this trigger feature would allow us to account not only for the failure to obtain consistent adaptation shifts with the semivowel [w] (Cooper & Blumstein, 1974), but also for the failure to obtain shifts for initial consonants after adaptation with VC syllables (Ades, 1974b), since the latter contain steady-state initial segments. A study by Tash (1974) indicates that if this proposed trigger feature exists it operates at the level of phonetic as opposed to auditory analysis.

PERCEPTUOMOTOR ADAPTATION TO SPEECH

Historical Perspective

The possibility that the perception and production of speech are subserved by a common mechanism has been considered over a period of centuries. According to Stevens and Halle (1967), the issue was raised over 300 years ago by G. de Cordemoy (1668)[7]:

> Lastly, I am to take notice, that there is so great a Communication and correspondency between the Nerves of the Ear, and those of the Larynx, that whensoever any sound agitates the Brain, there flow immediately spirits towards the Muscles of the Larynx, which duely dispose them to form a sound altogether like that, which was just not striking the Brain. And although I well conceive that there needs some *time* to facilitate those motions of the Muscles of the Throat, so the Sounds, which excite the Brain the first time, cannot be easily expressed by the Throat, yet notwithstanding I do as well conceive, that by virtue of repeating them it will come to pass, that the Brain, which thereby is often shaken in the same places, sends such a plenty of spirits through the nerves, that are inserted in the Muscles of the Throat, that at length they easily move all the cartilages, which serve for that action, as 'tis requisite they should be moved to form Sounds like those, that have shaken the Brain.

Almost 170 years later, von Humboldt (1836) expressed a similar strong belief in perceptuomotor processing for speech (see the passage cited by Stevens & House, 1972).

For a number of good reasons, the "strong" form of the motor theory of speech perception noted above, which posits that the sounds of speech are in fact perceived by direct reference to articulatory gestures, has been replaced in modern times by a "weaker" form (see Liberman *et al.*, 1967, for grounds on which this form is based), in which perception is mediated by a central processor believed to control both perception and articulation. The analysis-by-synthesis model of speech perception proposed by Stevens and Halle (Stevens, 1972; Stevens & Halle, 1967; Stevens & House, 1972) is the most explicit form of this theory, although no attempt has been made to provide anything approaching a direct test of its validity (Bailey & Haggard, 1973; Chistovich, Klass, & Kuz'min, 1963; Kozhevnikov & Chistovich, 1965). Our preliminary experiments in perceptuomotor adaptation have been designed to test the most general assumption underlying the analysis-by-synthesis model: namely, that the perception and production of speech do invoke a common mechanism at some stage of processing.

---

[7] I have tried in earnest to unearth still older proclamations on this topic but have met with no success thus far.

It now appears, however, that the experimental paradigm used to study this general assumption can be applied to study details of the mechanism as well.

Perceptuomotor Experiments

Cooper (1974d) designed a first experiment to determine whether perceptual adaptation might influence an aspect of speech production. The aspect of articulation chosen for study was the dimension of voice onset time (Lisker & Abramson, 1964). This temporal relation was selected both because (*a*) it can be measured from real speech waveforms with a reasonable degree of accuracy and speed, and (*b*) a sizable body of evidence had already been gathered regarding perceptual adaptation to the VOT dimension (see the previous discussion).

In the experiment, subjects were instructed to utter a given CV syllable, either [bi] or [pʰi], after listening to repetitions of either of these two syllables (VOTs,0 msec for [bi] and +80 msec for [pʰi]) or to repetitions of the isolated vowel [i]. Adaptation with the isolated vowel was designed to provide a base-line measure of VOT production values, to be compared with the values of VOT obtained after adaptation with the CV syllables [bi] and [pʰi]. During the periods of perceptual adaptation, subjects were required to hold their tongues firmly between their teeth and lips and were instructed to minimize subvocalization.[8]

An analysis of the utterances was carried out to determine whether the VOT values varied systematically as a function of perceptual adaptation. The speech waveforms were studied oscillographically, using a computer-controlled cursor to mark the onset of the release burst of the consonant and the onset of voicing for each utterances (Huggins, 1969). The time interval between these two marks was taken as the measure of VOT and was displayed on the oscilloscope screen to the nearest 100 μsec. Individual VOT measurements were estimated to be accurate within ± 1 msec, except in the case of [bi] utterances having VOT values near 0 msec (voicing onset simultaneous with the release burst), where the accuracy was reduced to about ± 3 msec.

The outcome of the experiment was as follows. A significant shift was obtained for the VOT distribution of the [pʰi] utterances after adaptation to [pʰi], as compared with the VOTs obtained in the base-line condition (adaptation with the vowel [i]). The direction of this adaptation shift was toward shorter VOT values, and the average magnitude of effect was 5.6 msec.

---

[8] It is recognized that subvocalization cannot be entirely prevented by these simple precautions. Yet, more sophisticated means of reducing subvocalization (Glassman, 1972) do not entirely eliminate subvocalization in any case; such procedures also introduce confounding factors that alter the subject's attention.

No systematic effect of adaptation was observed overall for the [bi] utterances, however. A look at the VOT distributions for the [bi] and [pʰi] utterances, based on a total of 640 utterances obtained from 16 subjects (see Figs. 7 and 8) reveals a difference between these utterances that may help to account for the difference in effectiveness of the adaptation procedure. Whereas the VOT values of the [pʰi] utterances are distributed in approximately Gaussian fashion under both test conditions, the distribution of the [bi] utterances does not approximate a Gaussian function and shows a very strong clustering of responses within the narrow VOT range between 0 and 20 msec. The distributional difference between the [bi] and [pʰi] utterances, also obtained in earlier measurements of VOT production under normal speaking conditions (Lisker & Abramson, 1964), was observed for the majority of individual subjects as well as for the group as a whole.

The clustering of the [bi] responses between 0 and 20 msec VOT indicates the presence of a stable target region for [bi] VOT production. Ohala (1970), among others, has pointed out that the relative stability of VOTs for voiced stops is a consequence of a simple mechanical coupling by airflow; voiceless stop VOTs, in contrast, are influenced by a number of additional factors, and it remains for us to determine whether one or a combination of these factors accounts for the adaptation effect. The possibility of studying voice-timing control factors that are manifest in the peripheral

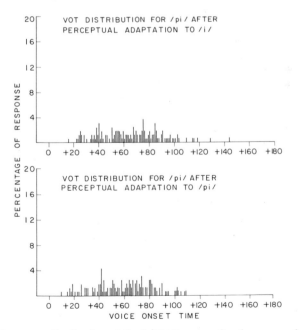

FIG. 7. Frequency distribution of the [pʰi] utterances for the group of 16 subjects. (From Cooper, 1974d.)

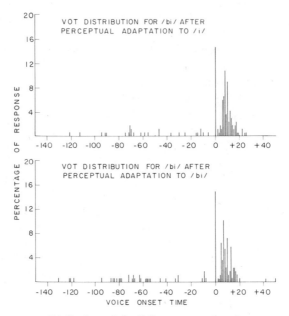

FIG. 8. Frequency distribution of the [bi] utterances for the group of 16 subjects. (From Cooper, 1974d.)

physiology of the vocal tract is being considered in this regard (Cooper & Nager, forthcoming).

It, of course, remains conceivable that adaptation effects did, in fact, occur for the [bi] utterances in the perceptuomotor study, but that these shifts were not systematic in direction across subjects. Some individuals did show fairly large shifts in VOT values after adaptation with [bi], as compared with the base line performance, although it was not clear whether such shifts represented an effect of adaptation or merely the extent of inherent base-line variability for VOT production. Further experiments, however, have revealed that these shifts are most probably a reflection of baseline variability rather than perceptuomotor adaptation (Cooper & Lauritsen, 1974).

The results obtained for the [pʰi] utterances of the perceptuomotor study provided initial support for the presence of direct interplay between speech perception and production. Most important, the effects for [pʰi] were shown not to be attributable to either (a) articulatory compensation for distorted perception or (b) voluntary mimicry of the adapting syllable (see Cooper, 1974d for details).

If perceptuomotor effects represented a compensation for perceptual shifts (Eimas & Corbit, 1973), we should expect the VOT values for [pʰi] to become longer. Rather the perceptuomotor effects are in the same direction as the same perceptual effects (i.e., after adaptation to [pʰ], stimuli with long-lag VOTs are perceived as having shorter VOTs and are produced with shorter VOTs), suggesting that both effects reflect the fatiguing of the same mechanism (see Cooper, 1974d, for details). The data from the perceptuomotor study also indicate that the effect obtained for the [pʰi] utterances cannot be accounted for by simple mimicry of the perceived adapting stimulus, since subjects' VOTs did not shift systematically with respect to the absolute VOT value of the [pʰi] adapting stimulus (+80-msec VOT). In particular, some subjects showing the overall shortening effect on VOT had values of VOT that were closer to the value of the adapting stimulus after adaptation, while others showing the same overall effect had VOT values further removed from the +80 value after adaptation. In addition to these results, a mimicry interpretation could not account for the crossed-adaptation results of Cooper and Lauritsen (1974).

Further experiments have been conducted to test the reliability and generality of the original perceptuomotor effects. In one series of experiments (Cooper & Lauritsen), we have obtained evidence that the perceptuomotor effect generalizes to [tʰi] utterances in a crossed-adaptation test. In this test, subjects listened to repetitions of [i], [pʰi], or [bi] as in the original perceptuomotor study, but were now required to utter the syllable [di] or [tʰi] after each minute of repetitive listening. After adaptation to [pʰi], it was found that the VOT values for the [tʰi] utterances were significantly shorter than in the control condition ($p < .01$, $N = 32$); the average magnitude of this crossed-adaptation effect was 3.2 msec, slightly larger than the effect obtained for [pʰi] utterances for the same subjects. The effect for the [tʰi] utterances not only provided further support for the existence of perceptuomotor interaction, but also indicated that this interaction operates during at least one particular stage of speech information processing—namely, the stage involved in the processing of *feature* information.

Since the completion of this work, Cooper and Nager (forthcoming) have found that the magnitude and consistency of the perceptuomotor adaptation effect can be enhanced by embedding the voiceless stop within a bisyllabic context (e.g., [rətʰí]) and that the magnitude of effect in this test situation is decidedly larger for alveolar as opposed to labial stops ([rətʰí] versus [rəpʰí] utterances showed mean adaptation effects of 6.5 and 2.7 msec of VOT respectively, $N = 22$). In addition, Cooper and Nager have proposed a general, yet explicit, neural model of the perceptuomotor system in order to provide a first step in describing the site and operation of the perceptuomotor adaptation effect and its relation to the effects obtained in "purely" perceptual adaptation studies. This model makes predictions about related voice-timing phenomena currently under study (see Cooper & Nager, forthcoming, for details).

A closely related set of experiments has been designed to test the possibility of obtaining a converse perceptuomotor adaptation effect; that is, an effect of speech production on speech perception. In these experiments (Cooper, Blumstein, & Nigro, forthcoming), we adapted subjects by requiring them to utter repetitions of a given CV syllable ([bæ], [mæ], [væ]) in a whispered voice for 1-min periods. During adaptation, subjects repeated the adapting syllable at a rate of about one repetition per second while listening to white noise over headphones. The presentation of noise served to prevent both auditory and bone-conducted feedback.

After each minute of articulatory adaptation, subjects were presented test syllables auditorily from the [bæ]–[dæ]–[gæ] place series, to be identified as either [b], [d], or [g]. Sizable adaptation effects were obtained after the repetitive articulation. These effects were virtually identical to the phonetic boundary shifts obtained in earlier perceptual adaptation tests along the same stimulus series (Cooper, 1974c).

VISUOAUDITORY ADAPTATION

The results of the perceptuomotor studies have encouraged us to try to find other instances of cross-modality adaptation to speech variables. One such attempt, involving visuoauditory adaptation, was undertaken recently to provide a convincing test of the presence of a phonetic (as opposed to auditory) component of the selective adaptation effects (see previous discussion). In the experiment (Cooper & Ebert, unpublished data), subjects were instructed to monitor visually presented words which contained either voiced or voiceless stop consonants (i.e., "bob"–"bog" or "pop"–"pot" were presented in a given session). These words were presented using capital and small letters in a rapid random sequence, and the subjects' task was to press alternate keys, depending on the particular word that was being presented, independent of whether that word was presented in capital or small print. This monitoring task was employed to encourage subjects to read the visually presented words. After 30 sec of this sort of visual adaptation and monitoring with words containing either voiced or voiceless stops, the subjects were presented syllables auditorily from a [ba]–[pʰa] series, to be identified as "B" or "P" as in earlier work. Using this procedure, consistent cross-modality effects of adaptation have been obtained, although the data obtained thus far are still preliminary and do not mirror the usual auditory adaptation effects in all major respects. In any event, the outcome of the experiment should be of some importance, since, to the extent that such visuoauditory effects can be shown to coincide with the effects obtained in regular auditory experiments, the case favoring a phonetic component of selective adaptation would be strengthened considerably.

The visuoauditory paradigm used here is of interest for another, more general, reason, in that this paradigm provides a fairly direct means of testing the hypothesis that a phonetic stage of encoding is involved during the process of normal reading (see for reviews Kavanagh & Mattingly, 1972; Smith, 1973). Whereas previous attempts to test this general hypothesis relied on word or phrase recognition tasks that are quite removed from the normal reading situation (Baron, 1973), the selective adaptation paradigm can be applied to the same problem in a more natural setting. In particular, full paragraphs can be used as the "adapting" stimuli.

Cooper and Provenzano (unpublished) have constructed paragraphs that are quite heavily weighted in either voiced or voiceless consonants and have used these paragraphs in a visuoauditory adaptation experiment:

> The following is an example used in this study.
> The fans crowded into the Toronto stadium to see the Leafs play the Philadelphia Flyers for the fifth time this season. A strain of revenge was evident among the Toronto team—four time losers. The first period saw three pucks fly into the Toronto net, scored by the skillful Flyers with just flicks of the wrist. A slap shot by Pierre Contreau, just traded from another team, went into the Toronto net untouched at the start of the second period. The furious fans started to scream and shout at the pitiful play of the Toronto players. Finally, in the third period, a fight started after the Toronto Center was tripped as he tried to slap the puck into the Flyer's net. Two Toronto players landed the first punches and were penalized and later suspended from play. The frustrated fans cleared the stadium quickly after the fight, effectively conceding Toronto's fifth straight loss.

This paragraph is heavily weighted in voiceless consonants such as [p], [t], [k], [f], and [s].

The subjects were instructed to read each of the paragraphs at normal speed and, as soon as each paragraph was completed, the subjects were tested auditorily on identification of stimuli from a [ba]–[pa] series. Preliminary data obtained in this visuoauditory experiment reveal effects that closely correspond to those obtained in the word-monitoring experiment discussed above, and we are actively continuing our work in this area. It is hoped that the outcome of the visuo-auditory experiments will help to determine whether normal reading typically involves a stage of phonetic encoding intermediate to the stage of (*a*) preliminary visual processing and (*b*) semantic–syntactic processing.

CONCLUDING REMARKS

It is believed that the selective adaptation technique will continue to be useful for investigating aspects of the speech-processing system, so long as researchers can isolate and deal with individual components of the effect and study their controlled interaction. The conditions of the foregoing proviso are far easier to state than to meet in actuality. Nevertheless, the proviso must be met if the technique is to help resolve some of the outstanding questions in speech-information processing. These questions, to which much of our future research will be directed, include the following:

1. Which auditory cues are processed as such during the preliminary stages of speech perception?
2. Are these auditory cues processed serially or in parallel?
3. Are these cues processed independently of each other or in a contingent manner?
4. Which *phonetic* features are extracted as such during speech perception? Are these features processed serially? Are these features processed independently of each other?
5. Are auditory and phonetic information processed serially *with respect to each other* (see Wood, Chapter 3 of this volume, who has studied this problem using acoustic cues to pitch versus place of articulation)? Does Wood's analysis apply to the case of auditory versus phonetic information when both types of information serve to cue a phonemic distinction (e.g., VOT versus voicing)?
6. What is the site and nature of the perceptuomotor interface?

Our planned model of the flow of information during speech processing will, in large part, rest on the answers we can obtain to these six questions.

The projected use of the adaptation technique should allow researchers to put these and other problems of speech processing to a more critical test than has been possible in the past. Almost as a direct consequence, current hypotheses about speech processing will be more quickly refuted than in the past. We must surely regard this increase in the hypothesis turnover rate as a welcome professional hazard, and join our colleagues in linguistics who readily admit that the average half-life of a linguistic theory is about 19 minutes, except perhaps when it is formulated on a Friday afternoon.

ACKNOWLEDGMENTS

This work was supported by NIH Training Grant No. NIH-5-T01-GM01064-12 to the Department of Psychology, M.I.T. Special thanks are due to Kenneth N. Stevens, W. Francis Ganong, Alvin M. Liberman, Hans-Lukas Teuber, and Anthony E. Ades for many helpful comments.

REFERENCES

Abercrombie, D. *Elements of general phonetics*. Chicago: Aldine, 1967.

Ades, A. E. A bilateral component in speech perception? *Journal of the Acoustical Society of America,* 1974, **55,** 610–616. (a)

Ades, A. E. How phonetic is selective adaptation? Experiments on syllabic position and vowel environment. *Perception & Psychophysics,* 1974, **16,** 61–66. (b).

Appley, M. H. (Ed.) *Adaptation-Level theory*. New York: Academic Press, 1971.

Bailey, P. Perceptual adaptation for acuostical features in speech. *Speech perception: Report on research in progress in the Department of Psychology, The Queen's University of Belfast, Northern Ireland,* 1973, **2.2,** 29–34.

Bailey, P. J., & Haggard, M. P. Perception and production: Some correlations on voicing of an initial stop. *Language & Speech,* 1973, **16,** 189–195.

Barlow, H. B. Dark and light adaptation. In D. Jameson & L. M. Hurvich (Eds.), *Handbook of Sensory Physiology,* Vol. VII/4. Berlin: Springer-Verlag, 1972.

Baron, J. Phonemic stage not necessary for reading. *Quarterly Journal of Experimental Psychology,* 1973, **25,** 241–246.

Bocca, E., & Calearo, C. Central hearing processes. In J. Jerger (Ed.), *Modern developments in audiology*. New York: Academic Press, 1963.

Chistovich, L. A., Klass, Iu. A., & Kuz'min, Iu. I. The process of speech sound discrimination. Research Translation ETR 63-10, Air Force, Cambridge Research Laboratories, Bedford, Massachusetts, 1963.

Chomsky, N., & Halle, M. *The sound pattern of English*. New York: Harper & Row, 1968.

Cooper, W. E. Selective adaptation for acoustic cues of voicing in initial stops, *Journal of Phonetics,* 1974, **2,** 303–313.   (a)

Cooper, W. E. Contingent feature analysis in speech perception. *Perception & Psychophysics,* 1974, **16,** 201–204.   (b)

Cooper, W. E. Adaptation of phonetic feature analyzers for place of articulation. *Journal of the Acoustical Society of America,* 1974, **56,** 617–627.   (c)

Cooper, W. E. Perceptuo-motor adaptation to a speech feature. *Perception & Psychophysics,* 1974, **16,** 229–234.   (d)

Cooper, W. E., & Blumstein, S. E. A 'labial' feature analyzer in speech perception. *Perception and Psychophysics,* 1974, **15,** 591–600.

Cooper, W. E., Blumstein, S. E., & Nigro, G. Articulatory effects on speech perception: A preliminary report, forthcoming.

Cooper, W. E., & Lauritsen, M. Feature processing in the perception and production of speech. *Nature,* 1974, **252,** 121–123.

Cooper, W. E., & Nager, R. M. Perceptuo-motor adaptation to speech: An analysis of bisyllabic utterances and a neural model, forthcoming.

de Cordemoy, G. *A philosophical discourse concerning speech*. London: J. Martin, 1668.

Delattre, P. C., Liberman, A. M., & Cooper, F. S. Acoustic loci and transitional cues for consonants. *Journal of the Acoustical Society of America,* 1955, **27,** 769–773.

Eimas, P. D. Speech perception in early infancy. In L. B. Cohen & P. Salapatek (Eds.), *Infant perception*. New York: Academic Press. (to appear).

Eimas, P. D. Auditory and linguistic processing of cues for place of articulation by infants. (forthcoming).

Eimas, P. D., & Corbit, J. D. Selective adaptation of linguistic feature detectors. *Cognitive Psychology,* 1973, **4,** 99–109.

Eimas, P. D., Cooper, W. E., & Corbit, J. D. Some properties of linguistic feature detectors. *Perception & Psychophysics,* 1973, **13,** 247–252.

Engen, T. Olfactory psychophysics. In L. M. Beidler (Ed.) *Handbook of sensory physiology.* Volume IV/1. Berlin: Springer-Verlag, 1971.

Fant, G. *Speech sounds and features.* Cambridge, Massachusetts: MIT Press, 1973.

Fidell, L. S. Orientation specificity in chromatic adaptation of human 'edge-detectors.' *Perception & Psychophysics,* 1970, **8,** 235–236.

Glassman, W. E. Subvocal activity and acoustic confusions in short-term memory. *Journal of Experimental Psychology,* 1972, **96,** 164–169.

Goldstein, L. M., & Lackner, J. R. Alterations of the phonetic coding on speech sounds during repetition. *Cognition,* 1974, **2,** 279–297.

Haggard, M., Ambler, S., & Callow, M. Pitch as a voicing cue. *Journal of the Acoustical Society of America,* 1970, **47,** 613–617.

Halle, M., Hughes, G. W., & Radley, J.-P. A. Acoustic properties of stop consonants. *Journal of the Acoustical Society of America,* 1957, **29,** 107–116.

Harris, C. S., & Gibson, A. R. Is orientation-specific color adaptation in human vision due to edge-detectors, after-images, or "dipoles?" *Science,* 1968, **162,** 1506–1507.

Held, R., & Shattuck, S. R. Color- and edge-sensitive channels in the human visual system: Tuning for orientation. *Science,* 1971, **174,** 314–316.

Helson, H. *Adaptation-level theory: An experimental and systematic approach to behavior.* New York: Harper, 1964.

Huggins, A. W. F. A facility for studying perception of timing in natural speech. *Quarterly Progress Report of the Research Laboratory of Electronics, M.I.T.,* 1969, **95,** 81–83.

von Humboldt, W. *Über die Verschiedenheit des menschlichen Sprachbaues,* 1836. (1960 fascimile edition of the 1st German edition of 1836, Ferdinand Dümmlers, Bonn.)

Jakobson, R., Fant, C. G. M., & Halle, M. *Preliminaries to speech analysis.* Cambridge, Massachusetts: MIT Press, 1963.

Jameson, D., & Hurvich, L. M. Color adaptation: Sensitivity, contrast, and after-images. In D. Jameson & L. M. Hurvich (Eds.), *Handbook of sensory physiology,* Vol. VII/4. Berlin: Springer-Verlag, 1972.

Kavanagh, J. F., & Mattingly, I. G. (Eds.) *Language by ear and by eye.* Cambridge, Massachusetts: MIT Press, 1972.

Kenshalo, D. R. The cutaneous senses. In J. W. Kling & L. A. Riggs (Eds.), *Woodworth & Schlosberg's experimental psychology* (3rd ed.). New York: Holt, 1971.

Kimura, D. Cerebral dominance and the perception of verbal stimuli. *Canadian Journal of Psychology,* 1961, **15,** 166–171.

Klatt, D. H. Voice-onset time, frication and aspiration in word-initial consonant clusters. *Quarterly Progress Report of the Research Laboratory of Electronics, M.I.T.,* 1973, **95,** 81–83.

Klatt, D. H. An acoustic theory of terminal catalog speech synthesis and a control strategy for the replication of a natural utterance. (Forthcoming).

Kozhevnikov, V. A., & Chistovich, L. Speech: Articulation and perception, *Joint Publication Research Services, U.S. Dept. of Commerce,* 1965, **30,** 543.

Ladefoged, P. *Preliminaries to linguistic phonetics*. Chicago: Univ. of Chicago Press, 1971.

Lashley, K. S. The problem of serial order in behavior. In L. A. Jeffress (Ed.), *Cerebral mechanisms in behavior*. New York: Wiley, 1951.

Liberman, A. M. Some results of research on speech perception. *Journal of the Acoustical Society of America*, 1957, **29**, 117–123.

Liberman, A. M., Cooper, F. S., Shankweiler, D. P., & Studdert-Kennedy, M. Perception of the speech code. *Psychological Review*, 1967, **74**, 431–461.

Liberman, A. M., Delattre, P. C., Cooper, F. S., & Gerstman, L. J. The role of consonant–vowel transitions in the perception of the stop and nasal consonants. *Psychological Monographs*, 1954, **68**, 1–13.

Liberman, A. M., Harris, K. S., Hoffman, H. S., & Griffith, B. C. The discrimination of speech sounds within and across phoneme boundaries. *Journal of Experimental Psychology*, 1957, **54**, 358–368.

Lisker, L., & Abramson, A. S. A cross-language study of voicing in initial stops: Acoustical measurements. *Word*, 1964, **20**, 384–422.

Lisker, L., & Abramson, A. S. Some effects of context on voice onset time in English stops. *Language & Speech*, 1967, **10**, 1–28.

Lisker, L., & Abramson, A. S. The voicing dimension: Some experiments in comparative phonetics. In *Proceedings of the Sixth International Congress of Phonetic Sciences, Prague, 1967*. Prague: Academia, 1970.

Mattingly, I. G., Liberman, A. M., Syrdal, A. K., & Hawles, T. Discrimination in speech and nonspeech modes. *Cognitive Psychology*, 1971, **2**, 131–157.

Mayhew, J. E. W., & Anstis, S. M. Movement after effects contingent on color, intensity, and pattern. *Perception & Psychophysics*, 1972, **12**, 77–85.

McCollough, C. Color adaptation of edge-detectors in the human visual system. *Science*, 1965, **149**, 1115–1116.

Ohala, J. J. Aspects of the control and production of speech. *UCLA Working Papers in Phonetics*, 1970, **15**.

Peterson, L. R., & Johnson, S. T. Some effects of minimizing articulation on short-term retention. *Journal of Verbal Learning & Verbal Behavior*, 1971, **10**, 346–354.

Pfaffmann, C., Bartoshuk, L. M., & McBurney, D. H. Taste psychophysics. In L. M. Beidler (Ed.), *Handbook of sensory physiology*, Vol. IV/2. Berlin: Springer-Verlag, 1971.

Pisoni, D. B. On the nature of categorical perception of speech sounds. Unpublished doctoral dissertation, University of Michigan, 1971. (Also in *Supplement to Status Report on Speech Research*, Haskins Laboratories, New Haven, Connecticut, November, 1971.)

Port, D. K., & Preston, M. S. Early apical stop production: A voice onset time analysis. *Haskins Status Report on Speech Research*, **SR-29/30**, 1972, 125–149.

Preston, M. S. Some comments on the developmental aspects of voicing in stop consonants. In D. L. Horton & J. J. Jenkins (Eds.), *Perception of Language*. Columbus, Ohio: Charles Merrill, 1971.

Riggs, L. A., & Wooten, B. R. Electrical measures and psychophysical data on human vision. In D. Jameson & L. M. Hurvich (Eds.), *Handbook of sensory physiology*, Vol. VII/4. Berlin: Springer-Verlag, 1972.

Sawusch, J. R., & Pisoni, D. B. Category boundaries for speech and nonspeech sounds. Paper presented at the 86th Meeting of the Acoustical Society of America, Los Angeles, California, November 1, 1973.

Sawusch, J. R., Pisoni, D. B., & Cutting, J. E. Category boundaries for linguistic and nonlinguistic dimensions of the same stimuli. Paper presented at the 87th Meeting of the Acoustical Society of America, New York City, April 25, 1974.

Small, A. M. Auditory adaptation. In J. Jerger (Ed.), *Modern developments in audiology*. New York: Academic Press, 1963.

Smith, F. (Ed.) *Psycholinguistics and reading*. New York: Holt, Rinehart & Winston, 1973.

Smith, P. T. Feature-testing models and their application to perception and memory for speech. *Quarterly Journal of Experimental Psychology*, 1973, **25**, 511–534.

Stevens, K. N. Segments, features, and analysis by synthesis. In J. F. Kavanagh & I. G. Mattingly (Eds.), *Language by eye and ear: The relationships between speech and reading*. Cambridge, Massachusetts: MIT Press, 1972.

Stevens, K. N. The potential role of property detectors in the perception of consonants. Paper presented at the Symposium on Auditory Analysis and Perception of Speech, Leningrad, USSR, August, 1973.

Stevens, K. N., & Halle, M. Remarks on analysis by synthesis and distinctive features. In W. Wathen-Dunn (Ed.), *Models for the perception of speech and visual form*. Cambridge, Massachusetts: MIT Press, 1967.

Stevens, K. N., & House, A. S. Speech perception. In J. Tobias (Ed.), *Foundations of Modern Auditory Theory*, Vol. II. New York: Academic Press, 1972.

Stevens, K. N., & Klatt, D. H. Role of formant transitions in the voiced–voiceless distinction for stops. *Journal of the Acoustical Society of America*, 1974, **55**, 653–659.

Studdert-Kennedy, M. Speech perception. In J. Lass (Ed.), *Contemporary issues in experimental phonetics*. Springfield, Illinois: Thomas, 1974.

Studdert-Kennedy, M., & Shankweiler, D. Hemispheric specialization for speech perception. *Journal of the Acoustical Society of America*, 1970, **48**, 579–594.

Studdert-Kennedy, M., Shankweiler, D., & Pisoni, D. B. Auditory and phonetic processes in speech perception: Evidence from a dichotic study. *Cognitive Psychology*, 1972, **3**, 455–466.

Summerfield, A. Q., & Haggard, M. P. Articulatory rate versus acoustical invariants in speech perception. Paper presented at the 83rd Meeting of the Acoustical Society of America, Buffalo, New York, April 18, 1972.

Tash, J. B. Selective adaptation of auditory feature detectors in speech perception. *Research on speech perception*, Department of Psychology, Indiana University, Progress Report No. 1, 33–81.

Ward, W. D. Auditory fatigue and masking. In J. Jerger (Ed.), *Modern developments in audiology*. New York: Academic Press, 1963.

Warren, R., & Gregory, R. An auditory analogue of the visual reversible figure. *American Journal of Psychology*, 1958, **71**, 612–613.

3

A NORMATIVE MODEL FOR REDUNDANCY GAINS IN SPEECH DISCRIMINATION

Charles C. Wood
Walter Reed Army Institute of Research

AUDITORY AND PHONETIC PROCESSES IN SPEECH PERCEPTION: SERIAL OR PARALLEL?

An important concept in recent speech-perception research is the distinction between auditory and phonetic levels of processing. Although this distinction has been made on intuitive grounds by a number of investigators (Fant, 1967; Fry, 1956; Liberman, Cooper, Shankweiler, & Studdert-Kennedy, 1967; Stevens & Halle, 1967; Stevens & House, 1972), it has been developed most extensively in the recent empirical and theoretical work of Studdert-Kennedy (in press a, b; Studdert-Kennedy & Shankweiler, 1970; Studdert-Kennedy, Shankweiler, & Pisoni, 1972). In brief summary, the auditory level is assumed to perform an analysis of the acoustic speech signal resulting in a corresponding set of nonlinguistic parameters such as the frequency spectrum of the signal, its amplitude, and changes in these parameters over time. In contrast, the phonetic level is assumed to perform abstract linguistic processes by which the particular acoustic cue or complex of cues for a given phonetic feature are extracted from the output of the auditory level.

Empirical support for the general distinction between auditory and phonetic processes has been obtained in a number of different experimental paradigms.[1] These results include:

[1] The references listed for each category are intended to be illustrative, not exaustive. For a comprehensive review and critical analysis of these and related experiments, see Studdert-Kennedy (in press b).

1. Error patterns and ear superiorities in dichotic listening tasks (Studdert-Kennedy & Shankweiler, 1970; Studdert-Kennedy *et al.,* 1972).
2. The "phoneme boundary effect" in discrimination among certain speech stimuli, a result obtained in accuracy data (Mattingly, Liberman, Syrdal, & Halwes, 1971; Pisoni, 1971, 1973), reaction time data (Pisoni & Tash, 1974), and average evoked potentials (Dorman, 1974).
3. Differential accuracy and ear superiorities for temporal-order-judgment of auditory and phonetic dimensions in dichotic tasks (Day, Cutting, & Copeland, 1971).
4. Differential interactions between auditory and phonetic dimensions in speeded classification tasks (Day & Wood, 1972).
5. Unilateral differences in average evoked potentials during classification of auditory and phonetic dimensions (Wood, Goff, & Day, 1971; Wood, 1975).
6. The relative effectiveness of various speech, speech-like, and non-speech stimuli in producing systematic phoneme boundary shifts in selective adaptation experiments (Ades, 1973, 1974; Bailey, 1973; Cooper, 1974, in press; Eimas & Corbit, 1973, Eimas, Cooper, & Corbit, 1973).

Although the distinction between auditory and phonetic processes in speech perception has considerable empirical support, a great deal remains to be determined concerning the specific processes performed by auditory and phonetic levels, as well as the nature of the interaction between them. To this end, Wood (1974) sought to determine whether auditory and phonetic levels are organized according to a strict sequential hierarchy, or whether some capability for simultaneous or parallel processing of auditory and phonetic information is available to the listener.[2]

The general supposition that linguistic processes are superimposed upon the general auditory system has been both implicit and explicit to varying degrees in a number of theoretical accounts of speech perception. For example, Stevens and House (1972) suggest:

> Certain concepts are common to almost all theories of speech perception. All acoustic signals undergo some common peripheral processing, and up to a certain point in the auditory system, the nature of this early processing is the same whether the signal is speech or is not speech. As a consequence

---

[2] Following Nickerson (1971), the terms "simultaneous" and "parallel" are used in the present paper to indicate ". . . that the processes in question are proceeding concurrently *relative to the time scale on which they are measured,* which is to admit the possibility of intermittent switching of attention between one process and another on a more microtemporal scale [p. 277]."

of this processing, the signal is transformed into some kind of neural space–time pattern, and it is assumed that all subsequent analyses and decisions with regard to the signal are based on observations or transformations of this pattern. In the case of speech signals, the listener presumably focuses on certain aspects of these patterns, and then processes them further in order to reach an organized linguistic description [p. 9].

In addition, however, Stevens and House and a number of other investigators have emphasized the likelihood of departures from a strict sequential or hierarchical organization: "Does the decoding proceed in cascade fashion with phonetic segments and features identified first, then morphemes, then larger syntactic units, in some ordered sequence? Or is there some sort of parallel computation in which decoding at all of these levels may occur simultaneously [p. 10]?" Similarly, Studdert-Kennedy (in press a) presents a view of the speech perception process

> . . . that entails, conceptually, at least these stages of analysis: 1) auditory, 2) phonetic, 3) phonological, 4) lexical, syntactic, and semantic. These stages form a conceptual hierarchy but in a working model must be both successive and simultaneous: tentative results from higher levels feed back to lower levels not only to permit correction of earlier decisions in light of later contradictions but also to permit partial determination of phonetic shape by phonological, syntactic, and semantic rules and decisions [p. 16].

For related discussions of serial and parallel processing in speech perception, see Liberman, Cooper, Shankweiler, and Studdert-Kennedy (1967), Lehiste (1972), Studdert-Kennedy (in press b), and Wickelgren (1972).

In attempting to distinguish between serial and parallel organizations of auditory and phonetic levels, Wood (1974) employed a two-choice speeded classification task similar to that previously used by Garner and Felfoldy (1970). Subjects received blocks of trials in which synthetic consonant–vowel (CV) syllables varied between two levels on a specified target dimension. By pressing one of the two response buttons, they were required, on each trial, to identify as rapidly as possible which level of the target dimension had been presented. Two stimulus dimensions were compared: an auditory (nonlinguistic) dimension, fundamental frequency (104 versus 140 Hz), and a phonetic dimension, place of articulation of the initial stop consonant ([b] versus [g]). For convenience, these two dimensions will be referred to as pitch and place, respectively. The two levels on the place and pitch dimensions were combined orthogonally to produce a stimulus set of four synthetic syllables: [bæ]–104 Hz, [bæ]–140 Hz, [gæ]–104 Hz, and [gæ]–140 Hz. The vowel context [æ] and all other acoustic parameters of the four stimuli were matched so that only the two target dimensions could be used to distinguish between stimuli.

TABLE 1
Representative Stimulus Sets for Control
and Correlated Conditions

	Condition	
Dimension	Control	Correlated
Place	[bæ] −104 Hz	[bæ] −104 Hz
	[gæ] −104 Hz	[gæ] −140 Hz
Pitch	[bæ] −104 Hz	[bæ] −104 Hz
	[bæ] −140 Hz	[gæ] −140 HZ

Response time (RT) for identification of each target dimension was obtained under three different conditions:

1. a single-dimension *control* condition, in which only the target dimension to be identified varied in the stimulus sequence;
2. a two-dimension *orthogonal* condition, in which both the target dimension and the irrelevant nontarget dimension varied independently;
3. a *correlated* condition, in which both dimensions again varied but were completely correlated or redundant.

The two conditions most important to the distinction between serial and parallel processing are the control and correlated conditions shown in Table 1. The control conditions provide an estimate of the base-line RT for the classification of each dimension alone, with the other dimension held constant.[3] In the correlated condition, both the target dimension and the redundant nontarget dimension provide sufficient information for a correct response. The outcome of interest is whether the additional information provided by the redundant dimension can be used to facilitate performance.

A strict serial organization of auditory and phonetic levels would require that auditory processing be completed before phonetic processing could begin. Thus, the serial model requires that RT for a given dimension in the correlated condition be no faster than the RT in the corresponding control condition. In contrast, given certain assumptions to be discussed in detail later, a class of parallel models predicts a significant decrease in RT (usually termed a "redundancy gain") in the correlated conditions relative to the control conditions for both dimensions.

[3] For simplicity, Table 1 presents only one of the two possible stimulus sets for each control condition. Half the subjects received the nontarget dimension held constant at the levels shown in Table 1 and half received the opposite levels.

TABLE 2
Mean RT (msec) for Place and Pitch in Control and Correlated Conditions[a]

Dimension	Condition	
	Control	Correlated
Place	386.8	342.8
Pitch	381.4	346.1

[a] From Wood (1974).

As shown in Table 2, the results of this experiment clearly reject the strict serial model. For the place dimension there was a decrease of 44.0 msec in the correlated condition relative to the control, and the corresponding decrease for pitch was 35.3 msec. Additional analyses of the data ruled out a number of possible ways in which redundancy gains could be obtained with an underlying serial model, including speed–accuracy trade-offs, selective serial processing, and differential transfer in favor of the correlated condition (for details, see Wood, 1974).

These results allow rejection of a strict serial or sequential organization of auditory and phonetic levels. Instead, the redundancy gains suggest that listeners possess the capability for some form of shared, simultaneous, or parallel processing of auditory and phonetic information. The remainder of this chapter is devoted to a more detailed examination of the processes that underlie such redundancy gains in speech discrimination.

The next two sections present a brief review of redundancy gains in previous multidimensional discrimination experiments and outline three process models that have been proposed to account for such results. The following section describes a normative model that enables the magnitude of the redundancy gain and the form of the redundant-dimension RT distribution to be predicted from empirical RT distributions for single dimensions. The final section compares the empirical redundancy gains obtained for auditory and phonetic dimensions to those predicted by the normative model.

REDUNDANCY GAINS IN DISCRIMINATION: A BRIEF REVIEW

To clarify the implications of the redundancy gains obtained by Wood (1974) for the organization of auditory and phonetic levels, it will be useful to consider previous experiments in which redundancy gains have been obtained.[4] Two experimental paradigms have typically been employed (*1*) absolute judgment tasks in which the primary dependent variable is response accuracy; and (*2*) speeded classification tasks in which accuracy is near perfect and the primary dependent variable is response speed.

In a now classic absolute judgment experiment, Eriksen and Hake (1955) employed three visual dimensions: hue, size, and brightness of color patches. Each dimension had 20 possible values or levels, with corresponding response categories 1–20. For judgment of the single dimensions alone, average information transmission (contingent uncertainty between stimuli and responses) was 2.75 bits. For correlated presentation of pairs of dimensions (i.e., hue–size, hue–brightness, and size–brightness), average information transmission increased to 3.43 bits. Finally, when all three dimensions were varied in correlated fashion, information transmission increased further to 4.11 bits. Thus, additional information provided by redundant dimensions produced clear performance facilitation in the form of increased accuracy of response. In another absolute judgment experiment, Lockhead (1966) obtained similar results for judgment of line length and line position. Average information transmission for length alone was 1.07 bits, for position alone .99 bits, and for correlated length and position 1.22 bits. Under more difficult viewing conditions the corresponding values were .19, .47, and .58 bits, respectively.

In contrast to the experiments of Eriksen and Hake (1955) and Lockhead (1966) in which clear redundancy gains were obtained, Garner and Lee (1962) found no gain for absolute judgment of redundant patterns of ✕'s and ◯'s. The possibility that this discrepancy could be related to differences in the nature of the stimulus dimensions between the Eriksen and Hake (1955), Lockhead (1966), and Garner and Lee (1962) experiments has been extensively discussed elsewhere (Garner, 1970, 1972, 1974; Garner & Felfoldy, 1970; Lockhead, 1966), and will not be considered in detail here.

A second major source of evidence concerning the effect of redundant dimensions on discrimination performance is based on speeded classification experiments. In contrast to the absolute-judgment task, performance in the speeded classification paradigm is speed- rather than accuracy-limited, and the primary dependent variable is the response time for classification in the single-dimension and redundant-dimension conditions.

---

[4] In a review of the effects of redundancy on discrimination, Garner (1972) has suggested a number of distinct ways in which redundancy can improve performance, depending upon the nature of performance limitations. The data considered in this paper correspond most closely to Garner's "redundancy that increases dimensional discriminability."

Available speeded classification experiments have employed either discrete RT tasks or card-sorting tasks in which time for sorting decks of stimulus cards is measured. Morton (1969a) compared sorting times for three different decks of stimulus cards: a digit deck, in which the six alternative stimuli were the single digits 1–6; a numerosity deck, in which the six alternative stimuli were one through six $\times$'s; and a redundant deck in which the six stimuli were the linearly redundant combinations of the two single dimensions (five 5's, six 6's, etc.). Sorting times for the redundant deck were consistently faster than those for either single dimension. Garner (1969) performed a similar experiment using distance between a pair of dots, orientation of the pair, and position of the pair as stimulus dimensions in a card-sorting task. Redundancy gains in the form of decreased sorting times were obtained for two- and three-dimensional redundant pairings. Finally, in an extensive series of card-sorting experiments, Garner and Felfoldy (1970) investigated single dimension and redundant bidimension performance for a number of different pairs of stimulus dimensions. A significant redundancy gain was obtained for classification of value and chroma of Munsell color chips when the two dimensions varied in a single chip. In contrast, no gain was obtained for the same two dimensions when they were presented on separate adjacent chips. Together with evidence from direct similarity scaling (Hyman & Well, 1968), free-classification (Handel & Imai, 1972), and speeded classification data for orthogonal stimulus dimensions, these results led Garner and Felfoldy (1970) to propose two general classes of stimulus dimensions termed "integral" and "separable" (see Garner, 1974, for a comprehensive review).

Only one discrete RT experiment directly analogous to that of Wood (1974) has been reported.[5] Biederman and Checkosky (1970) compared RT for classification of brightness and size of visual stimuli in two conditions analogous to the control and correlated conditions previously described. Significant redundancy gains were obtained under both low- and high-discriminability conditions. In the low-discriminability condition the

---

[5] "Same–different" RT experiments are related to the question of redundancy gains in both methodological and theoretical terms (cf. Egeth, 1966; Hawkins, 1969; Nickerson, 1971; Saraga & Shallice, 1973). In these experiments, pairs of stimuli are presented and subjects are required to indicate whether they were "same" or "different" according to preestablished criteria. Particularly relevant to the issue of redundancy gains is the observation that "different" RTs are typically faster for stimulus pairs differing in multiple stimulus dimensions than for those differing in a single dimension (Nickerson, 1971). However, because of a number of methodological differences between the same–different and redundancy gain experiments, the same–different data are not considered further at this time.

average redundancy gain was 17 msec; the average gain in the high-discriminability condition was 6 msec. The results of this experiment are considered further in the context of the normative model to be presented later.

THREE PROCESS MODELS

Three broad classes of process models have been proposed to account for the improvement in discrimination performance produced by redundant dimensions. Since the principal goal of the present analysis is a more complete understanding of the redundancy gains in RT data for auditory and phonetic dimensions, the models are presented in a form appropriate for RT rather than accuracy data. Although the exact form of the models necessarily differs for the two different types of experiment, it should be emphasized that their underlying assumptions are very similar.[6]

The first two models to be considered have been discussed previously by a number of investigators, both for tasks involving dimensional redundancy and those involving redundancy produced by the addition of discrete stimulus elements (see also references in Footnote 5). The models are similar in that each assumes that information about component dimensions is processed simultaneously and independently. They differ in the locus at which information about each component is combined to produce a single response. The terminology of Morton (1969a) is employed for these models in the present paper. The third model involves a different set of assumptions, the most important of which is an emphasis on holistic processes rather than the independent processing of component dimensions.

Decision Combination Model

In addition to the basic assumption of simultaneous and independent processing of component dimensions, the decision combination model assumes that the completion times for the component processes are independent random variables. The categorization process leading to a response is assumed to be initiated as soon as a decision criterion is reached on

[6] Any theoretical analysis of redundancy gains must ultimately account for the obtained facilitation in both accuracy and RT data. Only in the past few years (cf. Garner & Felfoldy, 1970; Lockhead, 1972) have these two sets of data been integrated into a single conceptual framework. Current experiments in this laboratory are investigating the relation between response speed and accuracy for redundant and single dimension tasks in a single paradigm. A speeded classification task similar to that used by Wood (1974) is combined with a "deadline" or "forced-RT" procedure (cf. Green & Luce, 1973; Schouten & Bekker, 1967) to produce empirical speed–accuracy trade-offs for redundant and single-dimension conditions. These experiments should permit a more direct analysis of redundancy gains in speed and accuracy than has been possible to date.

either of the component dimensions.[7] If the distributions of the component processes overlap in time, the RT for redundant dimensions will be faster on average than that for either single dimension. Accuracy models related to the decision combination model have been discussed by Eriksen and Hake (1955), Garner and Flowers (1969), Green and Swets (1966), Hake, Rodwan, and Weintraub (1966), Levy and Kaufman (1973), and Wickelgren (1967).

Evidence Combination Model

This model also assumes simultaneous and independent processing of component dimensions. However, instead of multiple independent categorization processes, a single categorization process is assumed, with information about the component dimensions integrated before categorization. Since multiple sources of information about the correct response are accumulating instead of a single source, a decision criterion would be reached more rapidly with redundant dimensions than with either single dimension alone. Similar accuracy models have been discussed by Garner and Flowers (1969), Green and Swets (1966), Morton (1969b), and Taylor, Lindsay, and Forbes (1967).

Holistic Model

A model based on holistic processing has been proposed by Lockhead to account for redundancy gains with integral dimensions in both accuracy and RT data (Lockhead, 1970, 1972). Instead of assuming independent processes for the component dimensions as do the two models just presented, this model assumes that the stimulus dimensions are represented as orthogonal continua in a Euclidean psychological space. According to this model, the subject's task in identifying a stimulus ". . . is one of locating the multidimensional stimulus in that space without the requirement that the space be analyzed according to its separate dimensions. . . [Lockhead, 1970; pp. 2–3]." To distinguish even further between this model and the parallel processing models, Lockhead (1972) emphasizes: "This is not parallel processing; an integral stimulus is a single thing and there is no requirement for independent decisions on the separate dimensions [p. 415]." Redundancy gains in accuracy or response time for redundant multidimensional stimuli arise naturally from the characteristics

[7] This form of model is typically termed "self-terminating" (cf. Biederman, 1972; Biederman & Checkosky, 1970; Egeth, 1966; Hawkins, 1969), with the implication that processing of the other dimensions in a stimulus is terminated when a decision on one component is reached. However, in a strict sense self-termination is not required, since processing of all dimensions may continue to completion after a response is initiated. Rather, the only necessary requirement appears to be that a response be possible based on the outcome of the earliest component completed.

of the multidimensional Euclidean space: Pairs of redundant stimuli are separated further in this space than pairs of stimuli differing only on the component dimensions. For the bidimensional case, the familiar Pythagorean relation holds and the distance between the points in this space for redundant pairings is $\sqrt{2}$ greater than the distance between the corresponding points for single dimensions. Thus, this holistic model accounts for redundancy gains in both accuracy and RT data simply on the basis of increased discriminability of the redundant stimulus set. A similar discriminability-based account of redundancy gains for integral dimensions has been suggested by Garner (1970, 1972, 1974; Garner & Felfoldy, 1970).

A NORMATIVE MODEL BASED ON DECISION COMBINATION

As already mentioned, the redundancy gains for auditory and phonetic dimensions allow rejection of a completely serial or sequential organization of auditory and phonetic processes. However, the data presented thus far cannot distinguish between alternative explanations of the obtained redundancy gains represented by the decision combination, evidence combination, and holistic models discussed in the preceding section. Because these three models imply very different organizations of auditory and phonetic processes, a more detailed investigation of the redundancy gains in the Wood (1974) experiment was undertaken in the context of these models.

The initial intent was to derive quantitative predictions from each model not only for the exact magnitude of the predicted redundancy gains, but also for the complete RT distributions in the redundant task. Such predictions would permit far more powerful analyses of redundancy gains in RT data than have heretofore been possible. However, it became clear immediately that such detailed predictions were not easily forthcoming for either the evidence combination or the holistic models without a far more stringent set of assumptions than those already outlined. As noted by Morton (1969a), the particular difficulty with the evidence combination model is that predictions about the exact form of the RT distributions and the magnitude of the redundancy gain would require detailed specification of the single-dimension evidence accumulation processes, their rates, and the exact nature of the evidence combination algorithm. Similarly, the holistic model in its simple form makes only the qualitative prediction that RT should be related to stimulus discriminability, regardless of whether such discriminability is produced by unidimensional or multidimensional stimulus differences. Thus, direct comparison of the magnitude of the redundancy gain or the form of the redundant RT distributions predicted by the holistic model cannot be made without further specification of the exact quantitatve relation between stimulus discriminability and RT. However, a possible indirect test of the discriminability interpretation is discussed later.

In light of these difficulties with directly applying the evidence combination and holistic processing models, the following analysis is based on the use of the decision combination model as a normative model. The term "normative model" in this context requires further clarification. Following Garner and Morton (1969) and Garner (1974) a distinction is made between descriptive or process models on one hand and normative models on the other. In a discussion of the concept of perceptual independence, Garner and Morton (1969) suggest:

> The rather special role of the normative model has perhaps been less well understood, however, since models are often accepted or rejected on the basis of the fit of the data to a particular model. But the special role of the normative model is not to describe a perceptual process but to provide a norm against which results are evaluated. Thus we should not ask whether the model is right or wrong but rather to what extent the experimental results conform to the criterion of independence which the particular model implies. This is not to say that normative models cannot be wrong; rather it is to say that the basis of their being wrong (or right) is not so much in fitting the data as in correctly reflecting the underlying concepts or processes which the experimenter intends them to reflect. Further, normative models may be more or less useful not insofar as data fit a particular model but insofar as the model helps clarify the nature of the process when the data do not fit the model [p. 234].

Thus, the procedure to be presented based on the decision combination model is not intended to be a literal description of the way in which redundant dimensions are processed. Nor is it intended to imply that the decision combination model as any greater validity as a process model than the evidence combination, holistic, or any other model. Rather, the procedure presented here is intended as a normative tool that hopefully will lead to a clarification of the conceptual issues involved and a more specific set of experimental questions to be investigated.

The present procedure was designed to employ the most simple possible set of assumptions based on the decision combination model (cf. Biederman & Checkosky, 1970; Hawkins, 1969; Morton, 1969a):

1. Processing of component dimensions can be initiated and proceed simultaneously, with the completion times for the component processes distributed as independent random variables.
2. The subject's response on each trial in a redundant task is based upon whichever component process is completed first on that trial.

Let a and b represent the completion times for the component processes corresponding to the two single dimensions. Based on the independence assumption, the predicted probability of completion (C) for redundant dimensions at a given time t following stimulus onset is a joint probability of the form

$$P(C = t) = P(a = t)P(b > t) + P(b = t)P(a > t). \qquad (1)$$

Let $f(t)$ and $g(t)$ represent the completion time distributions for the two single dimensions. In discrete form, the distribution for redundant dimensions, $h(t)$, may be written

$$h(t_i) = f(t_i) \sum_{j=i}^{n} g(t_j)$$

$$+ g(t_i) \sum_{j=i}^{n} f(t_j) - f(t_i)g(t_i). \qquad (2)$$

One simplifying assumption is necessary to apply Eq. (2) to empirical data. In the preceding description the distributions have been hypothetical completion time distributions, not empirical RT distributions. In order to apply the model, the empirical RT distributions in the single-dimension conditions are employed as the best available estimates of the unobservable completion-time distributions. This use of empirical RT distributions as inputs to Eq. (2) requires the assumption that other components of RT distributions such as peripheral stimulus processing and response execution be roughly constant in the single dimension and redundant conditions.

Before applying this procedure to the data of Wood (1974) it will be useful to outline briefly some major characteristics of the model's predictions based on simulated data. For simplicity, the results of these simulations are presented for normal component distributions. However, it is emphasized that applying the model to empirical data requires no assumptions about the form of the component distributions beyond their estimation by the empirical RT distributions.

The single most important generalization about the model's predictions is that both the magnitude of the predicted redundancy gain and the form of the predicted redundant-dimension RT distribution depend entirely upon the relation between the single-dimension RT distributions. One form of such dependence is illustrated in Fig. 1. The two single-dimension distributions are represented in this figure by crosshatched histograms, and the predicted redundant distribution is represented by the solid line. Figure 1a presents the results for completely identical and overlapping component distributions. Two features should be noted. The first is the obvious prediction of a decrease in mean RT for the redundant condition relative to the

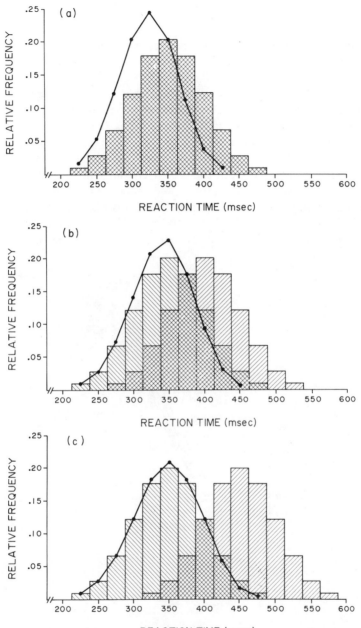

FIG. 1. Simulated data illustrating the predictions of the normative model. Single-dimension distributions are shown as diagonally crosshatched histograms, whereas the predicted redundant dimension distribution is shown as a solid line. Normal single-dimension distributions with $\sigma = 50$ msec were employed for this particular simulation. In (a) the single-dimension distributions have equal means of 350 msec. In (b) and (c) the mean of the faster single-dimension distribution remains at 350 msec, whereas the means of the slower distributions are equal to 400 and 450 msec, respectively.

67

single-dimension conditions, the redundancy gain. Less obvious, perhaps, is the prediction that the variance of the redundant dimension distribution should decrease significantly as well.

Figure 1b and 1c illustrates the critical role of the overlap between single-dimension distributions. The two distributions in Fig. 1a have equal means of 350 msec and equal standard deviations (σ) of 50 msec. Figure 1b and 1c retains these same distributions but displaces the mean of one distribution 1σ and 2σ (50 and 100 msec, respectively) relative to the other. This displacement has the clear effect of decreasing the magnitude of the predicted redundancy gain and causing the predicted redundant condition distribution to approximate more closely the distribution for the faster single-dimension condition. With the 100-msec difference between means shown in Fig. 1c, the predicted mean redundancy gain is on the order of

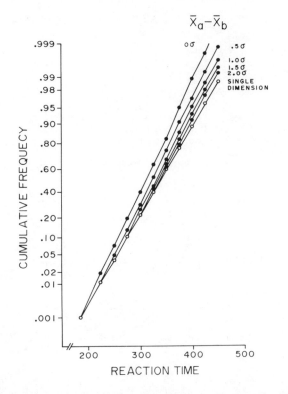

FIG. 2. Simulated data illustrating the effect of difference between means of single dimension distributions ($\bar{X}_a - \bar{X}_b$). Predicted redundant distributions are shown by filled circles. The faster single-dimension distribution is shown by open circles for comparison. Nomal single-dimension distributions with $\sigma = 50$ msec were employed.

1.2 msec, compared to the 27.4 msec maximal gain for completely over-lapping distributions of this type shown in Fig. 1a.

The importance of distributional overlap in the single dimension conditions is illustrated further in Fig. 2, which presents predicted distributions in cumulative form as a function of difference between means of the component distributions. The component distributions in this case are again normal with $\sigma = 50$ msec, and the mean of the faster single dimension conditions is again equal to 350 msec. As the difference between means of the component distributions increases from complete overlap (i.e., $\bar{X}_a - \bar{X}_b = 0\sigma$), the predicted gain decreases from a maximum and approaches the faster of the single dimension conditions. In the limiting case of zero overlap between component distributions, zero gain is the obvious result.

The effect of changes in the variance of the component distributions is shown in Fig. 3. The means of the single dimension distributions for

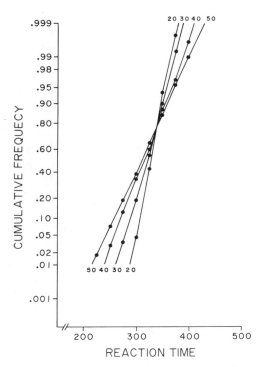

FIG. 3.   Simulated data illustrating the effect of variance of the single dimension distributions. The means of the single dimension distribution were held constant at 350 msec, whereas σ of both distributions was varied from 50 to 20 msec as indicated.

these predictions are again equal to 350 msec, and the $\sigma = 50$-msec distribution is identical to that for complete overlap in Fig. 2. The other predicted distributions illustrate the effect of jointly reducing the σ of both component distributions from 50 through 20 msec. These results further illustrate the importance of the form and overlap of the component distributions. Although the mean of the predicted redundant distribution remains relatively constant for all values of σ, its variance is directly proportional to the variance of the component distributions.

A number of additional simulations have been performed to investigate the effects of other variables on the predicted redundant condition RT distributions, including independent variation of the mean and variance of each component distribution and changes in the form of the component distributions holding mean and variance constant. Most of these results may be visualized by intuitively combining the principles illustrated in Figs. 1–3. An important feature of the model is that independent manipulations of these variables become possible with simulations, whereas they are almost always confounded in empirical RT distributions.

APPLICATION OF THE NORMATIVE MODEL TO REDUNDANCY GAINS FOR AUDITORY AND PHONETIC DIMENSIONS

In order to compare the redundancy gains obtained by Wood (1974) to those predicted by the normative model, across-subject RT distributions were first computed for the place and pitch single dimension (control) conditions. For each dimension, a separate distribution was computed (20-msec cell width) for each subject and converted from RT to unit normal (z) units. This procedure eliminated the possibility that subjects with different mean RTs would contribute disproportionately to different regions of the across-subject distribution. The two single-dimension distributions were then entered into Eq. (2) in the same fashion as the simulated data described earlier. For purposes of the comparison, the data from the correlated conditions for place and pitch dimensions were combined to form a single redundant-dimension distribution. The results of this comparison are shown in Table 3, which presents the means and standard deviations of the RT distributions in the faster single-dimension condition (i.e., pitch, see Table 2) and the obtained and predicted distributions for redundant dimensions.

From the simulated data already presented, it will be recalled that the model predicts both the mean and variability of the redundant dimension distribution will be decreased relative to the single dimension condition. This pattern is shown for the predicted distribution in Table 3, and is

TABLE 3
Means and Standard Deviations of Obtained and Predicted Redundant Dimension RT Distributions[a]

	Mean	Standard deviation
Faster single dimension	381.4	60.4
Redundant dimensions: obtained	344.4	51.6
Redundant dimensions: predicted	339.3	48.7

[a] Data from Wood (1974).

confirmed in the obtained data. However, the decreases in both the mean and standard deviation of the obtained distribution fall slightly short of those predicted by the model. Whereas the predicted mean redundancy gain is 42.1 msec, the obtained gain is 37.0 msec. Similarly, the predicted decrease in σ is 11.7 msec, whereas the obtained decrease is 8.8 msec. A comparison of the complete predicted and obtained RT distributions indicated that the major sources of disparity occurred in the upper tail of the distribution. Small, but consistently greater frequencies of long RTs were obtained than were predicted by the model. This observation was confirmed by a χ^2 comparison of the predicted and obtained distributions. When the complete distributions were compared, the value of the χ^2 statistic was sufficiently large to reject the null hypothesis of zero difference between distributions at the $p < .01$ level. In contrast, when the upper tail of the distribution ($> \bar{X} + 2\sigma$) was eliminated from the comparison, the value of the χ^2 statistic decreased to $.10 > p > .05$.

It should be clear that the use of this normative procedure need not be limited to redundancy gains for speech stimuli, but is appropriate for speeded classification tasks using other stimulus dimensions and sensory modalities.[8] As an example, an additional examination of the model for stimuli other than speech was made using the data of Biederman and Checkosky (1970). Although not considered here, the model is also logically appropriate for analysis of certain conditions in "same–different" RT experiments (cf. Footnote 5).

[8] The model is also appropriate, in principle, for card-sorting experiments of the type reported by Morton (1969a), Garner (1969), and Garner and Felfoldy (1970). However, since the typical datum in such experiments is the time taken to sort a deck of stimulus cards rather than a time for each single card, such experiments are less amenable to distributional analyses than discrete RT experiments.

One additional assumption was required for the Biederman and Checkosky (1970) data over that required for the Wood (1974) experiment. In the latter, the complete single-dimension distributions were available as inputs to Eq. (2). For the Biederman and Checkosky (1970) data, only the means and standard deviations of the RT distributions were reported and the full distributions had to be estimated. For simplicity, normal distributions were assumed, although it is probable that the actual distributions were somewhat skewed, as is typical for RT distributions. The normality assumption does not invalidate the comparison, however, since simulations have shown that small amounts of skewness have relatively minor effects on the magnitude of predicted redundancy gains when compared to normal distributions of equal mean and variance.

Predicted and obtained redundancy gains for the low- and high-discriminability conditions in the Biederman and Checkosky (1970) experiment are shown in Table 4. The pattern of results here is very similar to that presented for the Wood (1974) data. Although the obtained redundant-dimension data show reduced mean and variability relative to the faster single-dimension condition, the obtained redundancy gains fall slightly

TABLE 4

**Means and Standard Deviations of
Obtained and Predicted Redundant
Dimension RT Distributions**[a]

	Mean	Standard deviation
Low Discriminability Condition		
Faster single dimension	412	54
Redundant dimensions: obtained	395	36
Redundant dimensions: predicted	392	40
High Discriminability Condition		
Faster single dimension	382	37
Redundant dimensions: obtained	376	31
Redundant dimensions: predicted	368	29

[a] Data from Biederman and Checkosky (1970).

short of those predicted by the model. For the low-discriminability condition the predicted gain is 20 msec, whereas the obtained gain was 17 msec. Similarly, in the high-discriminability condition the predicted and obtained redundancy gains were 14 and 6 msec, respectively.

CONCLUSIONS

The normative model based on independent processing and categorization of component dimensions predicts slightly but consistently larger redundancy gains than those obtained empirically. As emphasized by Garner and Morton (1969), the value of a normative model should lie in its ability to clarify the reasons for failures of data to fit the model's predictions. How can the present results help to clarify the organization of auditory and phonetic processes in speech perception?

As already discussed, the data of Wood (1974) permit rejection of a strict serial organization of auditory and phonetic processes, suggesting instead that some form of shared or parallel processing is involved. The most important contribution of the normative model to clarification of such shared processing has been to reveal that strict independence of auditory and phonetic processes is apparently not met in empirical data. That is, there appears to be some form of nonindependence or correlation between the component processes for auditory and phonetic dimensions. However, such correlation could occur in two distinct forms which have very different implications for the underlying mechanisms involved. Following Garner and Morton (1969) and Garner (1972, 1974), the terms "state correlation" and "process correlation" are employed to describe these forms of correlation.

State correlation would exist in the present case if a subject's overall performance level fluctuated over time due to changes in alertness, attention, etc. Under such conditions the completion times for the auditory and phonetic dimensions would be empirically correlated, even though the auditory and phonetic processes could be functionally independent. In contrast, process correlation would refer in the present case to an actual interaction, correlation, or interdependence between auditory and phonetic processes.

Since state and process correlation have very different consequences for the nature of the underlying processes involved, it will be important in future work to attempt to distinguish between them. Garner and Morton (1969) have provided clear examples of the way in which these two forms of correlation may be distinguished in accuracy data, and parallel theoretical developments in the analysis of RT data are clearly required. The use of speed–accuracy trade-off experiments to compare redundant and single-dimension performance may be helpful in this regard (cf. Footnote 6).

Another approach to the problem of distinguishing between state and process correlation in RT data would be to estimate the degree of state correlation involved by empirically assessing the degree to which the data depart from statistical stationarity over time. Unfortunately, the conditions of the Wood (1974) experiment do not permit reliable estimates of stationarity to be made. Additional experiments might approach this question in two ways. One would be to employ blocks of trials sufficiently long to estimate departures from stationarity. A second would be to attempt to maximize the stationarity of the data by using extremely well practiced subjects, optimal payoff contingencies, etc. If the redundancy gains obtained under the latter conditions still fall short of those predicted by the normative model, then it becomes increasingly likely that some form of process correlation is involved.

The preceding discussion has implicitly assumed the validity of the "component-dimension" explanation of redundancy gains to the exclusion of the holistic or discriminability-based explanation outlined earlier (Garner, 1970, 1972, 1974; Garner & Felfoldy, 1970; Lockhead, 1970, 1972). Nevertheless, the importance of increased stimulus discriminability as an explanation for obtained redundancy gains remains to be determined. For example, it is quite possible that the correspondence between obtained and predicted redundancy gains in Tables 3 and 4 merely reflects the fact that many of the predictions of the normative model are readily interpretable in discriminability terms. In absence of clear quantative predictions from the discriminability model concerning magnitude of redundancy gains and forms of RT distributions, this possibility cannot be assessed directly. However, the normative model presented here may be able to provide evidence relevant to the discriminability explanation. For example, if a discriminability explanation were correct, then it should be possible to reproduce completely the effects of redundant dimensions merely by increasing the discriminability along a single dimension (Garner, 1970; Nickerson, 1971). By comparing the effects of single- and multidimensional changes in discriminability with those predicted by the normative model, it may be possible to distinguish further between discriminability and component dimension explanations of redundancy gains. Experiments are currently under way to examine this possibility.

Finally, the implications of the present results may be summarized by reference to the tentative organization of auditory and phonetic processes proposed as a working hypothesis by Wood (1974). This organization involves both serial and parallel processing and includes the following three components: (a) a common "peripheral" component for the transduction and preliminary analysis of all acoustic signals; (b) a "central" auditory component for the additional processing of nonlinguistic auditory information; and (c) a "central" phonetic component for the extraction of phonetic features from the results of the preliminary auditory analysis. The two central components would be capable of functioning in parallel, but both would be dependent upon the output of the preliminary auditory analysis.

The issue of state versus process correlation raised by the present results directly concerns the relationship between the central auditory and phonetic components. Does the obtained correlation between auditory and phonetic dimensions arise solely from state correlation, implying that the auditory and phonetic processes operate independently? Or are auditory and phonetic processes in some way functionally interdependent resulting in process correlation? If process correlation is in fact involved, how does it arise? Must the central auditory and phonetic components actually interact, or would a common input from the peripheral auditory stage be sufficient to produce apparent process correlation? Any detailed attempts to answer these questions must await both empirical and theoretical advances in the analysis of auditory and phonetic processes in speech perception. Together with other experimental approaches (cf. Pisoni & Tash, 1974; Studdert-Kennedy & Shankweiler, 1970; Studdert-Kennedy et al., 1972), the analysis of redundancy gains for various linguistic and nonlinguistic dimensions appears to be a useful approach to such questions.

REFERENCES

Ades, A. E. Some effects of adaptation on speech perception. *MIT Research Laboratory of Electronics Quarterly Progress Report,* 1973, **111,** 121–129.

Ades, A. E. How phonetic is selective adaptation? Experiments on syllable position and vowel environment. *Perception & Psychophysics,* 1974, **16,** 61–66.

Bailey, P. Perceptual adaptation for acoustical features in speech. *Speech Perception* (Department of Psychology, Queen's University, Belfast), 1973, **2,** 29–34.

Biederman, I. Human performance in contingent information-processing tasks. *Journal of Experimental Psychology,* 1972, **93,** 219–238.

Biederman, I., & Checkosky, S. F. Processing redundant information. *Journal of Experimental Psychology,* 1970, **83,** 486–490.

Cooper, W. E. Perceptuo-motor adaptation to a speech feature. *Perception & Psychophysics,* 1974, **16,** 229–234.

Cooper, W. E. Adaptation of phonetic feature analyzers for place of articulation. *Journal of the Acoustical Society of America,* in press.

Day, R. S., Cutting, J. E., & Copeland, P. M. Perception of linguistic and nonlinguistic dimensions of dichotic stimuli. *Haskins Laboratories Status Report on Speech Research,* 1971, **SR-27,** 193–197.

Day, R. S., & Wood, C. C. Interactions between linguistic and nonlinguistic processing. *Journal of the Acoustical Society of America,* 1972, **51,** 79(A).

Dorman, M. F. Auditory evoked potential correlates of speech sound discrimination. *Perception & Psychophysics,* 1974, **15,** 215–220.

Egeth, H. E. Parallel versus serial processes in multidimensional stimulus discrimination. *Perception & Psychophysics,* 1966, **1,** 245–252.

Eimas, P. D., & Corbit, J. D. Selective adaptation of linguistic feature detectors. *Cognitive Psychology,* 1973, **4,** 99–109.

Eimas, P. D., Cooper, W. E., & Corbit, J. D. Some properties of linguistic feature detectors. *Perception & Psychophysics,* 1973, **13,** 247–252.

Eriksen, C. W., & Hake, H. W. Multidimensional stimulus differences and accuracy of discrimination. *Journal of Experimental Psychology,* 1955, **50,** 153–160.

Fant, G. Auditory patterns of speech. In W. Wathen-Dunn (Ed.), *Models for the perception of speech and visual form.* Cambridge, Massachusetts: MIT Press, 1967. Pp. 111–125.

Fry, D. B. Perception and recognition in speech. In M. Halle, H. G. Lunt, & C. H. van Schoonevelt (Eds.), *For Roman Jakobson.* The Hague: Mouton, 1956. Pp. 169–173.

Garner, W. R. Speed of discrimination with redundant stimulus attributes. *Perception & Psychophysics,* 1969, **6,** 221–224.

Garner, W. R. The stimulus in information processing. *American Psychologist,* 1970, **25,** 350–358.

Garner, W. R. Information integration and form of encoding. In A. W. Melton & E. Martin (Eds.), *Coding processes in human memory.* Washington, D.C.: Winston, 1972.

Garner, W. R. *The processing of information and structure.* Potomac, Maryland: Erlbaum, 1974.

Garner, W. R., & Felfoldy, G. L. Integrality of stimulus dimensions in various types of information processing. *Cognitive Psychology,* 1970, **1,** 225–241.

Garner, W. R., & Flowers, J. H. The effect of redundant stimulus elements on visual discrimination as a function of element heterogeneity, equal discriminability, and position uncertainty. *Percepton & Psychophysics,* 1969, **6,** 216–220.

Garner, W. R., & Lee, W. An analysis of redundancy in perceptual discrimination. *Perceptual & Motor Skills,* 1962, **15,** 367–388.

Garner, W. R., & Morton, J. Perceptual independence: Definitions, models, and experimental paradigms. *Psychological Bulletin,* 1969, **72,** 233–259.

Green, D. M., & Luce, R. D. Speed-accuracy trade off in auditory detection. In S. Kornblum (Ed.), *Attention and performance—IV.* New York: Academic Press, 1973.

Green, D. M., & Swets, J. A. *Signal detection theory and psychophysics,* New York: Wiley, 1966.

Hake, H., Rodwan, A., & Weintraub, D. Noise reduction in perception. In K. R. Hammond (Ed.), *The psychology of Egon Brunswick.* New York: Holt, 1966.

Handel, S., & Imai, S. The free classification of analyzable and unanalyzable stimuli. *Perception & Psychophysics,* 1972, **12,** 108–116.

Hawkins, H. L. Parallel processing in complex visual discrimination. *Perception & Psychophysics,* 1969, **5,** 56–64.

Hyman, R., & Well, A. Perceptual separability and spatial models. *Perception & Psychophysics,* 1968, **3,** 161–165.

Lehiste, I. The units of speech perception. In J. H. Gilbert (Ed.), *Speech and cortical functioning.* New York: Academic Press, 1972.

Levy, R. M., & Kaufman, H. M. Sets and subsets in the identification of multidimensional stimuli. *Psychological Review,* 1973, **80,** 139–148.

Liberman, A. M., Cooper, F. S., Shankweiler, D., & Studdert-Kennedy, M. Perception of the speech code. *Psychological Review,* 1967, **74,** 431–461.

Lockhead, G. R. Effects of dimensional redundancy on visual discrimination. *Journal of Experimental Psychology,* 1966, **72,** 95–104.

Lockhead, G. R. Identification and the form of multidimensional discrimination space. *Journal of Experimental Psychology,* 1970, **85,** 1–10.

Lockhead, G. R. Processing dimensional stimuli: A note. *Psychological Review,* 1972, **79,** 410–419.

Mattingly, I. G., Liberman, A. M., Syrdal, A. K., & Halwes, T. Discrimination in speech and nonspeech modes. *Cognitive Psychology,* 1971, **2,** 131–157.

Morton, J. The use of correlated stimulus information in card sorting. *Perception & Psychophysics,* 1969, **5,** 374–376. (a)

Morton, J. The interaction of information in word recognition. *Psychological Review,* 1969, **76,** 165–378. (b)

Nickerson, R. S. Binary-classification reaction time: A review of some studies of human information-processing capabilities. *Psychonomic Monograph Supplement,* 1971, **4**(17, Whole No. 65).

Pisoni, D. B. On the nature of categorical perception of speech sounds. Doctoral Dissertation, University of Michigan, 1971. (Appeared as a supplement to *Haskins Laboratories Status Report on Speech Research,* 1971.)

Pisoni, D. B. Auditory and phonetic memory codes in the discrimination of consonants and vowels. *Perception & Psychophysics,* 1973, **13,** 253–260.

Pisoni, D. B., & Tash, J. Reaction times to comparisons within and across phonetic categories. *Perception & Psychophysics,* 1974, **15,** 285–290.

Saraga, E., & Shallice, T. Parallel processing of the attributes of single stimuli. *Perception & Psychophysics,* 1973, **13,** 261–270.

Schouten, J. F., & Bekker, J. A. M. Reaction time and accuracy. In A. F. Sanders (Ed.), *Attention and performance.* Amsterdam: North-Holland Publ., 1967.

Stevens, K. N., & Halle, M. Remarks on analysis of synthesis and distinctive features. In W. Wathen-Dunn (Ed.), *Models for the perception of speech and visual form.* Cambridge, Massachusetts: MIT Press, 1967. Pp. 88–102.

Stevens, K. N., & House, A. S. Speech Perception. In J. V. Tobias (Ed.), *Foundations of modern auditory theory,* Vol. II. New York: Academic Press, 1972. Pp. 1–62.

Studdert-Kennedy, M. The perception of speech. In T. A. Sebeok (Ed.), *Current trends in linguistics,* Vol. XII. The Hague: Mouton, in press. (a)

Studdert-Kennedy, M. Speech perception. In N. J. Lass (Ed.), *Contempory Issues in experimental phonetics,* Springfield, Illinois: Thomas, in press. (b)

Studdert-Kennedy, M., & Shankweiler, D. Hemispheric specialization for speech perception. *Journal of the Acoustical Society of America,* 1970, **48,** 579–594.

Studdert-Kennedy, M., Shankweiler, D., & Pisoni, D. Auditory and phonetic processes in speech perception: Evidence from a dichotic study. *Cognitive Psychology,* 1972, **3,** 455–466.

Taylor, M. M., Lindsay, P. H., & Forbes, S. M. Quantification of shared capacity processing in auditory and visual discrimination. In A. F. Sanders (Ed.), *Attention and performance.* Amsterdam: North-Holland Publ., 1967.

Wickelgren, W. A. Strength theories of disjunctive visual detection. *Perception & Psychophysics,* 1967, **8,** 331–337.

Wickelgren, W. A. Discussion paper on speech perception. In J. H. Gilbert (Ed.), *Speech and cortical functioning.* New York: Academic Press, 1972.

Wood, C. C. Parallel processing of auditory and phonetic information in speech perception. *Perception & Psychophysics,* 1974, **15,** 501–508.

Wood, C. C. Levels of processing in speech perception. Neurophysiological and information-processing analyses. *Journal of Experimental Psychology: Human Perception and Performance,* 1975, **104,** 3–20.

Wood, C. C., Goff, W. R., & Day, R. W. Auditory evoked potentials during speech perception. *Science,* 1971, **173,** 1248–1251.

4

DICHOTIC LISTENING AND PROCESSING PHONETIC FEATURES

David B. Pisoni
Indiana University

For over a hundred years it has been known that the left hemisphere of man is specialized for various types of linguistic processes. Evidence supporting this view has come from a variety of sources including both clinical and experimental studies of normal and brain-damaged subjects (Geschwind, 1970; Milner, 1971). However, only within the last decade have investigators begun to identify some of the stages and operations that underlie this asymmetric representation of language in the brain (Studdert-Kennedy, 1975a, b; Studdert-Kennedy & Shankweiler, 1970; Wood, 1973).

Some of the strongest support for specialized neural processes in normal subjects has been obtained in dichotic listening experiments (Kimura, 1961, 1967; Shankweiler & Studdert-Kennedy, 1967; Studdert-Kennedy & Shankweiler, 1970). In this paradigm, pairs of stimuli are presented simultaneously to right and left ears, and listeners are asked to identify, discriminate, or recall these sounds. Depending on the types of stimuli employed, two main findings have been repeatedly observed. First, if the pairs of stimuli are linguistic, such as words, digits, or syllables, subjects usually report the stimulus presented to the right ear more accurately than the stimulus presented to the left ear (Bartz, Satz, Fennell, & Lally, 1967; Kimura, 1961; Shankweiler & Studdert-Kennedy, 1967). Second, if the pairs of stimuli are nonlinguistic such as melodies, tones, sonar signals, or environmental sounds, the opposite effect is observed, namely, subjects report the left ear stimulus more accurately than the right ear stimulus (Curry, 1967; Kimura, 1964; Shankweiler, 1966).

Most investigators have assumed that the right ear advantage (REA) for linguistic stimuli is a reflection of the general asymmetry of cerebral dominance for language function (Bryden, 1967; Kimura, 1961, 1967; Studdert-Kennedy & Shankweiler, 1970). Explanations of the REA have generally been as follows: First, it is assumed that there is a functional prepotency of the contralateral auditory pathways from right ear to left hemisphere. This is supported by physiological evidence, which indicates that the contribution of the contralateral pathways is greater than the ipsilateral pathways (Bocca, Calearo, Cassinari and Migliavacca, 1955; Rosenzweig, 1951). Second, under dichotic stimulation the left-ear signal undergoes a relatively greater "loss" than the right ear signal because it must first travel to the right hemisphere before it is transmitted to the left hemisphere via the corpus callosum. There is also evidence that the ipsilateral pathways are occluded or inhibited during dichotic stimulation (Milner, Taylor & Sperry, 1968). However, at the present time, the exact locus of the REA still remains unspecified. It could occur immediately before, during, or immediately after the interface between auditory processing and initial phonetic analysis. Studdert-Kennedy and Shankweiler have further argued that the REA observed under dichotic stimulation reflects the operation of a "specialized" speech processor in the language-dominant hemisphere, and is not simply due to additional auditory processing capacities. They claim that both cerebral hemispheres are capable of processing the auditory information in the speech signal but only the language-dominant hemisphere is involved in the identification and recognition of phonetic features in the stimuli.

Support for the notion of a unilateral phonetic processor in the language-dominant hemisphere rests on several general findings about the relations between speech and language function (see Liberman, 1972; Mattingly & Liberman, 1969; Wood, 1973; Wood, Goff, & Day, 1971). However, most of the experimental evidence to date deals primarily with the types of interactions that have been observed between left- and right-ear dichotic speech inputs. In the present chapter I consider two of these dichotic interactions in some detail—the "feature sharing advantage" and the "lag effect." Both findings are central to a number of recent theoretical efforts in speech perception and have been the focus of a great deal of recent research (Benson, 1974; Blumstein, 1974; Speaks, Gray, Miller, Rubens, & Walker, 1974; Studdert-Kennedy, Shankweiler, & Pisoni, 1972).

The plan of this chapter is as follows: First, I consider the distinction between auditory and phonetic stages of processing, since this underlies much of the work to be described. Second, I review the feature-sharing advantage and lag effect in dichotic listening experiments. Third, I present the results of several recent dichotic recognition masking experiments that have examined these types of interactions in more detail. Fourth, I propose a rough model of some of the stages involved in phonetic processing and show how the model can account for the types of feature interactions observed between dichotic speech inputs. Finally, I briefly consider the relation between the right ear advantage and the lag effect in dichotic listening.

AUDITORY AND PHONETIC STAGES OF PROCESSING

Although the distinction between phonetic structure and higher levels of analysis is commonly accepted in linguistic theory, the distinction between auditory (i.e., acoustic structure) and phonetic levels of analysis has not been widely recognized. The auditory stage may be thought of as the first level of analysis between the acoustic signal and perceived message (cf. Studdert-Kennedy, 1975a). At this level, the acoustic waveform is transformed (i.e., recoded) into some "time-varying" neurological pattern of events in the auditory system. Acoustic information, such as spectral structure, fundamental frequency, intensity, and duration is extracted by the auditory system. All subsequent stages of analysis beyond the auditory stage of analysis are thought to be abstract and based on an analysis of these initial auditory features. The phonetic level, the second stage of analysis, is assumed to be closely related to the first stage. Here, segments and features necessary for phonetic classification are abstracted or derived from the auditory representations of the acoustic signal. At the output of this stage, the continuously varying auditory stimulus has become transformed into a sequence of discrete phonetic segments. Information about the feature specification of these phonetic segments in the form of an abstract distinctive feature matrix is then passed on to higher levels of processing for phonological and syntactic analysis.

Thus, we may think of the auditory level as that portion of the speech-perception process which is "nonlinguistic." It includes processes and mechanisms that operate on speech and nonspeech signals alike. On the other hand, processes and mechanisms at the phonetic level are assumed to perform a linguistic abstraction process, whereby a particular phonetic feature is identified or recognized from some configuration of auditory features (i.e., acoustic cues) in the acoustic input. The details of this process are central to all current theories of speech perception (Bondarko *et al.,* 1970; Fant, 1973; Liberman, Cooper, Shankweiler, & Studdert-Kennedy, 1967; Massaro, 1972; Stevens & House, 1972; Studdert-Kennedy, 1975a, b).

There is still little agreement among investigators as to exactly how auditory and phonetic features are processed during speech perception. Nevertheless, the general "lack of invariance" between the acoustic signal and segments in the linguistic message establishes that the recognition process cannot be a simple one-to-one matching of phonetic features in long-term memory with acoustic features in the speech stimulus (Liberman *et al.,* 1967). As a result, a number of investigators have suggested that speech sound perception may involve specialized neural mechanisms that may not be employed in the perception of other auditory signals (Liberman *et al.,* 1967; Stevens & House, 1972).

One broad aim of dichotic listening experiments has been to provide evidence for the existence of some type of specialized speech processing mechanism (Milner, 1962; Sparks & Geschwind, 1968). Recent work employing the selective adaptation paradigm to study feature detectors in speech perception has also been aimed in this direction (see for example, Cooper, 1974, this volume; Eimas & Corbit, 1973; Eimas, Cooper, & Corbit, 1973). However, a second related aim of dichotic listening experiments has been to study the more general processes of speech and language function. Specifically, a number of recent experiments have been concerned with defining the stages of processing and describing the types of operations that take place at each of these stages. In this sense, dichotic listening is simply one of a number of experimental techniques that can be used to study the processing of speech sounds.

The concern in this chapter is not primarily with the nature of the REA in dichotic listening nor with its magnitude under various experimental conditions. The literature is much too extensive to even attempt to review it here coherently. Moreover, some efforts have already been made along these lines in several recent papers (see, for example, Berlin, Lowe-Bell, Cullen, Thompson, & Loovis, 1973; Berlin & McNeil, 1975; Studdert-Kennedy & Shankweiler, 1970). Rather, auditory and phonetic feature interactions between dichotic inputs are examined in order to begin to describe some of the stages of processing by which phonetic features are identified.

FEATURE-SHARING ADVANTAGE

The feature-sharing advantage refers to a gain in identification for dichotic pairs of consonant vowel (CV) syllables that share phonetic features (e.g., place or voicing). The effect is shown in Fig. 1, which is based on data from Studdert-Kennedy and Shankweiler (1970). The probability that both initial stop consonants will be correctly identified is greater if the two consonant segments shared the place feature (e.g., [ba]–[pa]) or the voicing feature (e.g., [ba]–[da]) than if neither feature was shared (e.g., [ba]–[ta]). This interaction was interpreted by Studdert-Kennedy and Shankweiler as providing evidence that both dichotic inputs converge on

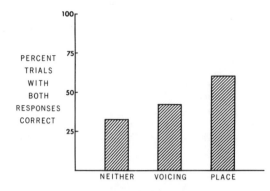

FIG. 1.   The percentage of trials on which both responses were correct as a function of the consonant feature shared by the dichotic CV pairs. (After Studdert-Kennedy, Shankweiler, & Pisoni, 1972.)

a single phonetic processing center before the extraction of phonetic features. The authors suggested that "duplication of the auditory information conveying the shared feature value gives rise to the observed advantage [Studdert-Kennedy & Shankweiler, 1970, p. 589]." This conclusion seemed reasonable at the time. Since the same vowel (i.e., [a]) was used in each syllable, auditory and phonetic features were redundant.

The context-conditioned dependence of consonant cues on vowel context should be emphasized here. One of the best-known facts about phonetic perception is that the acoustic cues for a particular consonant segment, especially stop consonants, vary as a function of vowel context, position in the syllable, stress, speaking rate and speaker.[1] Thus, when the vowel is the same, particularly with synthetic stimuli, the acoustic cues that underlie a consonant feature are also the same. The acoustic cues for a particular consonant feature vary only when vowel context or some additional parameter is manipulated. Thus, although the feature sharing advantage was originally thought to be due to commonality of the auditory features in the two inputs, the effect could also be due to shared phonetic features. To test this hypothesis we studied the feature sharing advantage under two conditions (Studdert-Kennedy, Shankweiler, & Pisoni, 1972). In one condition, vowel context remained the same for both dichotic inputs, in the other condition vowel context was varied. Schematized spectrographic patterns of the stimuli which illustrate this comparison are shown in Fig. 2. Eight CV syllables were formed from all possible combinations of the four

[1] Throughout this chapter I use the terms "acoustic cue" and "auditory feature" somewhat interchangeably since there is a one-to-one mapping of acoustic cue to auditory feature.

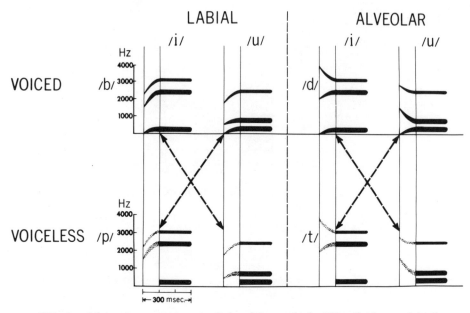

FIG. 2.   Schematic spectrograms of the eight synthetic CV syllables used in the feature sharing experiment. (After Studdert-Kennedy, Shankweiler, & Pisoni, 1972.)

stop consonants ([b, p, d, t]) and the two vowels ([i, u]). As shown in this figure, all within column pairs (e.g., [bi–pi, bu–pu, di–ti, du–tu]) share both place of articulation (i.e., labial, alveolar) and the following vowel. These pairs have identical formant transitions and, therefore, the same auditory features underlie the phonetic feature of place of articulation. The cross-column pairs which are shown by the arrows ([bi–pu, bu–pi, di–tu, du–ti]) also share place of articulation but contrast on the vowel. Thus, these pairs have different formant transitions and, therefore, different auditory features cue the same phonetic feature. As in the earlier experiment, CV syllables that have the same vowel share both phonetic and auditory features. Pairs that contrast on the vowel shared only phonetic features. The results of that experiment replicated the earlier feature-sharing results; correct performance for both stimuli is greater for dichotic pairs that share a feature in common. But of most interest was the finding that there was no effect of vowel context on correct recognition. Thus, we concluded that the feature sharing advantage was due to the shared phonetic features in the two inputs and not shared auditory features. The feature sharing advantage is assumed to have a phonetic rather than auditory basis. These results suggested to us at the time that the feature sharing advantage arises after phonetic analysis during output or response organization—"activation of a feature processor for one response facilitates its activation for another temporally contiguous response [Studdert-Kennedy, Shankweiler, & Pisoni, 1972, p. 463]."

The feature sharing advantage in dichotic listening may be considered to be a facilitatory effect at the phonetic feature level. Features in both inputs have been recognized and appear to be present in short-term memory. This idea is supported by the presence of "blend" and feature reversal errors in subjects' responses. Both types of errors occur when the features in a stimulus presented to one ear are incorrectly combined with the features in the other ear. For example, a "blend" error occurs if [ba] and [ka] are presented dichotically and the subject reports [ga]; the voicing feature from [ba] is combined with the place feature of [ka] to produce a response having both component features. A feature reversal error occurs when the subject reports [ba] and [ta] when the input stimuli were [pa] and [da]; all the component features of the input stimuli are present in the responses but the features have been recombined incorrectly.

Theoretical interest in these types of phonetic interactions is twofold. First, they provide additional support for the idea that phonetic features are recognized more or less independently during perceptual processing. This stage of processing, however, should be distinguished from the earlier stage where auditory features are processed. Current evidence suggests that auditory features are not processed independently of each other (Haggard, 1970; Holloway, 1971; Sawusch & Pisoni, 1974; Smith, 1973). A second reason for interest in these feature interactions is that they indicate that recombination of the component features from each stimulus must have a common locus, presumably after phonetic processing in the language-dominant hemisphere. Indeed, most of the support for a unilaterally represented phonetic processor rests on these types of phonetic feature interactions (Studdert-Kennedy & Shankweiler, 1970). If recombination of the component features occurred separately for each ear, there would be little possibility for the phonetic features from each ear to recombine in the form of blend and feature reversal errors.

LAG EFFECT

The second type of interaction to be considered is the so-called "lag effect" in dichotic listening. This effect occurs when the dichotic inputs are presented with varying temporal delays. Studdert-Kennedy, Shankweiler, and Schulman (1970) reported that subjects identify the second or lagging syllable of a dichotic pair of temporally overlapping stimuli more accurately than the leading syllable. The effect is shown in Fig. 3, which has been replotted from the original report. As shown here, performance is better on the lagging syllable than the leading syllable. When the same

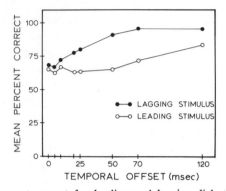

FIG. 3. Mean percent correct for leading and lagging dichotically presented CV syllables. (Based on the data from Studdert-Kennedy, Shankweiler, & Schulman, 1970.)

syllables were mixed and the signal presented monotically to one ear, the lag effect was reversed; the leading syllable was now reported more accurately than the lagging syllable. Studdert-Kennedy *et al.* (1970) originally interpreted the lag effect as a form of "interruption" of speech processing presumably occurring at a central level of perceptual analysis. They suggested that, "the lag effect is tied to speech, and, specifically, to those components of the speech stream for which a relatively complex decoding operation is necessary [Studdert-Kennedy, Shankweiler, & Schulman, 1970, p. 601]." Indeed, the lag effect has been used as evidence to support the general argument that speech perception engages specialized processes that differ from those of nonspeech auditory perception (Liberman, Mattingly, & Turvey, 1972).

The lag effect appears to be a variation of a more general result obtained in backward recognition masking experiments: A second stimulus can impede the processing of a preceding stimulus (Kahneman, 1968; Massaro, 1972; Turvey, 1973). As used in the speech perception literature, the lag effect actually deals with the relative difference between forward and backward masking; there appears to be more dichotic backward masking than forward masking for CV syllables.

A number of recent dichotic experiments have shown that the lag effect may not be peculiar to speech sounds, since it has been obtained with nonspeech timbres, vowels, and other sounds. For example, Darwin (1971), using a directed attention paradigm, has reported a lag effect for stimuli that differ only in fundamental frequency. With ±25-msec offsets between stimuli, listeners reported the second stimulus more often than the first. Although Porter, Shankweiler, and Liberman (1969) initially failed to obtain a lag effect for steady-state vowels, Kirstein (1971) obtained the effect with slightly different procedures. Since the lag effect has been found with speech as well as nonspeech stimuli, it seems reasonable to suppose that this type of dichotic interaction has an auditory rather than phonetic basis. The interaction between the inputs may occur at the auditory feature level prior to phonetic analysis.

We may think of the lag effect as a form of interference in dichotic listening, but what is the locus and nature of this form of interference? At what stage in the information processing system does the interference arise? The dichotic recognition masking experiments to be described were aimed at these questions.

If the masking that underlies the lag effect occurs at an early stage of processing prior to auditory analysis any CV syllable should interfere with the processing of a preceding syllable. This is essentially a stop-processing or interruption hypothesis. On the other hand, if the lag effect occurs after auditory analysis, only certain types of stimulus contrasts should produce interference. These masking experiments indicate that interference is not found equally for all stimulus contrasts. The greatest interference occurs on trials that contain CV syllables that do not share phonetic features. Thus, the feature sharing advantage and the lag effect provide evidence for distinct auditory and phonetic feature interactions in dichotic listening. Furthermore, these types of interactions provide some basis for formulating a rough model of the stages of processing in phonetic perception.

DICHOTIC RECOGNITION MASKING

The method used to study the feature sharing advantage and the lag effect was a dichotic-recognition-masking paradigm. Two CV syllables, a target and a mask, were presented on each trial. The syllables differed in the consonant, the vowel, and their relative times of onset. The subjects' task was always to identify the target stimulus in an ear-monitoring paradigm and to ignore the masking stimulus. Figure 4a shows the general arrangement of the target and masking stimuli used in the backward-masking experiments. For the forward-masking experiments, the configuration of target and mask was simply reversed. In backward masking, the subject identified the first stimulus, in forward masking he identified the second stimulus.

With this technique the processing of a target stimulus may be probed by a masking stimulus at various stimulus onset asynchronies and thereby provide us with some information about the temporal course of perceptual processing of the target sound (Massaro, 1972, 1974). The targets and masks used in these experiments were always drawn from different stimulus ensembles as shown in Fig. 4b. There were two voiced targets, [ba] and

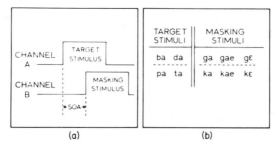

FIG. 4. Arrangement of target and masking stimuli in the dichotic backward masking paradigm (a) and the targets and masks (b) used in the experiments. Targets and masks drawn from the same row share the feature of voicing, whereas targets and masks drawn from different rows contrast on voicing. (After Pisoni & McNabb, 1974.)

[da], and two voiceless targets [pa] and [ta]. The six masks used were selected so that they either shared or contrasted with the auditory and phonetic feature composition of the targets. As in the Studdert-Kennedy, Shankweiler, and Pisoni experiment, the vowel context was varied in order to manipulate the auditory features which underlie a particular phonetic feature. However, the phonetic feature studied in these experiments was voicing, whereas in the previous experiment the feature was place of articulation. We should note here that the place feature in stop consonants is cued primarily by rapid transitional changes in the spectrum (Liberman, Delattre, Cooper, & Gerstman, 1954). On the other hand, the voicing feature is cued primarily by the timing of the onset of first formant relative to the second formant (Liberman, Delattre, & Cooper, 1958).[2]

By varying the vowel context the overall spectral composition of the target and mask could also be manipulated. For example, the target–mask pair [ba]–[ga] shares the voicing feature (+voicing) and the vowel. The pair [ba]–[gæ] still shares the voicing feature but now differs in the vowel. Half of all trials in these experiments contained pairs of stimuli that shared the voicing feature; half contained pairs that contrasted on voicing.

Two comparisons are of interest here as a function of time. First, is there a difference in recognition between pairs of stimuli that share or contrast on the voicing feature? Second, what is the effect of the vowel in the mask on identification of the target? The latter comparison should permit us to specify the locus of the interactions between the dichotic inputs.

[2] The voicing feature in the present experiments is cued by voice onset time (VOT), the temporal interval between the release of stop closure and the onset of laryngeal pulsing. Since VOT is a temporal cue, manipulating vowel context does not necessarily entail a strict independence between auditory feature and phonetic feature as was the case with the place cue.

For example, if the vowel context of the mask has no effect on the identification of the target, we would conclude that the interaction between the inputs occurred at the phonetic level. This would be anticipated if the consonant segments had already been abstracted from the syllables. On the other hand, if the vowel context systematically affects target identification, this would indicate that, at least, some component of the interaction occurs at an earlier stage of analysis either before or during phonetic processing.

Backward Masking

In the first experiment, backward masking was examined for shared and nonshared trials as a function of stimulus onset asynchrony (SOA). The main results are shown in Fig. 5, averaged over the three vowel contexts. Voiced and voiceless targets have also been combined in this figure. Performance was consistently higher for pairs that shared voicing than pairs that contrasted on voicing. Performance is relatively stable for shared pairs at all SOA values, whereas performance improves steadily for nonshared pairs as SOA increased. When we scored the data for correct recognition of the voicing feature alone, performance in the shared condition was virtually perfect. For example, if [ba] was the target and the subject responded with [da], this was scored as a correct response of the voicing feature; stimulus and response were both (+voiced). In contrast, performance for the voic-

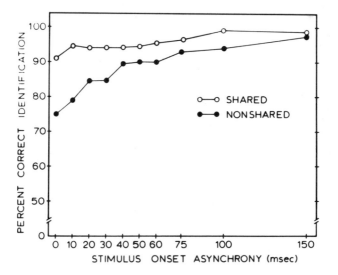

FIG. 5.   Percentage of correct identifications of target stimuli for shared and nonshared trials as a function of stimulus onset asynchrony. The data are averaged over the three vowel-masks. (After Pisoni & McNabb, 1974.)

ing feature on the nonshared trials remained the same as in the previous analysis of correct responses.

The effect of vowel context of the mask on shared and nonshared trials is shown separately for each of the three vowel conditions in Fig. 6. The influence of the vowel is restricted primarily to the nonshared pairs. Performance on these trials was lowest for [a] vowel masks, highest for [ɛ], and midway between the two for [æ]. Identification in the shared condition is consistently higher under each vowel condition than in the nonshared condition.

The main results of this experiment suggest that the feature sharing advantage and the interference obtained in the lag effect are distinct types of interactions between dichotic speech inputs, presumably occurring at different levels of analysis. Overall performance is affected by both SOA and vowel context of the mask. However, the difference between shared and nonshared trials still maintains itself under these conditions.

These results replicate and extend the previous findings on the feature sharing advantage reported by Studdert-Kennedy and Shankweiler (1970) and Studdert-Kennedy *et al.* (1972). As noted earlier, these findings were interpreted as evidence that the feature sharing advantage occurred on the output side of phonetic analysis during response organization. However, in the present experiment the feature sharing advantage still occurs and with considerable magnitude when only one response is required. Thus, we can infer from this result that the feature sharing advantage probably lies somewhere before response organization after the features have been identified. We will return to a more detailed account of the feature sharing advantage later on.

These results also provide some insight into the type of interaction underlying the lag effect. For nonshared trials we observe that performance

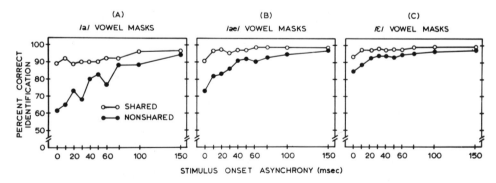

FIG. 6.   Percentage of correct identifications of target stimuli for shared and non-shared trials under each vowel mask. (After Pisoni & McNabb, 1974.)

increases as the interval between the onset of the target and mask is increased. Increases in SOA provide increases in processing time for recognition of the auditory features in the target stimulus. Since recognition of the target stimuli is affected systematically by the vowel context of the masking syllable, one component of the interaction must occur before phonetic analysis, while the auditory features in the syllables are still being processed. If the interaction occurred after the consonant features had been abstracted from the target, the vowel context should not have affected the identification of the target. These results suggest that the locus of the interference underlying the lag effect occurs at an auditory feature level.

At first glance, the results of this experiment present somewhat of a paradox: similarity in the consonant voicing feature (i.e., voice onset time) reduces interference, similarity in the vowel increases interference. The latter effect is not difficult to understand. We have only to suppose that the more similar the vowels of the target and mask, the more likely the two syllables are to "fuse" or integrate into one perceptual unit, so that the listener has difficulty assigning the correct auditory features to the appropriate stimulus (see also Cutting, 1972). This account of the vowel effect argues against a strict interruption or stop-processing explanation. If the second stimulus simply terminated the readout of auditory features from the first stimulus, vowel similarity should not have had any effect on target recognition. Any speech stimulus should have terminated processing. In addition, we would not expect to find an interaction between the phonetic feature composition of the consonant targets and the vowel context of the mask. Both findings suggest an account of masking based on some form of integration at an auditory level. Auditory features from both stimuli merge together to form a composite stimulus which is then made available for subsequent phonetic analysis. Thus, variations in the degree of backward masking can be accounted for by variations in "acoustic confusability" due to overall spectral composition of target and mask. We are going to assume that the vowel effect is due to relatively low-level binaural interaction in the auditory system (see Colburn & Durlach, in press; Durlach & Colburn, in press).

But how are we to account for the apparent lack of interference for pairs of stimuli that share the voicing feature? Before attempting an account of the absence of masking in this condition, we consider another experiment, where mask intensity is manipulated. If auditory factors are the principal determinants of variations in the degree of backward masking, we would expect intensity variations to have an effect on both shared and nonshared trials as well as the variations in spectral composition. Intensity as a gross physical parameter should also have its effect at relatively early stages of processing.

We carried out another backward masking experiment where the intensity of the mask differed from the target by 0, +10, or +20 dB. Figure 7 shows the results of this experiment for shared and nonshared trials as a function of SOA for each mask intensity level. These functions are averaged over all vowel contexts. Note that the effect of mask intensity is clearly present for both shared and nonshared trials; performance on the target systematically decreased as mask intensity increased. The difference in recognition between shared and nonshared trials is, however, still present under all three intensity conditions.

When the data were scored separately by voicing, treating a response as correct if voicing was correct, the intensity effect for the shared trials disappears. This result is shown in Fig. 8 which is based on the data from the [a] vowel mask condition. Thus, increased mask intensity for shared pairs apparently has its main effect on the place feature that is cued by relatively rapid spectral changes during the very early portion of the syllable. In contrast, correct identification of the voicing feature for the nonshared pairs decreases systematically as mask intensity is increased.

A clue to understanding the absence of interference for shared pairs is provided by an examination of the feature errors. Table 1 displays the proportions of voicing and place feature errors for shared and nonshared trials in the conditions yielding maximum masking, namely, a +20-dB mask intensity with target and mask vowels identical. The main point to note in this table is that, whereas place errors are roughly the same when the voicing feature is shared as when it is not, voicing errors are sharply increased in the nonshared condition. In other words, the feature-sharing advantage is confined to the particular feature shared. The previous studies by Studdert-Kennedy and Shankweiler (1970) and Studdert-Kennedy *et al.* (1972) failed to observe this because they did not score the subject's

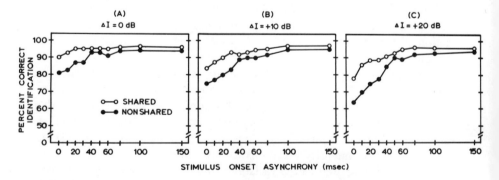

FIG. 7.   Percentage of correct identifications of target stimuli for shared and nonshared trials at each of three mask-intensity levels. (After Pisoni & McNabb 1974.)

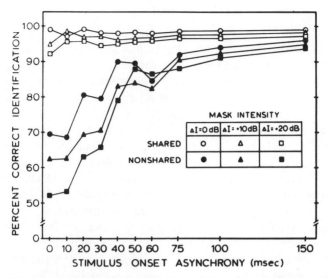

FIG. 8. Percentage of correct identifications of the voicing feature on shared and nonshared trials as a function of mask intensity from the [a] vowel mask condition. (After Pisoni & McNabb 1974.)

TABLE 1
Proportions of Voicing and Place Errors under
Voicing Shared and Nonshared Conditions for the
+20-dB [a] Vowel Masks[a]

	Feature	Voicing shared	Voicing nonshared
Voicing	Voiced	.05	.31
	Voiceless	.03.	.16
Place	Labial	.16	.12
	Alveolar	.03	.04

[a] From Pisoni and McNabb (1974).

response by feature but only by total response. Thus, if a subject makes a voicing error on a nonshared trial, his response must contain the voicing feature of the mask. The high rate of errors on voicing is then due to the fact that the voicing feature of the mask interacts with the voicing feature of the target. This result should be emphasized, since it clearly suggests that the feature sharing advantage occurs at the phonetic feature level and not earlier.

Forward Masking

The backward recognition masking results could be explained by a simple masking or interruption hypothesis (Massaro, 1972, 1974). The second stimulus terminates the readout of auditory features from the preceding stimulus. However, some complexities arise when we consider the case of forward recognition masking. In this experiment, subjects identify the second stimulus rather than the first. The forward masking experiment is important for several reasons. First, if the interference between target and mask were due strictly to interruption, no forward masking would be anticipated, since processing time for the target is unlimited. Second, the presence of forward masking would lend additional support to the integration hypothesis outlined earlier. The target and masking stimuli merge to form a composite stimulus containing auditory features of both stimuli.

In this forward-masking experiment, all stimuli and experimental conditions were identical to the first backward-masking experiment described earlier, except that a new group of subjects was employed. The main results are shown in Fig. 9 averaged over the three vowel contexts. The difference in correct identification of the targets between shared and nonshared trials is quite similar to that found in the earlier backward masking experiments. Performance improves steadily as a function of SOA for both types of trials. The effect of the vowel context is shown separately again for each vowel in Fig. 10. The effect of the vowel on target identification is remarkably similar to that found in the backward masking case; overall performance is inversely related to the spectral composition of the vowel context of the target and masking syllables.

We can summarize the results of these experiments quite simply. First, forward- and backward-masking functions appear to be essentially the same. Differences in relative onset of target and mask, spectral similarity, and mask intensity influence the overall level of performance for both shared and nonshared trials. Furthermore, shared and nonshared trials continue to show differences in performance under these experimental manipulations. These results suggest several stages at which dichotic speech inputs can interact. In order to describe these interactions in more detail we consider a rough model of the stages of processing in phonetic perception.

STAGES OF PROCESSING

Taken together, the forward and backward dichotic masking results provide some insight into the recognition process. Earlier, I described the distinction between auditory and phonetic stages of processing. However, based on the present findings, this dichotomy appears to be much too gross, and additional stages are required. Figure 11 shows a qualitative model

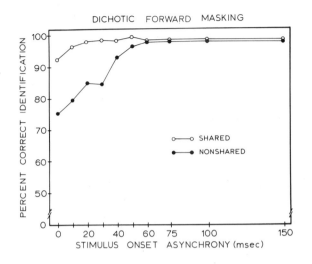

FIG. 9.   Percentage of correct identifications of target stimuli in forward-masking condition for shared and nonshared trials as a function of stimulus onset asynchrony.

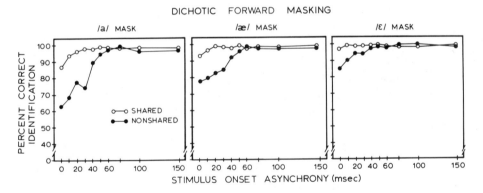

FIG. 10.   Percentage of correct identifications of target stimuli in forward-masking condition under each vowel condition.

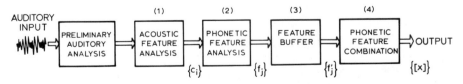

FIG. 11.   Stage model of levels of processing in phonetic recognition. Auditory input is processed progressively through several levels of analysis.

of the stages of processing involved in phonetic recognition. Auditory input first undergoes preliminary auditory analysis. The output is assumed to be some type of spectral display in terms of frequency, time, and intensity. Sensory input is then processed progressively through several levels of analysis. Processing stages have been arranged here serially only for convenience, since insufficient experimental evidence exists to argue for parallel or serial processing between these stages at the present time (see Wood, 1974, Chapter 3 of this volume).

Acoustic feature analysis is the first stage of the recognition process. Here, auditory features of the speech signal are identified by a system of individual auditory feature detectors (Cooper, Chapter 2; Stevens, 1973). For example, in the case of a simple CV syllable, we assume that specialized detectors will respond selectively to some of the following types of auditory information:

(*a*) presence or absence of a rapid change in the spectrum; (*b*) direction, extent and duration of a change in the spectrum; (*c*) duration and intensity of noise; (*d*) frequency of noise segment or burst; (*e*) presence or absence of the fundamental frequency from the beginning of the syllable; (*f*) abrupt rise in the frequency of the fundamental at the transition from consonant to steady-state vowel. The output of acoustic feature analysis is some set of acoustic cues or auditory features, $\{c_i\}$, which forms the input to the next stage of processing.

In Stage 2, *phonetic feature analysis,* we assume that a set of decision rules is employed to map multiple auditory features into phonetic features. It is asumed that this is a many-to-one mapping where several different auditory features provide information about a particular phonetic feature (e.g., see Hoffman, 1958; Liberman, Delattre, & Cooper, 1958). Rather than assuming that a "phonetic processor" exists as a distinct physiological mechanism, I prefer, at the present time, to describe its function simply in terms of decision rules. Decisions about a particular feature are based on auditory information distributed across the whole syllable (Liberman, 1970; Massaro, 1971; Studdert-Kennedy, 1975a, b). It is at this stage that processing becomes lateralized in the language-dominant hemisphere. The output of acoustic feature analysis, $\{c_i\}$, from each hemisphere converge for phonetic feature analysis. The output of phonetic feature analysis is a set of abstract phonetic features $\{f_j\}$.

Phonetic features are subsequently maintained in Stage 3, the *feature buffer*. This may be thought of as a holding mechanism, which maintains decisions about the feature composition of a particular syllable. We distinguish the output of the feature buffer, $\{f_j'\}$, from the input, $\{f_j\}$, since information can be lost by interference or decay, and confusion among features can result. There are two reasons for postulating a feature buffer.

First, not all phonetic features are assumed to be processed (i.e., recognized) at the same rate. Second, some memory process is needed to preserve or maintain phonetic features more or less independently for subsequent stages of linguistic processing.

Feature information is then used in Stage 4, *phonetic feature combination,* where individual features are recombined to form discrete phonetic segments (i.e., phonemes). The output of Stage 4 is a phonetic segment, [X], where the feature specification is, for example, some form of an abstract distinctive feature matrix. This information is passed on to higher levels of linguistic analysis (i.e., phonological).

The model as I have described it is still preliminary, and a number of details remain to be worked out. However, the model can account in a qualitative way for a number of the dichotic listening results discussed so far. For example, the feature sharing advantage probably arises after phonetic feature analysis in the feature buffer. Redundant features do not have to be maintained separately in the buffer and there is less chance of confusion. The feature reversal and blend errors described earlier probably result from confusions among features in the buffer before recombination into phonetic segments. Since these errors involve only the loss of local sign (i.e., ear of origin) it is clear that the features have been identified and they are being maintained in some form independent of context.

Forward and backward masking appears to arise before acoustic feature analysis. Since relative onset time, spectral similarity, and mask intensity all effect overall performance for both shared and nonshared trials, it seems safe to assume that these gross physical parameters affect processing at relatively early stages. Thus, the advantage for sharing a phonetic feature must occur relatively late in the processing sequence, since the difference between these two pairs is still present regardless of large acoustic differences between the target and masking stimuli.

THE RIGHT EAR ADVANTAGE AND THE LAG EFFECT

Throughout most of this chapter, I have focused on the interactions between dichotic speech inputs and essentially ignored asymmetries between the ears. In this section I deal briefly with the right ear advantage for speech stimuli and its relation to the lag effect.

Weeks (1973) has called attention to an apparent paradox between the right ear advantage (REA) and the lag effect in dichotic listening experiments. Most investigators have assumed that the REA is due to some loss of information from the left-ear input. Loss may result from the additional time necessary for the left-ear input to reach the dominant hemisphere since the signal must transverse a longer distance via the corpus callosum. Weeks (1973) has called this a queueing or "delay" hypothesis. It is assumed that the ipsilateral input from the left ear arrives at the dominant hemisphere some time later than the contralateral input from the right ear. However, loss of information from the left ear may also be due to some impairment in the ipsilateral signal as a result of interhemispheric transfer. This is the currently favored explanation of the REA, which has been coined the "degradation hypothesis" by Weeks. Feature extractors in the dominant hemisphere receive a poorer or more degraded signal from the ipsilateral ear.

The apparent paradox between the REA and the lag effect is as follows: Both the delay and degradation hypotheses of the REA assume that the left-ear stimulus arrives at the dominant hemisphere some time later than the right-ear stimulus. Thus, there is an inherent temporal asymmetry, and masking should occur between left- and right-ear stimuli. The left-ear stimulus should interrupt the processing of the right-ear stimulus. However, available evidence indicates that the REA and lag effect are more or less independent of each other (Berlin *et al.,* 1973; Kirstein, 1970, 1971). Thus, the interpretation of the lag effect as a form of interruption of processing through backward masking is in serious conflict with the interpretation of the REA in terms of some inherent delay of the left-ear stimulus. This paradox can be resolved easily, however, by assuming, as I have in this chapter, that the lag effect results from integration of the two dichotic inputs. Thus, the two dichotic stimuli are not functionally independent of each other and, therefore, each hemisphere probably receives a different composite of both stimuli. The interference underlying the lag effect arises, therefore, prior to the stage at which the REA occurs. Several experiments that deal with this particular problem are currently in progress.

FINAL REMARKS

In this chapter I have tried to show how dichotic listening techniques can be used to study some of the more general processes in speech perception. A good part of the recent dichotic listening literature has focused on the types of auditory and phonetic interactions that occur between dichotic speech inputs. These interactions appear to occur at a number of different processing stages, and provide some insight into the general organization of information processing in speech perception. However, we are a long way off from a really well-developed model of the speech perception process. Many details still need to be worked out and many of the conclusions arrived at through dichotic listening experiments will need to be evaluated in other experimental paradigms. In the future, however, we can probably expect to see an increase in the use of various types of brain-damaged subjects in speech perception experiments. These experiments should help to bridge the gap between our knowledge of underlying physiology of speech and language function and the processes we have imparted to little boxes that have appeared in such ever-increasing proclivity over the last few years.

ACKNOWLEDGMENTS

The research reported in this paper was supported by NIMH Research Grant MH-24027-01 to Indiana University. Preparation of the manuscript was supported in part by a Faculty Fellowship from the Office of Research and Advanced Studies, Indiana University. I am very grateful to S. D. McNabb for help and assistance in all phases of this work and to M. Studdert-Kennedy and J. R. Sawusch for critical comments and suggestions.

REFERENCES

Bartz, W. H., Satz, P., Fennell, E., & Lally, J. R. Meaningfulness and laterality in dichotic listening. *Journal of Experimental Psychology,* 1967, **73,** 204–210.

Benson, P. Phonetic and auditory features in dichotic listening. Paper presented at the 87th Meeting of the Acoustical Society of America, New York, New York, April, 1974.

Berlin, C. I., Lowe-Bell, S. S., Cullen, J. K., Thompson, C. L., & Loovis, C. F. Dichotic speech perception: An interpretation of right-ear advantage and temporal offset effects. *Journal of the Acoustical Society of America,* 1973, **53,** 699–709.

Berlin, C. I., & McNeil, M. R. Dichotic listening. In N. J. Lass (Ed.), *Contemporary issues in experimental phonetics.* Springfield, Illinois: Thomas, 1975.

Blumstein, S. The use and theoretical implications of the dichotic technique for investigating distinctive features. *Brain & Language,* 1974, **1,** 337–350.

Bocca, E., Calearo, C., Cassinari, V., & Migliavacca, F. Testing "cortical" hearing in temporal lobe tumors. *Acta Oto-laryngologica,* 1955, **45,** 289–304.

Bondarko, L. V., *et al.* A model of speech perception in humans. *Working Papers in Linguistics No. 6.* Computer & Information Science Research Center, Ohio State University, Columbus, Ohio. Technical Rept. 70-12, 1970.

Bryden, M. P. An evaluation of some models of laterality effects in dichotic listening. *Acta Oto-laryngologica,* 1967, **63,** 595–604.

Colburn, H. S., & Durlach, N. I. Models of binaural interaction. In E. C. Carterette & M. P. Friedman (Eds.), *Handbook of perception.* Vol. IV. New York: Academic Press, 1975. (In press.)

Cooper, W. E. Adaptation of phonetic feature analyzers for place of articulation. *Journal of the Acoustical Society of America,* 1974, **56,** 617–627.

Curry, F. K. W. A comparison of left-handed and right-handed subjects on verbal and non-verbal dichotic listening tasks, *Cortex,* 1967, **3,** 343–353.

Cutting, J. E. A preliminary report on six fusions in auditory research. *Haskins Laboratories Status Report on Speech Research,* **SR-31/32,** 1972, 93–107.

Darwin, C. J. Dichotic backward masking of complex sounds. *Quarterly Journal of Experimental Psychology,* 1971, **23,** 386–392.

Durlach, N. I., & Colburn, H. S. Binaural phenomena. In E. C. Carterette & M. P. Friedman (Eds.), *Handbook of perception.* Vol. IV. New York: Academic Press, 1975. (In press.)

Eimas, P. D., Cooper, W. E., & Corbit, J. D. Some properties of linguistic feature detectors. *Perception & Psychophysics,* 1973, **13,** 247–252.

Eimas, P. D., & Corbit, J. D. Selective adaptation of linguistic feature detectors. *Cognitive Psychology,* 1973, **4,** 99–109.

Fant, G. *Speech sounds and features.* Cambridge, Massachusetts: MIT Press, 1973.

Geschwind, N. The organization of language and the brain. *Science,* 1970, **170,** 940.

Haggard, M. P. The use of voicing information. *Speech Synthesis & Perception* (University of Cambridge, London), 1970, **2,** 1–15.

Hoffman, H. S. A study of some cues in the perception of the voiced stop consonants. *Journal of the Acoustical Society of America,* 1958, **30,** 1035–1041.

Holloway, C. M. A test of the independence of linguistic dimensions. *Language & Speech,* 1971, **14,** 326–340.

Kahneman, D. Method, findings, and theory in studies of visual masking. *Psychological Bulletin,* 1968, **70,** 404–425.

Kimura, D. Some effects of temporal lobe damage on auditory perception. *Canadian Journal of Psychology,* 1961, **15,** 156–165.

Kimura, D. Left–right differences in the perception of melodies. *Quarterly Journal of Experimental Psychology,* 1964, **16,** 355–358.

Kimura, D. Functional asymmetry of the brain in dichotic listening. *Cortex,* 1967, **3,** 163–178.

Kirstein, E. F. Selective listening for temporally staggered dichotic CV syllables. *Journal of the Acoustical Society of America,* 1970, **48,** 95(A).

Kirstein, E. F. Temporal factors in perception of dichotically presented stop consonants and vowels. Unpublished doctoral dissertation. Storrs, Connecticut: University of Connecticut, 1971.

Liberman, A. M. The grammars of speech and language. *Cognitive Psychology,* 1970, **1,** 301–323.

Liberman, A. M. The specialization of the language hemisphere. Paper presented at the Intensive Study Program in the Neurosciences at Boulder, Colorado, July, 1972.

Liberman, A. M., Cooper, F. S., Shankweiler, D. S., & Studdert-Kennedy, M. Perception of the speech code. *Psychological Review,* 1967, **74,** 431–461.

Liberman, A. M., Delattre, P. C., & Cooper, F. S. Some cues for the distinction between voiced and voiceless stops in initial position. *Language & Speech,* 1958, **1,** 153–167.

Liberman, A. M., Delattre, P. C., Cooper, F. S., & Gerstman, L. J. The role of consonant–vowel transitions in the perception of the stop and nasal consonants. *Psychological Monographs,* 1954, **68,** 1–13.

Liberman, A. M., Mattingly, I. G., & Turvey, M. T. Language codes and memory codes. In A. W. Melton & E. Martin (Eds.), *Coding processes in human memory.* Washington, D.C.: Winston, 1972. Pp. 307–334.

Massaro, D. W. Preperceptual images, processing time, and perceptual units in auditory perception. *Psychological Review,* 1972, **79,** 124–145.

Massaro, D. W. Perceptual units in speech recognition. *Journal of Experimental Psychology,* 1974, **102,** 199–208.

Mattingly, I. G., & Liberman, A. M. The speech code and the physiology of language. In K. N. Leibovic (Ed.), *Information proceesing in the nervous system.* Berlin and New York: Springer-Verlag, 1969. Pp. 97–117.

Milner, B. Laterality effects in audition. In V. B. Mountcastle (Ed.), *Interhemispheric relations and cerebral dominance.* Baltimore: Johns Hopkins Univ. Press, 1962. Pp. 177–195.

Milner, B. Interhemispheric differences in the localization of psychological processes in man. *British Medical Bulletin,* 1971, **27,** 272–277.

Milner, B., Taylor, L., & Sperry, R. W. Lateralized suppression of dichotically presented digits after commissural section in man. *Science,* 1968, **161,** 184–185.

Pisoni, D. B., & McNabb, S. D. Dichotic interactions and phonetic feature processing. *Brain & Language,* 1974, **1,** 351–362.

Porter, R. J., Shankweiler, D., & Liberman, A. Differential effects of binaural time differences on perception of stop consonants and vowels. *Proceedings of the 77th Annual Meeting of the American Psychological Association.* Washington, D.C.: American Psychological Association, 1969. Pp. 15–16.

Rosenzweig, M. R. Representations of the two ears at the auditory cortex. *American Journal of Physiology,* 1951, **167,** 147–158.

Sawusch, J. R., & Pisoni, D. B. On the identification of place and voicing features in synthetic stop consonants. *Journal of Phonetics,* 1974, **2,** 181–194.

Shankweiler, D. P. Effects of temporal-lobe damage on perception of dichotically presented melodies. *Journal of Comparative & Physiological Psychology,* 1966, **62,** 115–119.

Shankweiler, D., & Studdert-Kennedy, M. Identification of consonants and vowels presented to left and right ears. *Quarterly Journal of Experimental Psychology,* 1967, **19,** 59–63.

Smith, P. T. Feature-testing models and their application to perception and memory for speech. *Quarterly Journal of Experimental Psychology,* 1973, **25,** 511–534.

Sparks, R., & Geschwind, N. Dichotic listening in man after section of neocortical commissures. *Cortex,* 1968, **4,** 3–16.

Speaks, C., Gray, T., Miller, J., Rubens, A., & Walker, M. Interference with processing dichotic pairs of CV syllables after temporal-lobe lesion. Paper presented at the 87th Meeting of the Acoustical Society of America, New York, New York, April, 1974.

Stevens, K. N. The potential role of property detectors in the perception of consonants. Paper presented at the Symposium on Auditory Analysis and Perception of Speech, Leningrad, USSR, August, 1973.

Stevens, K. N., & House, A. S. Speech Perception. In J. Tobias (Ed.), *Foundations of modern auditory theory,* Vol. II. New York: Academic Press, 1972. Pp. 1–62.

Studdert-Kennedy, M. The perception of speech. In T. A. Sebeok (Ed.), *Current trends in linguistics.* Vol. XII. The Hague: Mouton, 1975.   (a)

Studdert-Kennedy, M. Speech perception. In N. J. Lass (Ed.), *Contemporary issues in experimental phonetics.* Springfield, Illinois: Thomas, 1975.   (b)

Studdert-Kennedy, M., & Shankweiler, D. Hemispheric specialization for speech perception. *Journal of the Acoustical Society of America,* 1970, **48,** 579–594.

Studdert-Kennedy, M., Shankweiler, D., & Pisoni, D. B. Auditory and phonetic processes in speech perception: Evidence from a dichotic study. *Cognitive Psychology,* 1972, **3,** 455–466.

Studdert-Kennedy, M., Shankweiler, D., & Schulman, S. Opposed effects of a delayed channel on perception of dichotically and monotically presented CV syllables. *Journal of the Acoustical Society of America*, 1970, **48**, 599–602.

Turvey, M. T. On peripheral and central processes in vision: Inferences from an information-processing analysis of masking with patterned stimuli. *Psychological Review*, 1973, **80**, 1–52.

Weeks, R. A. A Speech perception paradox?: The right-ear advantage and the lag effect. *Haskins Laboratories Status Report on Speech Research*, **SR-33**, 1973, 29–35.

Wood, C. C. Levels of processing in speech perception: Neurophysiological and information-processing analyses. Unpublished doctoral dissertation. New Haven: Yale University, 1973. (Also appears in *Haskins Laboratories Status Report on Speech Research*, **SR-35/36**, 1973.)

Wood, C. C. Parallel processing of auditory and phonetic information in speech perception. *Perception & Psychophysics*, 1974, **15**, 501–508.

Wood, C. C., Goff, W. R., & Day, R. S. Auditory evoked potentials during speech perception. *Science*, 1971, **173**, 1248–1251.

PART II
CONTEMPORARY APPROACHES TO JUDGMENT

N. John Castellan, Jr.
Harold R. Lindman

In the past dozen years, increasing emphasis has been placed on cognitive factors in judgment. Although much early emphasis was placed upon the simple stimulus–response link in judgment (see Bock & Jones, 1968, for an extensive treatment of such work) as far back as the 1930s psychologists like Brunswik were urging that greater emphasis be placed on the information processing and cognitive aspects of judgment. While it is difficult to point to a distinct starting point for the modern trend in research in judgment, it is certainly clear that today major emphasis is placed upon cognitive functioning.

Whereas reasons for the change are not clear, at least one was because the older approaches did not help much in the understanding of judgment processes in ecologically relevant areas such as medical decision making and interpersonal learning.

In these introductory remarks it is not our purpose to provide a comprehensive overview of developments in the area—this has been done in two excellent reviews, one by Slovic and Lichtenstein (1973) and the other by Rapoport and Wallsten (1972). Their important surveys cover developments prior to about 1971. At this point, our purpose is to distinguish certain characteristics of research paradigms that can provide insight into the variety of problems and approaches in the area of cognitive judgment.

Two major threads wind through the chapters by Birnbaum, Dawes, and Pitz. One can be characterized by concern with the process of judgment and the capabilities of the judge, and the other is characterized by concern with the task. These two features cannot be considered adequately in isolation, but it is possible to focus briefly on some representative aspects of each.

PROCESSING IN JUDGMENT

There are many approaches to the study of information processing in judgment. The chapter by Birnbaum deals with a dual processing of physical sensations and expectancies. As Birnbaum points out, the processing of contextual stimuli has played a role in the study of illusions and is an important part of theories like Helson's adaptation-level theory. One of the important points about Birnbaum's approach is that the subject makes a judgment based upon current information available in the stimulus object, and a comparison of the current object with some internal representation.

Other expectancy models in judgment also postulate the covert comparison of a stimulus with some internal representation. Such a model was proposed by Castellan and Edgell (1973) in which, rather than make a simultaneous comparison of stimulus object and representation as Birnbaum does, a successive comparison of object and representation was proposed. Such models consider responses to be point estimations of response tendencies, and observed variability is considered to be part of the response generation process. Closely related to this is the medical judgment model proposed by Wortman (1970, 1972). In a more formal context, Garner (1974) has conducted extensive and systematic research on the processing of stimuli which are well encoded by subjects.

In the chapter by Pitz, it is assumed that the subject is well aware of the uncertainty of the stimulus information, and estimates the variability by specifying a special confidence internal ("tertile" in Pitz's terminology). The sort of research in which the subject estimates variability grows out of the Bayesian tradition in psychology in which the subject is often asked to estimate probabilities and uncertainties. (See Lee, 1971, for a comprehensive review of this research.) The recent work on cascaded inference is a promising extension of this approach.[1]

FOCUS ON TASK

The work of Dawes focuses on the importance of task description in developing explanations in judgment. This focus is important because, in

---

[1] The interested reader should consult the special issue of *Organizational Behavior and Human Performance* published in December 1973, which was devoted entirely to this approach.

many situations, the task description is so crude that one cannot tell how well a subject is actually performing. Certain linear models have been helpful in gaining an understanding of the task situation. One such model, the "lens model" (Castellan, 1973; Hursch, Hammond, & Hursch, 1964; Tucker, 1964) has been especially useful. This model requires that both the task and the subject be described in the same terms so that the subject's behavior, relative to the environment, can be assessed. Whereas it has been pointed out by Dawes in this volume and elsewhere (Dawes & Corrigan, 1974) that there are limitations on the usefulness of linear models, the limited benefits derived are often sufficient to make significant contributions to an understanding of the judgment process.

Others have focused on the task in order to study judgment, using a task analysis to see to what extent a subject's behavior can be modified by changing the description given the subject concerning his performance (see, e.g., Castellan, 1974). In another situation, Einhorn (1970) proposed models which attempt to match the model of judgment to the general goals dictated by the judgment task itself.

Focusing on the task has both practical and theoretical implications for the study of behavior. These three chapters all come out of what might be considered a pessimistic tradition about human judgmental ability under uncertainty. Dawes' contribution comes from a long series of studies in which subjects' judgments in situations presumably requiring complicated analysis are no better than simple linear models. The tradition of Pitz is even more pessimistic. Early attempts to use models of optimal decision strategies to understand choices under uncertainty have been shown to be futile by more recent studies indicating that people cannot always make consistent, let alone optimal, choices even in apparently simple situations (Lichtenstein & Slovic, 1971; Lindman, 1971; Tversky, 1969). Other studies, involving people's ability to evaluate and manipulate probabilistic evidence, have shown even greater deficiencies in human judgment (Kahneman & Tversky, 1972; Tversky & Kahneman, 1973). Even perceptual research—one source for Birnbaum's contribution—indicates that people frequently misjudge their perceptions.

Nevertheless, each of these papers sounds an optimistic note about human judgment. They suggest that the failure might be more often in the researchers than in the judges. Although human judgments are probably seldom, if ever, optimal, they can be much better than the literature indicates if (1) the task is clear and understandable; (2) the feedback and payoffs are such that "optimal" judgments are clearly superior; and (3) personal variables (such as the expectancies or hypotheses entertained by the subject) that are not part of the formal experimental situation are taken into account.

REFERENCES

Bock, R. D., & Jones, L. V. *The measurement and prediction of judgment and choice.* San Francisco: Holden-Day, 1968.

Castellan, N. J., Jr. Comments on the 'Lens Model' and the analysis of multiple-cue judgment tasks. *Psychometrika,* 1973, **38,** 87–100.

Castellan, N. J., Jr. The effect of different types of feedback in multiple-cue probability learning. *Organizational Behavior and Human Performance,* 1974, **11,** 44–64.

Castellan, N. J., Jr., & Edgell, S. E. An hypothesis generation model for judgment in nonmetric multiple-cue probability learning. *Journal of Mathematical Psychology,* 1973, **10,** 204–222.

Dawes, R. M., & Corrigan, B. Linear models in decision making. *Psychological Bulletin,* 1974, **81,** 95–106.

Einhorn, H. J. The use of nonlinear, noncompensatory models in decision making. *Psychological Bulletin,* 1970, **73,** 221–230.

Garner, W. R. *The processing of information and structure.* Hillsdale, New Jersey: Lawrence Erlbaum Assoc., 1974.

Hursch, C. J., Hammond, K. R., & Hursch, J. L. Some methodological considerations in multiple-cue probability studies. *Psychological Review,* 1964, **71,** 42–60.

Kahneman, D., & Tversky, A. Subjective probability: A judgment of representativeness. *Cognitive Psychology,* 1972, **3,** 430–454.

Lee, W. *Decision theory and human behavior.* New York: Wiley, 1971.

Lichtenstein, S., & Slovic, P. Reversals of preferences between bids and choices in gambling decisions. *Journal of Experimental Psychology,* 1971, **89,** 46–55.

Lindman, H. Inconsistent preferences among gambles. *Journal of Experimental Psychology,* 1971, **89,** 390–397.

Rapoport, A., & Wallsten, T. S. Individual decision behavior. *Annual Review of Psychology,* 1972, **23,** 131–176.

Slovic, P., & Lichtenstein, S. Comparison of Bayesian and regression approaches to the study of information processing in judgment. In L. Rappoport & D. A. Summers, (Eds.), *Human judgment and social interaction.* New York: Holt, 1973. Pp. 16–108.

Tucker, L. R. A suggested alternative formulation in the developments by Hursch, Hammond, and Hursch, and Hammond, Hursch, and Todd. *Psychological Review,* 1964, **71,** 528–530.

Tversky, A. Intrasitivity of preferences. *Psychological Review,* 1969, **76,** 31–49.

Tversky, A., & Kahneman, D. Judgment under uncertainty: Heuristics and biases. *Oregon Research Institute,* 1973, **13,** No. 1.

Wortman, P. M. Cognitive utilization of probabilistic cues. *Behavioral Science,* 1970, **15,** 329–336.

Wortman, P. M. Medical diagnosis: An information-processing approach. *Computers and Biomedical Research,* 1972, **5,** 315–328.

5
EXPECTANCY AND JUDGMENT

Michael H. Birnbaum
University of Illinois

Many psychologists seeking explanations of behavior have found judgment to be a rewarding area of investigation. Judgment is a pervasive aspect of human behavior: we say the evening was "pleasantly warm," the man was "tall," his intentions were "not very good," the girl was "extremely beautiful," and she loved him "very much." Judgments even characterize the occupations of physician, lawyer, politician, editor, and the activities of voter, motorist, juror, athlete, and consumer.

The ubiquity of judgmental behaviors identifies judgment as an important problem. More important, perhaps, is the fact that judgments are often public events. They are easily obtained and easily quantified by ordinary rating scales. What meaning one can apply to the numbers obtained in this way is, of course, an important empirical issue (Birnbaum, 1974a,b). But judgment is clearly one area of psychology in which the dependent variable and the problem to be explained are closely allied.

It will be helpful to introduce several empirical themes and methodological ideas that are basic to the present discussion. The first is that judgments are *relative* (Helson, 1964; Parducci, 1968, 1974). So-called "absolute" judgments depend upon the *context*, or stimulus array. The man is judged "tall" because his height exceeds that of a majority of the other men in the context. A 6-ft 2-inch man might be judged "tall" at a cocktail party, but "short" in the context of professional basketball players.

Another fundamental theme is that judgments often require *information integration* (Anderson, 1970b, 1971, 1974a,b); that is, the effects of many

107

stimuli combine to form overall impressions. For example, subjects might be asked to form an impression of a person described as "sincere, intelligent, malicious, and obnoxious." Such a person would probably be judged low on a scale of likeableness (Birnbaum, 1974a). It is assumed that in order to form this impression, the meanings or *values* of the words are combined by an *integration* process to create an impression of likeableness, and this impression is transformed to an overt response ("dislike very much") by a *judgment* process. These processes have been investigated by means of an approach known as *functional measurement* (Anderson, 1970b), in which psychological measurements are derived in accord with the model to be tested. Separation of the stimulus valuation, information integration, and response formation processes can be achieved through extensions of functional measurement methods (see e.g., Birnbaum, 1974a; Birnbaum & Veit, 1974a,b).

A final theme is that man is an active processor of his uncertain, probabilistic environment, an *intuitive statistician* (Brunswik, 1956; Brunswik & Herma, 1951), whose reactions can adapt to changing relationships. Brunswik proposed that the subject's utilization of stimulus cues in perception depends on the predictive value of the cue, and that the pattern of intercorrelations among stimulus events is an important determinant of behavior. For example, a stimulus that produces a trapezoidal retinal image may be either a rectangle viewed from an angle or a trapazoid. The organism must make a "best bet," based on the predictive power of cues.

This chapter views man as dealing with his environment partly through the formation of expectancies that can be compared with actual outcomes or events. The formation of expectancies and the process of comparison are considered fundamental properties of perceptual and judgmental systems. Expectancies can be thought of as the predictions of an intuitive statistician, based on subjective correlations between stimulus cues and events. The combination of cues to form expectancies as well as the comparison of events with expectancies can be studied in terms of information integration. Finally, the relations among events define a context, which can be manipulated to produce predictable effects on judgments.

A THEORY OF EXPECTANCY

Through general experience, organisms are presumed to learn to predict events from correlated cues. As R. L. Gregory and other psychologists have noted, it is useful to conceptualize perception as an *hypothesis* that accounts for sensations. According to this analogy, sensation is to perception as data is to theory. Just as scientific hypotheses yield experimental predictions, perceptions yield sensory predictions.

These predictions or "expectancies" can be thought of as being similar to a statistician's best-fit predictions, since the deviations between perceptual experiences and expectancies should be minimal. Why should the organism form expectancies? It is not enough of an answer to say, *For the same reason that the statistican does,* because the statistician's behavior also deserves explanation.

Perhaps the beginning of an answer can be seen by considering the normative requirements of an organism that lifts objects of varied size, weight, and substance. Suppose you were trying to design a robot that could lift objects in a coordinated fashion. Once designed, the robot is a model of behavior. Of course, the robot should contain a feedback system that allows continuous correction and adjustment of its operations. However, one can also see the advantages of a system that would allow the robot to predict from cues, such as size, the correct forces to apply to move the objects to specified locations. In addition, the robot should be flexible enough to adapt its predictions to a new size–weight relationship in a changing environment.

A statistician could suggest a simple starting point for the robot. It should plot a scatter diagram of weight as a function of size, plotting a separate point for each object. If the objects were all made of the same substance, the correlation would be unity. But in any reasonable environment, such as the set of table-top objects, size and weight will be positively, but imperfectly, correlated. The problem is to predict weight based on size, minimizing the deviations between expectancies and events. The linear regression equation provides a simple solution,

$$\hat{Z}_Y = r_{XY} Z_X , \tag{1}$$

where $\hat{Z}_Y$ is the standard score of the predicted value $(\hat{Y})$, r_{XY} is the correlation between X and Y, and Z_X is the standard score of X. This formula predicts weight as a linear function of size, minimizing the squared deviations between obtained and predicted weight, $(Y - \hat{Y})^2$.

The statistical robot would apply a force of $\hat{Y}$ to an object of size X, and the robot's feedback mechanism would have to correct the force by the amount $(Y - \hat{Y})$. This statistical robot would soon adapt to an environment, requiring the feedback mechanism to do less work as the sample estimate of r_{XY} improved. But this robot would do badly in a changing environment. Suppose the robot were lifting objects of fixed size, all 100 gm in weight. Then $\hat{Y} = 100$ gm. If the robot were then to experience objects all of 200 gm, the robot's expectancy for weight (the average event) would begin to approach 200 as the 200-gm weights are averaged with 100 gm. But it would never reach 200. Even if the robot placed greater weight on more recent events, its predictions would never become unbiased in the new, 200-gm environment. One way the robot could overcome this difficulty would be to form new expectancies by taking a linear combination of the event (Y), the event-expectancy contrast $(Y - \hat{Y})$, and the previous expectancy $(\hat{Y})$. For example, if the robot lifted a 200-gm weight expecting 100 gm, the contrast would be $+100$ gm. Event (200) plus contrast (100) would be 300 gm; when averaged with the previous expectancy (100), the new expectancy would be exactly 200 gm. Thus, by forming new expectancies based on contrasts with previous events, it may be possible to adapt to a changing environment.

It would seem almost preposterous to propose that humans perform these statistical calculations in their heads or that they could even usefully introspect how they actually form expectancies. The preceding normative considerations provide a set of analogies, a framework for the discussion of perceptual expectancy, adaptation, and judgment. The statistical robot suggests a testable model of expectancy and judgment.

The model presumes that experiences are contrasted with expectancies. Judgments are given by the equation

$$J = E + a(E - E^*), \tag{2}$$

where J is the subjective value of the event, E is what the event would be apart from the expectancy effect, and E^* is the expectancy of the event based on predicting cues. The constant a reflects the magnitude of the contrast effect. Overt ratings are presumed to be a linear function of the subjective values J. Equation (2) gives a qualitative account of the size–weight illusion (Anderson, 1970a, 1972). Since larger objects would be expected to be heavier, they are judged lighter than smaller objects of the same weight. Equation (2) also explains why blind dates are doomed to failure. In order to get a friend to agree to a blind date, E^* must be made large; but the greater E^*, the less the judgment of satisfaction when the friend actually meets the date.

Birnbaum and Veit (1973) proposed that expectancies depend upon the subjective correlation R_{EP} between the event E and the predictor P:

$$E^* = R_{EP} \cdot P, \tag{3}$$

where E^* is the expectancy for the event. Equation (3) is analogous to Eq. (1), except Eq. (3) involves subjective correlation and subjective stimulus values. The subjective correlation is assumed to depend on prior experience and the actual correlation between events in the experimental situation; it need not be equal to the actual correlation in a given situation.

EXPERIMENTAL ILLUSTRATION

A recent experiment done in collaboration with Ken Hagen illustrates the essential ideas of the present theory. Consider the lever in the upper portion of Fig. 1. On each trial, the subject's task is to press at point A, lifting a weight at one of three positions (distances from the fulcrum, B), and judge the force ("effort") required to do so.

If the *same* weight were moved from position 1 to position 3, the actual force required at point A would increase with increasing distance from the fulcrum. However, in this experiment, *different* weights are placed at different locations on different trials to alter the subjects' expectancies. The lower panel of Fig. 1 illustrates the experimental design; each symbol represents a different type of stimulus presentation. The three solid circular points in each row represent different actual weights that, when individually

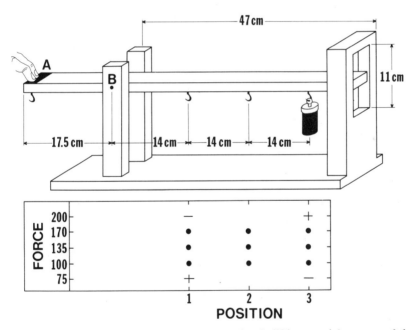

FIG. 1.   The lever: The subject presses at point A, lifting a weight at one of three distances from the fulcrum at point B. The task on each trial was to rate effort required to move lever. The lower panel shows the experimental design. Each symbol represents a stimulus presentation. Ordinate values represent the force in gram equivalents that would be required at point A to balance the lever. Solid circles represent test presentations that were the same for all correlation conditions; plus and minus signs represent contextual presentations for the positive and negative conditions, respectively.

placed at the appropriate position, would balance a constant force at point A (indicated by the ordinate value). The weights are all identical in appearance.

Figure 1 also depicts the additional, contextual trials that are presented to change the subjective correlation for different groups of subjects. Subjects in the positive correlation condition are presented with many trials on which a large force (200 gm) is required to lift a weight at the far position or a small force (75 gm) is required for a weight at the near position (see plus signs in Fig. 1). Presumably, after a number of trials they learn to expect greater forces at farther positions. However, subjects in the negative correlation condition are presented with trials that require a large force (200 gm) to lift a weight at the near position or a small force (75 gm) to lift a weight at the far position (minus signs in Fig. 1); consequently, they should expect that objects placed at the nearer positions will require greater forces to lift. Subjects in the zero correlation condition are given both types of presentations. All groups receive the test trials (solid circles in Fig. 1); every other trial is a contextual presentation for the appropriate correlation condition. Thus, the marginal distributions of forces and positions are the same for all groups, but the correlation between force and position is either positive, negative, or zero.

How will judgments of the force required at A depend on position when actual force is held constant? Equation (2) predicts that judgments reflect a contrast between force applied (E) and force expected (E^*), where E is presumed to depend on actual force and E^* is presumed to depend on position. Equation (3) predicts that the direction of the expectancy depends upon the subjective correlation between force and position. In the positive correlation, subjects should expect greater forces at farther positions; hence, judgments should vary inversely with distance. However, subjects in the negative correlation should have the opposite expectancy, and judgments should vary directly with position.

Each panel of Fig. 2 plots mean judgments for a different group (eight subjects), who experienced positive, zero, or negative correlations between position and force. Within each panel, mean judgments of effort are plotted as a function of distance from the fulcrum (position) with a separate curve for each level of actual force (labeled in gram equivalents).

The model predicts that reversing the subjective correlation should reverse the effect of position. Indeed, Fig. 2 shows that judgments vary *inversely* with position in the positive correlation, vary *directly* with position in the negative correlation, and show little effect of position in the zero correlation. When judgments are plotted separately for each subject as a function of position, the data for all eight subjects in the positive condition had negative slopes and for all eight subjects in the negative condition had

FIG. 2. Mean judgment of effort required at point A plotted as a function of position, with a separate curve for each level of actual force. Each panel shows results for a different group of subjects with a different correlation. When the correlation is positive, judgments vary inversely with position; when the correlation is negative, judgments vary directly.

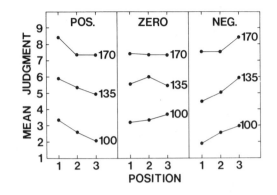

positive slopes. As predicted by the model, the effect of position can be reversed by manipulating the force–position correlation.

Equation (2) also predicts that the curves in each panel should be parallel, since the differences between the curves are a function of force only. The interaction between force and position, and the three-way interaction with correlation were nonsignificant, in agreement with Eq. (2). These results are consistent with the model, and add further support to the findings of Birnbaum and Veit (1973) and of Birnbaum, Kobernick, and Veit (1974) for the size–numerosity illusion.

Data for the size-numerosity illusion (Birnbaum *et al.,* 1974, Expt. I) are shown in Fig. 3. Judgments of the numerosity of dots vary inversely

FIG. 3. Results for the size–numerosity illusion: (a) mean judgments of numerosity as a function of the background size with a separate curve for each level of actual number of dots; (b) mean judgments averaged over levels of number, with separate curves for differerent groups who received different size–numerosity correlations. [From Subjective correlation and the size–numerosity illusion, by Michael H. Birnbaum, Marc Kobernick, & Clairice T. Veit, *Journal of Experimental Psychology,* 1974, **102,** 537–539. Copyright by the American Psychological Association. Reproduced by permission.]

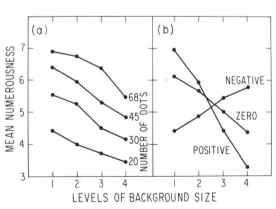

with the size of the background on which the dots appear. It is presumed that subjects expect more dots on larger backgrounds. Consistent with Eqs. (2) and (3), when the correlation between size and actual number is negative, the effect of size is reversed.

Birnbaum et al. (1974, Expts. I and II) found that subjective correlations estimated from Eq. (3) were monotonically related to the seven actual correlations. When the size–numerosity correlation was actually zero, it was found that the subjective correlation was positive, as if previous experience establishes a positive subjective correlation; that is, as if subjects expect more things to appear on larger backgrounds. In the lever experiment, the subjective correlation (slopes in Fig. 2) is very close to zero when the actual correlation is zero. Expectancies concerning the lever may be relatively weak, or it may be that psychomotor expectancies are labile so that the first series of trials in the zero correlation minimizes the effect of prior experience.

An interesting finding of Birnbaum et al. (1974, Expt. II) was that subjective correlations are easily reversed. In relatively few trials, it was possible to reverse the subjective correlation built up at the beginning of the experiment. An interesting problem for further work would be to examine trial-by-trial changes in expectancy and how each type of contextual trial affects subsequent judgments.

SYSTEXTUAL DESIGN

In the present model, the formation of expectancies depends on subjective correlations among events. This empirical proposition is similar to one that led Brunswik (1956) to question the generalizability of systematic research in psychology. It was argued that systematic design obscures the variation and covariation of the independent variables, and if this textured environment is an important determinant of behavior, then the results of systematic research must be ungeneralizable. Brunswik advocated representative design, in which experimental control of the independent variables is given up to achieve sampling of stimulus situations. Each subject is exposed to a context "representative" of the context to which generalization is desired. Poulton (1973) has taken a similar view, but rather than expose each subject to a representative context, he advocated complete between-subject designs to "avoid" context effects.

The present approach is that of *systextual design* (Birnbaum, 1972, 1974b; Birnbaum & Veit, 1973), in which the contextual features of the experimental design are systematically manipulated. Thus, the distributions of the independent variables and their joint distributions (covariances) can be manipulated while maintaining factorial designs (e.g., lower panel of

Fig. 1). This permits investigation of the empirical effects of context while maintaining experimental control.

The lever experiments (as well as the size–numerosity experiments) illustrate a contextual effect of a very general type. The effect of position depends on the experimental design used to measure it. It should be clear that the question, *What is the effect of position?* does not have an answer apart from context. Thus, the important finding is that the direction of the effect depends upon the *pattern* of other stimuli also presented.

Attempts to "avoid" context effects (Poulton, 1973), to sample "representative" contexts (Brunswik, 1956), or even to establish "standardized" contexts are not satisfactory. To investigate the effect of position on judgments of force, a complete between-subject design would use a different group of subjects for each position and force, and could easily find no main effects because judgments are relative. A standardized design might employ a factorial design in which force and position are uncorrelated, and could easily find no effect of position. Representative design would attempt to employ the ecological force–position correlation (positive) and would probably obtain results resembling the positive correlation condition. Between-subject designs simply confound treatments with contexts; standardized or representative designs hold context fixed at some arbitrary value. Hence, these designs do not avoid context effects; nor do they permit assessment of the effects of context. If experimental results are theorized to depend on the context, then systextual design seems appropriate. By manipulating the contextual correlation between force and position, systextual design reveals that the effect of position can be reversed by changing the context.

In another example of systextual design, Birnbaum (1974b) showed that one can use the lawfulness of context effects in psychophysics to derive context-invariant measures. Birnbaum's (1974b) treatment of Parducci's range–frequency theory describes responses as the composition of a context-independent psychophysical function and a context-dependent judgment function. Systematic manipulation of the stimulus distribution led to large context effects that could be separated from the distribution-invariant psychophysical function. It should be emphasized that neither the context-dependent ratings nor context-invariant psychophysical function has greater status, since prediction of judgments requires knowledge of the psychophysical function, the context, and the contextual theory.

Systextual design and functional measurement, together with appropriate theory, can not only lead to context-invariant measures but can also be used to derive measures of the context itself. An interesting feature of the present approach is that one can estimate subjective correlation, a measure of the context that represents an integration of many experiences. Subjective correlation might otherwise seem vague and ephemeral, but it is well-defined in the model and can be estimated by finding the slope of judgments as a function of position and reversing the sign.

ELABORATIONS

The present conception of expectancies is based on the finding that the effect of a cue can be reversed by manipulating its correlation with the judged event. A more general conception of expectancy would take the entire joint distribution into account. Perhaps each stimulus is compared with the distribution of expected events rather than with a single measure of central tendency. The distinction between this more general view and Eq. (2) is analogous to the distinction between Parducci's range–frequency theory (Birnbaum, 1974b; Parducci & Perrett, 1971; Parducci, 1974) and Helson's adaptation-level theory (Helson, 1964; Restle & Greeno, 1970). For example, each event might be judged partly on the basis of its rank in the expected distribution and its relative location in the range of expected values. Equation (2) could thus be tested against the distribution theory by varying the form of the conditional distributions.

An experiment on the size–weight illusion (Birnbaum & Veit, 1974b) has shown systematic deviations from Eq. (2). The effect of weight was less for larger objects than for smaller ones. If objects of all sizes are made of all substances, large objects would be expected to have a greater *range* of weights as well as a greater median weight. Consequently, if objects are judged relative to the expected distribution, the smaller objects should not only be judged heavier, but should also show a greater range of judgments as a function of weight. This interpretation, which could account for the results of Birnbaum and Veit (1974b), could be tested with the lever paradigm by varying the range of forces at different positions. The effect of actual force should be less for positions with greater ranges of weights placed on them. Consistent with this notion, Fig. 2 shows that the effect of actual force is less in the zero correlation condition where the range of weights at positions 1 and 3 is greater. A more convincing test would unconfound range, position, and correlation. This could be accomplished by using four different groups of subjects, who receive only one of the four types of additional contextual presentations.

The lever paradigm may be considered an experimental analogy to perceptual and social judgment. The lever and size–numerosity experiments are directly analogous to the size–weight illusion. More importantly, they are also analogous to a wide array of situations in which expectancies are part of the context that affects judgment. By studying situations in which the relevant variables seem under experimental control, the aim is to uncover basic principles that will have wide applicability for the understanding of judgment. When a theory attains a certain degree of success in a limited domain, its appeal for the discussion and interpretation of other phenomena is enhanced.

ACKNOWLEDGMENTS

This project was initiated at Kansas State University with the support of Bureau of General Research. The author thanks Bonnie G. Birnbaum, Barbara J. Rose, James C. Shanteau, and Clairice T. Veit for comments on an earlier draft.

REFERENCES

Anderson, N. H. Averaging model applied to the size–weight illusion. *Perception & Psychophysics,* 1970, **8,** 1–4.   (a)

Anderson, N. H. Functional measurement and psychophysical judgment. *Psychological Review,* 1970, **77,** 153–170.   (b)

Anderson, N. H. Information integration and attitude change. *Psychological Review,* 1971, **78,** 171–206.

Anderson, N. H. Cross-task validation of functional measurement. *Perception & Psychophysics,* 1972, **12,** 389–395.

Anderson, N. H. Cognitive algebra: Integration theory applied to social attribution. In L. Berkowitz (Ed.), *Advances in experimental social psychology,* Vol. 7. New York: Academic Press, 1974.   (a)

Anderson, N. H. Information integration theory: A brief survey. In D. H. Krantz, R. C. Atkinson, R. D. Luce, & P. Suppes (Eds.), *Contemporary developments in mathematical psychology,* Vol. 2. New York: Academic Press, 1974.   (b)

Birnbaum, M. H. Systextual design for stimulus variation and covariation. Paper presented at Conference on Human Judgment and Social Interaction, Boulder, Colorado, March, 1972.

Birnbaum, M. H. The nonadditivity of personality impressions. *Journal of Experimental Psychology Monograph,* 1974, **102,** 543–561.   (a)

Birnbaum, M. H. Using contextual effects to derive psychophysical scales. *Perception & Psychophysics,* 1974, **15,** 89–96.   (b)

Birnbaum, M. H., Kobernick, M., & Veit, C. T. Subjective correlation and the size–numerosity illusion. *Journal of Experimental Psychology,* 1974, **102,** 537–539.

Birnbaum, M. H., Parducci, A., & Gifford, R. K. Contextual effects in information integration. *Journal of Experimental Psychology,* 1971, **88,** 149–157.

Birnbaum, M. H., & Veit, C. T. Judgmental illusion produced by contrast with expectancy. *Perception & Psychophysics,* 1973, **13,** 149–152.

Birnbaum, M. H., & Veit, C. T. Scale convergence as a criterion for rescaling: Information integration with difference, ratio, and averaging tasks. *Perception & Psychophysics,* 1974, **15,** 7–15.   (a)

Birnbaum, M. H., & Veit, C. T. Scale-free tests of an additive model for the size–weight illusion. *Perception & Psychophysics,* 1974, **16,** 276–282.   (b)

Brunswik, E. *Perception and the representative design of experiments.* Berkeley: Univ. of California Press, 1956.

Brunswik, E., & Herma, H. Probability learning of perceptual cues in the establishment of a weight illusion. *Journal of Experimental Psychology,* 1951, **41,** 281–290.

Helson, H. *Adaptation-level theory.* New York: Harper & Row, 1964.

Parducci, A. The relativism of absolute judgment. *Scientific American,* 1968, **219,** 84–90.

Parducci, A. Contextual effects: A range-frequency analysis. In E. C. Carterette and M. P. Friedman (Eds.), *Handbook of perception,* Vol. II. New York: Academic Press, 1974.

Parducci, A., & Perrett, L. F. Category rating scales: Effects of spacing and frequency of stimulus values. *Journal of Experimental Psychology Monograph,* 1971, **89,** 427–452.

Poulton, E. C. Unwanted range effects from using within-subject experimental designs. *Psychological Bulletin,* 1973, **80,** 113–121.

Restle, F., & Greeno, J. G. *Introduction of mathematical psychology.* Reading, Massachusetts: Addison-Wesley, 1970.

6

THE MIND, THE MODEL, AND THE TASK

Robyn M. Dawes
Oregon Research Institute
  and
University of Oregon

In this chapter, I will discuss two tasks that cognitive psychologists have used in order to understand the information processing capabilities of their subjects. The method employed has been to develop formal models of the subjects' behavior, and to see how well such models represent the behavior. The major thesis of this chapter is that these models are primarily models of the task, and that they represent the subjects' behavior only because the subjects have acquired certain (simple) abilities that allow them to behave appropriately (not necessarily optimally) in the task situation. To quote Edwards (1971):

> Probably the most underrated psychologist of the 1937–1955 period was Egon Brunswik . . . he saw one thing very clearly that seems to have escaped all of his contemporaries except the very few who took the trouble to understand him. He saw that psychology is not only about people who emit behavior—it is also, perhaps more importantly, about the tasks that elicit that behavior. That is, he saw that the task-relevant characteristics of the environment are a necessary part of every process theory in psychology.
>
> That was a profound insight. Its consequences began to be felt only after World War II, and even now many deeply sophisticated psychological theorists fail to recognize how much effort they spend in modeling the task, and how little effort they spend in modeling the behavior of the subject in the task. Some theorists do understand this. Frank Restle, for example, once told me about an occasion in which he had tried some five totally different sets of assumptions about the subject, combined with the same

set of assumptions about the nature of the task—and obtained indistinguishable predictions. . . . Fame awaits the mathematical psychologist who can
figure out a satisfactory way to partition the predictive success of a model
between its task-describing components and its man-describing components.
My own guess is that most successful models now available are successful
exactly because of their success in describing tasks, not people [p. 640].

My conclusion is slightly different from that of Edwards. I do not wish
to separate people modeling from task modeling; rather I wish to stress
the importance of task modeling per se in understanding behavior.

The first task (Wiggins & Kohen, 1971) is one typical of many in which
subjects are asked to predict an outcome or output on the basis of multi-
variate coded input:

Each subject was asked to predict the actual first-year graduate grade
point averages of 90 profiles representing real psychology graduate students
at the University of Illinois who had entered between the years of
1965–1968. Each profile consisted of the following 10 cues: (a) Graduate
Record Examination (GRE)—Verbal; (b) GRE—Quantitative; (c)
GRE—Advanced; (d) cumulative undergraduate grade point average for
the last 2 years of college; (e) Astin (1965) ratings of selectivity of the
undergraduate school; (f) mean peer ratings received on a 5-point scale
for need Achievement; (g) Extraversion, and (h) Anxiety; (i) self-rating
on conscientiousness; and (j) sex of student. The peer ratings and self-
ratings were obtained at the end of the first semester of graduate work
for all first-year psychology students at the University of Illinois [p. 102].

(For a review of such tasks see Slovic & Lichtenstein, 1971; or Dawes
& Corrigan, 1974.)

The second task (Inhelder & Piaget, 1958) is chosen to be topologically
quite dissimilar from the first. It is typical of many presented by Piaget
and his followers to assess "formal operations." (See also Ripple & Rockcastle, 1964; Magary, Poulsen, Lubin, & Coplin, 1973.)

Three metal balls of different weights are placed on a disc at three different distances from its center. The disc is rotated faster and faster until
the balls roll off the disc because of centrifugal force. The problem is
to predict in what order they will leave their initial positions (and roll
off) and why [p. 211].

Psychologists studying their subjects' performance in the first task built
linear models of each, whereas those studying performance in the second
discussed it in terms of formal combinatorial logic. That is, as suggested
by Goldberg (1968, p. 485) in discussing tasks of the former type, the
psychologist: (a) searched for a formal (i.e., specifiable) model, which
(b) allowed the input information to be (c) transformed according to the

model in order to (d) "produce as accurately as possible a copy of the responses." In the first example, the linear model constructed is referred to as a "model of the man," whereas in the second, the combinatorial analysis is referred as "formal operational thinking." I hope to persuade you that the models might better be regarded as models of the tasks. This distinction is not merely semantic or metapsychological, but is basic to the analysis of what it is we are studying. The model of the task enables us to understand the task requirements—i.e., to answer questions of how the task is successfully completed. Understanding these task requirements, in turn, yields an understanding of the subject who performs in a more-or-less successful manner. This approach to studying cognition has been stressed previously by Simon (1969). What I hope to do here is to show that it can be fruitfully followed in two areas in which the investigators themselves have not emphasized the task requirements.

Performance on the first task was analyzed by building linear models of the subjects' predictions and an optimal linear model of the criterion (optimal in the least-squares sense). On the average, the subjects' linear models correlated .65 with their predictions; the optimal linear model correlated .69 with the criterion. Furthermore, on the average, the subjects' linear models correlated .50 with the criterion, whereas the subjects' predictions themselves correlated only .33 with the criterion. This incremental validity of model over prediction was interpreted as an instance of "bootstrapping" (Dawes, 1971; Goldberg, 1970; Wiggins & Kohen, 1971). Later, however, Dawes and Corrigan (1974) demonstrated that a weighting of the standardized variables that was arbitrary except for sign ("random linear models") yielded composites that also correlated about .50 with the criterion (.51 to be exact). Hence, the fact that the linear models of the subjects were linear models, rather than related to the particular behavior of the subjects, accounts for the incremental validity.

Now what exactly have we learned? First, we know that the task is one that is performed rather well by a linear model; it is performed best, of course, by a model whose weights are optimally chosen—but it is also performed well by a model whose weights are arbitrary except for sign. Second, we have learned that subjects' deviations from linear predictions do *not help them* in this task. The reason for this latter conclusion is that .33 is precisely equal to .51 times .65; that is, the average validity is precisely equal to the average correlation of linear models in general with the criterion times the average correlation between the subjects' predictions and their linear models; hence, the partial correlation between predictions and criterion partialing out "linearity" is zero. The conclusion is that the task is one in which linear models are appropriate, and that people can more or less grasp the essentials of the task.

Why are linear models appropriate? Because, as pointed out by Dawes and Corrigan (1974), the task is one in which each variable has a conditionally monotone relationship with the criterion; that is, higher values on each variable predict higher values on the criterion, irrespective of the pattern of values on the remaining variables. This condition, which is really a combination of independence and additivity (Krantz, Luce, Suppes, & Tversky, 1971), guarantees that linear models will do well in prediction. Len Rorer (reported in Dawes, 1968; Rorer, 1971, 1972) has demonstrated by computer simulation that conditionally monotone models are well approximated by linear ones.

[For example, Rorer investigated by computer simulation the degree to which $Y = X + Z$ is correlated with $Y = (X + Z)^2$ when X and Z are always positively valued. Using values 0, 1, 2, and 3 for X and Z with equal frequency, he obtained a correlation of .96 when X and Z themselves were uncorrelated. An analysis of variance revealed ω^2 values of .47 for X and Z and only .06 for XZ. Thus, a function that is both quadratic and multiplicative—i.e., "curvilinear" and "configural"—can be well approximated by a linear function when only positive values are considered. This result is similar to an earlier one of Yntema and Torgerson (1961) who obtained a correlation of .97 between the linear function $X + Z + W$ and the multiplicative function $XZ + XW + ZW$—again using only positive values. Rorer, however, investigated a much wider variety of conditionally monotone functions; for example, a hierarchically disjunctive[1] step function correlated .85 with its linear approximation. For further discussion see Rorer (1972).]

My conclusion is that we have learned that subjects know that the task is one in which each variable has a conditionally monotone relationship with the criterion and that they can respond with criterion values in a manner that more or less reflects this conditional monotonicity. They know that higher scores on the GRE, higher GPAs, and higher levels of achievement motivation are all related to higher first-year grades in graduate school; they use this information in the correct direction. In the absence of a trial-by-trial analysis, we do not even know that they integrate the information from diverse sources on a single trial. The model of the task helps us understand the conditional monotonicity inherent in it, and the fact that the sub-

---

[1] The values X, Z, and W are considered in turn. If the value of X is 0, the value of Y is 0; if the value of X is 3, the value of Y is 1. If the value of X is 1 or 2, the value of Z is considered; if the value of Z is 0 or 3, the value of Y is, respectively, 0 or 1—otherwise W is considered. Again, if the value of W is 0 or 3, the value of Y is, respectively, 0 or 1. If X, Z, and W all have values of 1 or 2, their values are added and Y is assigned the value 1 or 0 depending on whether the sum is greater or less than 4.5. Rorer's correlation of .85 was obtained when X, Z, and W were all uncorrelated.

jects as well can be represented by linear models indicates that they are responding somewhat appropriately.

We know of no better ways to predict the criterion than by a linear model. Since there is no alternative model for describing appropriate task mastery, it is not clear that we have discovered anything about the subjects' information processing, independent of the task. If, on the other hand, we had alternative models that could have described behavior appropriate to the given task situation, then the behavior of the subjects in conforming to one model rather than another would presumably allow us to make some generalization.[2] By analyzing the task itself in terms of the linear model, we understand what little knowledge is gained by building linear models of the subjects. But there is some knowledge gained; they do behave appropriately (not optimally) in a very simple way. They can understand and cope with conditional monotonicity, at least in this familiar context.

The emphasis in the preceding analysis is that subjects *can* pay attention to several dimensions and treat them in a conditionally monotone manner. People do not naturally do so in all situations; for example, Shepard (1964) has devised a judgment task in which subjects do not.

[*A caveat:* The preceding analysis impiles that subjects who are more linear should also be more accurate, because even linear models with randomly chosen coefficients do well (at least in comparison to clinical judges). Thus far, such a relationship has not been established either in the Wiggins and Kohen study (Nancy Wiggins, personal communication) or in a similar study by Goldberg (1970). I do not know why. Further data are currently being analyzed.]

Now let us consider the second problem—that of predicting the order in which balls will fall off the rotating disk. The centrifugal force f is proportional to mr, where m is the mass of the ball, and r is the distance from the center of the disk. Thus, as the rotation of the disk is accelerated, the heavier the ball is and the further from the center it is, the sooner it will roll off. Inhelder and Piaget (1958) describe this as a problem in "compensation." A heavy ball near the center may be displaced at the same time as a lighter ball near the edge of the disk.

Inhelder and Piaget describe the following sequence of reasoning from the young child to the adolescent:

1. The youngest child thinks the balls go off "because they want to."
2. At about 5 or 6 years old, the child understands that the speed of falling off is related to the weight of the ball and its distance from

[2] Analogously, when the only manipulanda in a Skinner box is a bar and the only change in the environment is the appearance of food pellets, it is not surprising that the pattern with which food pellets occur "shapes" bar-pressing behavior.

the center. Sometimes the child holds one factor responsible, sometimes the other. The child is unable to see that these factors are jointly involved.

3. The child is able to combine the two factors, but only if the two factors are working in the same direction, not in terms of compensation. Thus the child understands that a heavy ball near the edge falls off sooner than a light ball near the center.

4. If the experimenter holds one factor constant, the child is able to specify the relationship to speed to the other factor.

5. The child decides for himself to hold one factor constant and vary the other.

6. The child understands the principle of compensation: a change in one factor can be offset by a (reverse) change in the other. Finally (a stage not covered in the present analysis), the child is able to state the principle of compensation in terms of a metric relationship.

As Dawes (1974) has demonstrated, the simplest way to understand the subjects' behavior in this and similar tasks is to analyze the behaviors in terms of a *truth table*. (This example is chosen because it involves the most complicated analysis; for a simpler analysis of an easier task see Dawes, 1974.) Given two statements, p and q, both of which may be true or false, there are four possible combinations: pq, $p\bar{q}$ (that is, p and not q), $\bar{p}q$, and $\bar{p}\bar{q}$. Each of these combinations may itself be true or false. The result is $2^4 = 16$ possibilities which may be represented in a truth table—see Table 1. In Table 1, 1 and 0 represent truth and falsity, respectively. Logical relationships are specified in each column. For example, in Column 14, $p\bar{q}$ is absent. Such absence specifies the relationship that p implies q. In Column 6, only pq and $p\bar{q}$ are present. This pattern is equivalent to the assertion of p.

Consider two balls. Let p refer to the fact that the second ball is heavier than the first and let q represent the fact that the second is farther from the center of the disk. For appropriately chosen values of p and q, the two balls will fall off simultaneously, which may be represented by a 1, or at different times, represented by a 0. The adolescent discovers that for appropriately chosen values of p and q, $p\bar{q}$ or $\bar{p}q$ lead to the event that the balls roll off at the same time; that is, the adolescent behaves as if he were examining all the columns of the truth table and discovering that column 9 is the appropriate one. Hence, the subject learns the principle of compensation.

Dawes (1974) has demonstrated that the other experiments discussed by Piaget and Inhelder (1958) also may be analyzed by truth tables. In addition, the partial solutions proposed by the younger subjects—who fail

TABLE 1
Truth Table

	Column no.															
	1	2	3	4	5	6	7	8	9	10	11	12	13	14	15	16
pq	0	1	0	0	0	1	1	1	0	0	0	1	1	1	0	1
$p\bar{q}$	0	0	1	0	0	1	0	0	1	1	0	1	1	0	1	1
$\bar{p}q$	0	0	0	1	0	0	1	0	1	0	1	1	0	1	1	1
$\bar{p}\bar{q}$	0	0	0	0	1	0	0	1	0	1	1	0	1	1	1	1

to solve the problem—may also be analyzed in terms of truth tables (albeit incomplete ones). In Stage (2) the child is looking only at p and $\bar{p}$ in isolation or q and $\bar{q}$ in isolation. In Stage (3) the child looks at pq and $\bar{p}\bar{q}$, but ignores $p\bar{q}$ and $\bar{p}q$. In Stages (4) and (5), the child looks at p and $\bar{p}$ within a single value of q (i.e., he looks at pq and $\bar{p}q$ or $p\bar{q}$ and $\bar{p}\bar{q}$ but not both), and vice-versa, while only in Stage (6) does the child look at all four combinations: pq, $p\bar{q}$, $\bar{p}q$, and $\bar{p}\bar{q}$.

What have we learned from the subjects' responses to this task? As children grow older, they tend (learn?) to look at more possibilities. Hence, if a problem is solved best by considering all logical possibilities, the child does better as he or she grows older. Piaget and Inhelder talk about "formal operations" of children in such a situation, but Dawes (1974) has argued that what Piaget and Inhelder are finding is the *potentiality* or *ability* to understand the logic of combinations.

As in the previous example, the combinatorial—or truth table—model is the only one appropriate for solving the problem. Hence, the fact that subjects' behavior can be represented by this model limits the generality of the conclusion. Subjects *can*, as they grow older, behave appropriately in the situation, but to propose that the model is primarily one of the subject would imply that subjects engage in "formal thought" consistently. And they do not.

The last assertion is evident from a number of empirical studies, the simplest of which uses a task devised by Wason and Hughes (summarized in Wason, 1969). Their task appears to involve "formal thinking," but it nevertheless is not mastered by a vast majority of highly educated Western adults. Consider four index cards with an **a** printed on one card, a **b** on the second, a **2** on the third, and a **3** on a fourth. The experimenter places these cards on a table and makes the assertion that, *All the cards with a vowel on one side have an even number on the other*. The subject is then asked which cards should be turned over in order to check the validity of this assertion.

The correct answer is that the card with the **a** printed on it should be turned over (to check that there is indeed an even number on the other side) and the card with the **3** printed on it should be turned over (to check that there is *not* a vowel on the other side). Yet a vast majority of the subjects assert that the cards with the **a** and with the **2** should be turned over—even though anything on the other side of the card with the **2** is completely compatible with the statement. In fact, Wason (1968) reports that "from 60 to 75%" make the incorrect selection (of **2**) and that "only a minority select" **3**. He concludes that his results are "disquieting." To quote Wason:

> If Piaget is right (Inhelder & Piaget, 1958), then the subjects in the present investigation should have reached the stage of formal operations. A person who is thinking in these terms will take account of the possible and hypothetical by forming propositions about them. He will be able to isolate the variables in the problem and subject them to a combinatorial analysis. But this is exactly what the subjects in the present experiments singularly failed to do. The variables in the present task are abstract but they are distinct and susceptible to symbolic manipulation. Could it then be that the stage of formal operations is not completely achieved at adolescence, even among intelligent individuals? [p. 281.]

I have informally replicated Wason's results with subjects who have doctorates in mathematical psychology! Only one of five subjects correctly solved the task. (I feel constrained not to reveal the names of these mathematical psychologists, but they are all well-published and—at least in my biased estimation—highly regarded members of their field.)

What are we to conclude? (*a*) that the mathematical psychologists are incapable of formal thought; or (*b*) that Piaget and Inhelder have a mistaken conception of the nature of formal thought; or (*c*) that the subjects simply misunderstand the instructions.

I cannot accept the conclusion that mathematical psychologists are incapable of formal thought—nor that the results are based on verbal misunderstanding. That mathematical psychologists are capable of formal thought is self-evident. The verbal misunderstanding hypothesis rests on the conclusion that subjects make a biconditional inference when only the conditional one is appropriate. That is, the subjects interpret the statement *All the cards with the vowel on one side have an even number on the other* as meaning *Cards will have a vowel on one side if and only if they have an even number on the other*. Even under such an interpretation, however, the subjects should turn over the card with the **3** on it—a card which is selected by "only a minority."

My conclusion is that the model that Inhelder and Piaget propose is essentially a model of how best to solve the tasks that they devised for their subjects, and that they are finding how well children of various ages can think in terms of all logical possibilities. Moreover, as in the previous example, the subjects did not do as well as does the optimal model. From their verbal protocols, it is quite clear that these subjects think only more or less systematically about the problem, just as the earlier subjects were only more or less linear.

Brehmer (1973) has surveyed five tasks (involving "clinical judgment") that varied in the degree to which the criterion could be linearily predicted by an optimal model and in the degree to which subjects' behavior could be predicted from the linear model. The task with the higher multiple correlations between input and criterion also evoked higher linearity in the subjects' responses. Brehmer concludes (1973) that "this implies that the judgment process is not a characteristic of the clinician, but that it is a characteristic of the clinician-task system [p. 7]." I would go one step further and maintain that if there is only a single model (that the experimenter knows of) that describes appropriate task performance, then that model must be considered *primarily* a model of the task, rather than of the person. To quote Brehmer (1969) from an earlier study: "The general finding, in studies of clinical inference, that humans use information only in a linear, additive way might, therefore, be due to the fact that linear, additive tasks have been used rather than to characteristics of the human inference process [p. 503]."

I agree with Edwards and Brehmer that a great many models that are supposedly models of the subject might be better regarded as models of the task. Of course, I realize that task per se cannot produce behavior; neither linear models nor truth tables construct themselves.

What then have the two tasks shown? First, it is indisputable that children are more able to think in terms of logical possibilities the older they grow and that the ability to think systematically about such possibilities appears sometime around puberty. (But what possibilities are worth thinking about prior to that time?) Second, it appears incontrovertible that graduate students can attend to more than one dimension—perhaps simultaneously, perhaps sequentially—and treat each dimension in a conditionally monotone manner. But Piaget claimed that people acquire this ability sometime around the age of 6! And finally, the emphasis is on *can*. People do not always act all that smart.

ACKNOWLEDGMENTS

This research was supported in part by National Institute of Mental Health Grants MH-21216 and MH-12972, and by National Science Foundation Grant GS-32505. I would like to thank my ORI colleagues—in particular, Lewis Goldberg, Paul Hoffman, and Paul Slovic—for their critical comments of earlier versions of this paper.

REFERENCES

Brehmer, B. Cognitive dependence on additive and configural cue-criterion relations. *American Journal of Psychology,* 1969, **82,** 490–503.

Brehmer, B. Note on clinical judgment and the formal characteritsics of clinical tasks. *Umeå Psychological Reports,* 1973, No. 77 (Department of Psychology, University of Umeå, Sweden).

Dawes, R. M. Algebraic models of cognition. In C. A. J. Vlek (Ed.), *Algebraic models in psychology: Proceedings of the NUFFIC International Summer Session in Science.* The Hague: Netherlands Universities Foundation for International Cooperation, 1968.

Dawes, R. M. A case study of graduate admissions: Application of three principles of human decision making. *American Psychologist,* 1971, **26,** 180–188.

Dawes, R. M. An interpretation of some of Inhelder's and Piaget's findings. In J. F. Magary, M. K. Poulsen, & G. I. Lubin (Eds.), *Proceedings of the Third Invitational Interdisciplinary Seminar on Piagetian Theory and its Implications for the Helping Professions.* Los Angeles: UAP, Childrens Hospital of Los Angeles, 1974.

Dawes, R. M., & Corrigan, B. Linear models in decision making. *Psychological Bulletin,* 1974, **81,** 95–106.

Edwards, W. Bayesian and regression models in human information processing—a myopic perspective. *Organizational Behavior & Human Performance,* 1971, **6,** 639–648.

Goldberg, L. R. Simple models or simple processes? Some research on clinical judgments. *American Psychologist,* 1968, **23,** 483–496.

Goldberg, L. R. Man versus model of man: A rationale, plus some evidence, for a method of improving on clinical judgments. *Psychological Bulletin,* 1970, **73,** 422–432.

Inhelder, B., & Piaget, J. *The growth of logical thinking from childhood to adolescence.* London: Routledge & Kegan Paul, 1958.

Krantz, D. H., Luce, R. D., Suppes, P., & Tversky, A. *Foundations of measurement.* Vol. 1. New York: Academic Press, 1971.

Magary, J. F., Poulsen, M., Lubin, G. I., & Coplin, G. (Eds.), *Proceedings: Second Annual UAP Conference on Piagetian Theory and the Helping Professions.* Los Angeles: University Publishers, 1973.

Ripple, R. E., & Rockcastle, V. N. (Eds.), *Piaget rediscovered: A report of The Conference on Cognitive Studies and Curriculum Development.* Ithaca, New York: Cornell Univ. Press, 1964.

Rorer, L. G. A circuitous route to bootstrapping. In H. B. Haley, A. G. D'Costa, & A. M. Schafer (Eds.), *Conference on Personality Measurement in Medical Education.* Washington, D.C.: Association of American Medical Colleges, 1971.

Rorer, L. G. A circuitous route to bootstrapping selection procedures. *Oregon Research Institute Research Bulletin,* 1972, **12,** No. 9.

Shepard, R. N. On subjectively optimum selections among multi-attribute alternatives. In M. W. Shelly III & G. L. Bryan (Eds.), *Human judgment and optimality.* New York: Wiley, 1964.

Simon, H. A. *The sciences of the artificial.* Cambridge, Massachusetts: MIT Press, 1969.

Slovic, P., & Lichtenstein, S. Comparison of Bayesian and regression approaches to the study of information processing in judgment. *Organizational Behavior & Human Performance,* 1971, **6,** 649–744.

Wason, P. C. Reasoning about a rule. *Quarterly Journal of Experimental Psychology,* 1968, **20,** 273–281.

Wason, P. C. Regression in reasoning? *British Journal of Psychology,* 1969, **60,** 471–480.

Wiggins, N., & Kohen, E. S. Man versus model of man revisited: The forecasting of graduate school success. *Journal of Personality and Social Psychology,* 1971, **19,** 100–106.

Yntema, D. B., & Torgerson, W. S. Man–computer cooperation in decisions requiring common sense. *IRE Transactions of the Professional Group on Human Factors in Electronics,* 1961, **HFE-2**(1), 20–26.

7

BAYES' THEOREM: CAN A THEORY OF JUDGMENT AND INFERENCE DO WITHOUT IT?

Gordon F. Pitz
Southern Illinois University at Carbondale

After resting in peace and relative obscurity for most of the 200 years following his death, the ghost of the Reverend Thomas Bayes must be perturbed by the increasing use of his name in recent years. The seminal paper written by an obscure English clergyman (Bayes, 1763) was not published until after his death, but it has now become the center of some dispute in those disciplines concerned with inference and decision making. Much of the controversy properly concerns the foundations of statistics, and I shall ignore such issues here. Quite independent of the statistical issues, however, are those arguments related to the use of Bayes' theorem in theories of human inference. My purpose is to try to place Thomas Bayes' theorem in its proper context as an approach to the psychology of human inference.

Bayes' theorem is the cornerstone of that branch of statistics that is based on the personalist definition of probability (Savage, 1954), and gives that area its name. It was probably inevitable that psychologists would sooner or later see the importance of Bayesian statistics to theories of inference, and indeed the development of Bayesian theories of inference followed the development of Bayesian statistics by about 10 years. The statistical use of Bayes' theorem depends, of course, on the willingness of the statistician to define probabilities in terms of some person's beliefs. When probability is defined in this way, it becomes of interest to the psychologist, since the business of measuring beliefs is properly a part of his domain. When the statistician's interest in personal (or subjective) probabilities was coupled with the parallel development of utility theory by economists (von Neumann & Morgenstern, 1944), the result was the development of subjective expected utility (SEU) theory by psychologists (Edwards, 1955). Out of the tradition of SEU theory came the use of Bayes' theorem as a descriptive model for judgment and inference (Edwards & Phillips, 1964).

Bayes' theorem is, in effect, a rule for revising probabilities following the presentation of evidence. In case the reader has never been exposed to this rule, it is given as

$$P(H_i|E) = \frac{P(E|H_i)P(H_i)}{\sum\limits_{j=1}^{k} P(E|H_j)P(H_j)} . \tag{1}$$

We let H_i, $i = 1, \ldots, k$, be the possible hypotheses that are being entertained, and E be some piece of evidence. In Eq. (1), $P(H_i)$ is one's probability for H_i prior to observing E, and $P(E|H_i)$ is the probability of observing E when H_i is true.

The question is: Can Eq. (1) be said to describe the way in which individuals revise their beliefs following the presentation of relevant information? Before answering this question, one important point should be made about tests of SEU theory, in general. The theory is, in effect, a theory of rational behavior in the face of uncertainty, and in this sense, is related to those systems of deductive logic that are the basis for other forms of rational behavior. Indeed, the point has been made by Jeffreys (1961) that the theory of subjective probability governs the process of induction in the same way that symbolic logic governs the process of deduction. Now, if we wish to decide whether a subject is using a particular form of logic, it must be assumed that the subject understands the problem that has been presented. Clearly, this assumption leads to a circularity; if one wishes to find out whether a subject understands a problem, or perceives the problem in the same way that it is perceived by the experimenter, it is necessary to assume that the subject is using a known form of logical reasoning. Hence, given a failure by the subject to respond in a way that the experimenter considers appropriate, there is no way of determining whether this failure results from a lack of understanding of the problem or the use of a different system of logic. This point has been made by Smedslund (1970) with respect to the study of language and problem solving in young children. It applies equally to the study of decision making and inference when one attempts to evaluate a normative theory such as SEU.

Bayes' theorem as a rule for the revision of beliefs is a theorem derivable from the axioms of probability theory, which are an integral part of SEU theory. Hence, the preceding argument applies to studies of Bayes' theorem as a descriptive model of judgment. When a subject appears to have revised his beliefs in a manner different from that predicted by Bayes' theorem, it is impossible to know whether this failure is the result of a failure of the theory, or a failure on the part of the subject to understand the task as it has been described to him. Another way to make the same point is to note that there are enough degrees of freedom in Eq. (1) to account for any observed data. For example, the parameter k, the number of hypotheses entertained by the subject, is one that has rarely, if ever, been estimated from the data in the many studies comparing subjects' behavior with the predictions of Bayes' theorem. Yet there is a priori reason to believe that k may not be equal to the number of hypotheses explicitly mentioned in the description of the task.

This argument, of course, makes Bayes' theorem, taken in its most general form, theoretically empty; it can neither be supported nor disproved. Rather, it can be used as a working assumption that represents the starting point, not the finishing point, for a theory of inference. One may propose and test various stronger forms of the theory. The task for the psychologist is to find stronger assumptions that are psychologically meaningful, that is, are related in some way to everything else that is known about the process of opinion revision.

Why use Bayes' theorem as a theoretical framework, rather than some other? A number of reasons have been suggested, either explicitly or implicitly, and they depend in part on the intent of the researcher. In particular, it is important to distinguish between applications of Bayes' theorem to externally defined events, such as stimulus frequencies, and the use of Bayes' theorem to describe hypothetical subjective probabilities. A failure to make this distinction can lead to unwarranted criticisms and unfortunate misunderstandings.

There are at least two possible reasons for using Bayes' theorem with stimulus-defined quanties employed on the right-hand side of Eq. (1), an application that I shall call the "external" use of Bayes' theorem. One justification is based on a supposed analogy between the study of inference and the study of sensory psychophysics. Early studies of subjective probability sought meaningful stimulus variables that might be related to subjective probabilities in the same way that physical measures of the energy of a light source are related to perceived brightness. Bayes' theorem has sometimes been used in this fashion, with hypothetical constructs such as "conservatism" acting rather like a psychophysical power law (Stevens, 1957). Unfortunately, it is now apparent that conservatism is a construct that has little generality, and serves no useful explanatory purpose. The invariant relationships between external stimulus characteristics and subjective probabilities that will lead to useful theories of the judgment process remain to be discovered.

An entirely separate source of interest in the external application of Bayes' theorem stems from an interest in helping those whose business it is to make decisions. Such an interest has stimulated the comparison of unaided inference by a human with the normative prescriptions of a formal theory (Peterson & Beach, 1967). From a practical viewpoint, it is certainly useful to be able to identify the possible sources of error in human judgment. This research, however, does not, by itself, say much about the internal process of opinion revision.

There can be little quarrel with the reasons given for the external application of Bayes' theorem. However, much of the research in this tradition is based on a terminology that is somewhat misleading. The outcome of such research is frequently described as the comparison of an individual's subjective probabilities with "objective probabilities," a concept that is wholly foreign to the Bayesian approach. As pointed out by Phillips (1970), if a probability is to be defined as a measure of a person's belief, there can be no such thing as an objective probability that is different from that belief. Research using the external application of Bayes' theorem has typically involved the comparison of a subject's verbalized responses with calculations based on such characteristics of the external environment as a set of observed frequencies. This comparison is related to the process of revising subjective probabilities only in an indirect way. If beliefs are indeed revised according to Bayes' theorem, there is not a necessary reason why numerical responses should correspond to the results obtained from calculations based on external events. Observing a failure on the part of the subject to match some external criterion established by the experimenter is uninformative with respect to the issue of whether the subject's logic is at fault or his understanding of the problem differs from that of the experimenter.

Is it possible that, notwithstanding failures by the subject to match the external results of Bayes' theorem, the theorem still serves as a useful model for the inference process? This question is certainly worth exploring, and leads to what I shall call the "internal" application of Bayes' theorem. In an earlier paper (Pitz, 1974) I suggested a biological justification for SEU theory generally, which might be extended to Bayes' theorem. It is usually not unsafe to assume that the behavior of an organism in its environment has, through a process of natural selection, become maximally adaptive to that environment. Now, if Bayes' theorem does indeed represent the theoretically "best" way of revising beliefs, one might assume that this is the way in which humans have come to revise their beliefs. Unfortunately, this argument is weakened by the theoretical research that has demonstrated that a failure on the part of the subject to follow that normative theory usually leads to a very small penalty. This result has been called the "flat maximum" effect, and is discussed by von Winterfeldt and Edwards (1973). If theoretically optimal behavior is indeed very little better than many nonoptimal forms of behavior, it is possible that the learning process of a single individual, and the natural selection process that manifests itself in an entire species, would never be sensitive to such small effects.

It seems that the justification for the internal use of Bayes' theorem must eventually be made on the grounds of research strategy. There are a number of practical advantages to using a Bayesian approach to the study of inference and judgment. First, the formal properties of Bayes' theorem are well understood in a number of interesting special cases, the result of studies in such normative disciplines as statistics and operations research. Second, the generality of Eq. (1) permits a number of other theories to be rephrased in Bayesian terms. For example, Anderson's information integration theory (Anderson, 1971) can, if desired, be interpreted in terms of subjective probabilities. Published attempts to compare the Bayesian approach with information integration theory (e.g., Shanteau, 1972) have, in fact, used restricted versions of the Bayesian theory. It is indeed useful to know that certain restrictions that might reasonably be placed on the parameters of Eq. (1) are incompatible with observed data. However, it is best to avoid disputes over the relative superiority of Bayesian and other approaches that may, in the long run, turn out only to be disputes over terminology.

A case can be made for the argument that all human behavior will be found to be normative, provided one takes into account those outcomes that are of value to the subject (e.g., minimizing cognitive effort) and the constraints under which he is working (e.g., limited computational abilities, due, perhaps, to limits on the capacity of short-term memory). The advantage to this assumption is that much of the psychologist's effort can be directed toward an analysis of the task rather than the person, an approach that is apparently often successful (see Dawes, Chapter 6). This argument alone should stimulate renewed interest in a Bayesian theory of inference.

One reason why the general version of Bayes' theorem is difficult to use as a theory of inference is that internal beliefs must be translated into overt behavior through some response mechanism. It is unwise to take a number given by a subject as a direct measure of an internal state of belief (Pitz, 1970). The problem of inferring belief states from overt numerical responses is not necessarily of concern if one is using Bayesian theory in an external sense. Presumably much of the earlier literature comparing subjects' verbalized statements of probability with probabilities generated by Bayes' theorem was conceived in this spirit. However, if one's interest lies in the internal application of Bayes' theorem, it is necessary to deal directly with the process by which internalized beliefs are translated into overt responses. This can be done by constructing a model that includes assumptions about both internal processes and the response-generating mechanism. If the model is supported by the data, then both aspects of the model are jointly validated.

To date, there has been very little study of the response mechanisms that might be used in tasks that require a subject to give a numerical probability. Let us grant, for the time being, that subjective probabilities are revised in a manner specified by Bayes' theorem. Unfortunately, few people have ever been asked prior to an experiment to express their beliefs as numbers between zero and one. Indeed, outside the laboratory, rarely are they asked to describe their beliefs in any way other than through ill-defined adjectives such as "strong" and "weak." It is likely, then, that a subject's response tells us more about how he adapts to an unfamiliar task than it tells us about his beliefs.

One way to study internal states of belief is to make the response task as simple as possible, so that the part of the theory dealing with the response mechanism has a high probability of being accurate. For example, if one asks a subject to choose from among a small set of hypotheses, it might be reasonable to assume that the subject's choice is based upon the hypothesis he believes most likely to be correct. Such an approach is similar in spirit to the conjoint measurement analysis of subjective probabilities, which uses only ordinal level properties of the data (Wallsten, 1972). If one assumes that the relationship between the overt judgment and the internal belief is not necessarily linear, conjoint measurement methods can be used to test hypotheses about the composition rules used in aggregating evidence.

In one paper (Pitz, 1972), I attempted to show how hypotheses generated from earlier studies of probability estimation might be rephrased in terms applicable to a decision task, with some useful results. In the remainder of this paper I would like to describe two other ways in which subjective probabilities can be studied through reference to the decision process. First, I shall show how decisions can be used to measure parameters of subjective probability distributions for continuous quantities. Then I shall return to Bayes' theorem, and show how some very general implications of Eq. (1) can be tested by using a sequential decision task.

There are several situations in which it seems appropriate to describe a person's knowledge or beliefs in terms of probability distributions for continuous quantities. First, there are cases in which a subject has information about the true value of a quantity, yet cannot give a single exact value; he may be able to give only a "ball park" estimate. For example, a subject may be asked about the population of some country, the age of a well-known person, or the distance between two points. In all of these cases, it can be assumed that a subject uses any specific knowledge he has that he believes to be relevant. On the basis of this knowledge, he can decide that certain values are more or less likely to be correct. In other situations, a subject might need to predict a value for some continuous random quantity, such as the height of a randomly selected person. In these cases, there is no single correct answer, but the subject can presumably use his past experience with the heights of people to decide whether certain values are possible or likely.

In cases like these, a continuous subjective probability distribution might reasonably be used as a measure of the subject's uncertainty. The most direct method of measuring uncertainty in this way is to ask the subject to give an interval: two values for the quantity in question, the difference between which will be a measure of his uncertainty. There are a number of examples of this task in the literature: Stael von Holstein (1971) reported studies in which subjects were asked to give a range of values for quantities such as the proportion of law students enrolled at a university. These intervals were to have a fixed probability of including the true value. Peterson, Snapper, and Murphy (1972) asked weather forecasters to give credible interval forecasts of temperature. These forecasts used the median and quartiles of the forecaster's subjective probability distributions. An example that used randomly selected quantities is the study by Vlek (1973), who asked subjects for percentile judgments of the heights of men and women. A task related to the measurement of subjective probabilities was used by Beach and Solak (1969), who asked subjects to give statements of the degree of acceptable error in tasks that required numerical estimates.

While having subjects give an interval response is useful in measuring their uncertainty, problems arise in designing a task that is easily comprehended by the subject. The task can be made easier by asking for indifference judgments, having the subject define two or more events that he considers equally likely to be true. It is then not necessary to use any numerical statement of probability in defining the task for the subject. For example, the median of a subjective probability distribution can be defined as the value that divides all possible values into two equally likely regions. A value m, is the median for a qnantity, x, if the subject is indifferent between a bet that pays off if the true value of x is less than m and a bet that pays off is the true value of x is greater than m. The use of indifference judgments can clearly be extended to permit the definition of other fractiles. Any set of n values will define $n + 1$ possible regions in which the true value might be located. If three regions can be found that define four equally likely regions, then these values can be defined as the quartiles of the subjective probability distribution.

The more regions used to measure a subjective probability distribution, the greater the complexity of the task for the subject. A convenient compromise between complexity of task and amount of information extracted from the subject can be realized through the use of *tertiles*. Two values, T_1 and T_2, are tertiles if the subject believes that, for some quantity, X, the correct value is equally likely to be found in the three regions, (a) $X < T_1$,   (b) $X > T_2$,   (c) $T_1 \leq X \leq T_2$. From the two tertiles it is possible to derive measures of central tendency and uncertainty for the distribution, two measures that will conveniently summarize the main aspects of a subject's knowledge (Pitz, 1974).

Methods that require subjects to give direct numerical estimates for T_1 and T_2 suffer from the usual problems related to the interpretation of numerical responses. The problem may be somewhat less severe than in probability judgment studies; a subject is more likely to be acquainted with units such as miles, feet, and so on, than he is with units of the probability scale. Nevertheless, I shall show how one might obtain indirect estimates for the tertiles of a probability distribution by using only a decision task. Becker (1962) has pointed out how one could use decisions to measure subjective probabilities for a single event to any necessary degree of precision. The method to be described here is similar to Becker's in some respects, but it is more general.

The method works as follows: For a quantity, such as the population of Canada, a subject is given any two values, T_1 and T_2, which are not necessarily tertiles. There are, then, three regions in which the population might lie: less than T_1, greater than T_2, or in between T_1 and T_2. The subject may choose one of these three regions, earning, say, three points if he is correct. If he prefers, he may make a negative decision, a decision that one of the three regions does not contain the true value. A correct negative decision earns, say, two points. Suppose the subjective probabilities for the three regions are P_1, P_2, and P_3, and that they are ordered in magnitude, $P_3 < P_2 < P_1$. Clearly the subject should give either a "Yes 1" response (i.e., decide that the population *is* located in Region 1), or a "No 3" response. It is easy to show that he will maximize his expected payoff by giving a positive response if and only if $P_1 > 2P_2$.

The decisions made by the subject may be used to generate revised values of T_1 and T_2, and the process used iteratively to estimate the tertiles of the subjective probability distribution. Figure 1 illustrates how this method works, under the assumption that the decisions are based on the relative magnitudes of P_1, P_2, and P_3. Figure 1a illustrates a hypothetical probability distribution divided into three regions by T_1 and T_2.

Following a decision by the subject that the true value of X is located in Region 1, the values of T_1 and T_2 are shifted to the points shown in Fig. 1b. When the subject then selects Region 2, the values of T_1 and T_2 are shifted to those shown in Fig. 1c. Figure 2 shows one of a number of ways in which the magnitude of the shift, δ, is reduced as T_1 and T_2 converge. In this case a "Yes 2" decision is followed immediately by a "No 2" decision.

The magnitude of δ is gradually reduced as the process continues. In principle, T_1 and T_2 should converge at two values that make the subject's decision maximally difficult. At this point, T_1 and T_2 can be said to be tertiles for the subjective probability distribution. This method has been programmed for a PDP-12 computer. Figure 3 illustrates the changes in T_1 and T_2 over a series of trials for one particular subject who was tested by this program. The values shown are the running averages over five consecutive trials. In this experiment, the subject was making decisions about eight different uncertain quantities, with random presentation of quantities on each trial. In this way, the subject was not making a sequence of 18 consecutive decisions about Canada; the points shown in Fig. 3 were interspersed among other decisions. As for most subjects, the values of T_1 and

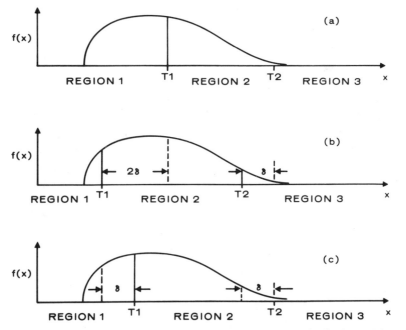

FIG. 1.   Example of a hypothetical subjective probability distribution, $f(x)$, and the shift in T_1 and T_2 values following (a) a "Yes 1" decision, and (b) a "Not 1" decision.

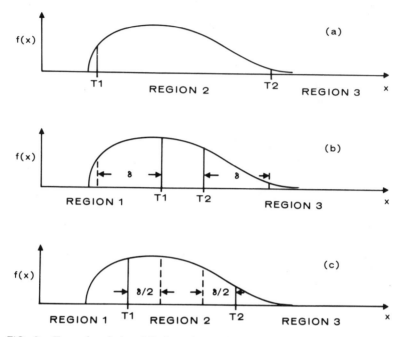

FIG. 2. Example of the shift in values of T_1 and T_2 following (a) a "Yes 2" decision, and (b) a "Not 2" decision.

T_2 converged within 10 or 15 trials. After that they often oscillate slightly, reflecting, perhaps, slight changes in the subject's beliefs over time. The data in Fig. 3, incidentally, come from the first subject to be run using this procedure.

The method described here has now been used in a number of studies designed to measure a subject's beliefs about a variety of quantities, ranging from the age of Golde Meir to the price of a hypothetical stock on the New York Stock Exchange. It seems clear now that tertiles estimated in this way are consistently different from tertiles obtained by asking subjects for direct specification of regions of indifference. Most important, the tertiles obtained through the decision process are usually closer together than those given directly. I have discussed (Pitz, 1975) a theoretical approach to uncertain knowledge that would predict this apparently greater degree of certainty in the decision-based task. Of course, it is pointless to ask which method gives the "true" tertiles. Rather, one must seek theoretical explanations for the difference in terms of the underlying decision process.

While of some interest in its own right, the study of subjective probability is of most interest when examined in the context of changes in beliefs

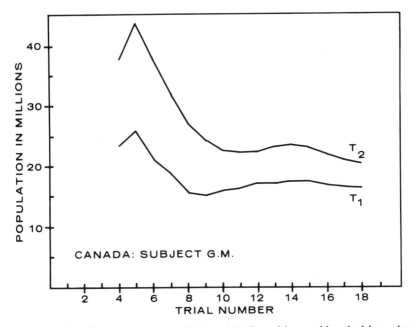

FIG. 3.   Example of convergence of T_1 and T_2 for subject making decisions about the population of Canada. Points shown are running averages over five successive trials.

following the presentation of information. I would like to show that one can also study the process of opinion revision by studying decision behavior. I have already referred to an earlier experiment (Pitz, 1972), in which a decision task was used to test hypotheses about the way in which subjects perceived and used several items of simultaneously presented information. Other experiments have examined decision behavior when information was presented sequentially (e.g., Pitz & Reinhold, 1968). We have conducted a number of studies recently that were designed to explore further the sequential decision-making process. I shall say a little about one such series of experiments, which was based on ideas suggested by Bayes' theorem.

Suppose Bayes' theorem is used to decide between two possible hypotheses, H_1 and H_2, following the presentation of a sequence of information. The decision can be based on a ratio of the two posterior probabilities, the posterior odds, which may be expressed as the product of a prior odds and a likelihood ratio. Suppose two items of information, E_1 and E_2, are presented; then the posterior odds following E_1 must be multiplied by the likelihood ratio for E_2. This second likelihood ratio, L_2, is

$$L_2 = \frac{P(E_2|H_1, E_1)}{P(E_2|H_2, E_1)} . \tag{2}$$

Note that, in Eq. (2), it is necessary to take account of the fact that the first event has already occurred in evaluating the conditional probability of the second. In some cases, however, each item of information is *conditionally independent* of every other; i.e., the probability of an event's occurrence, given a fixed hypothesis, does not depend upon the occurrence of earlier events. In this case the likelihood ratio for the second event may be written as

$$L_2 = \frac{P(E_2|H_1)}{P(E_2|H_2)}, \tag{3}$$

in which explicit reference to the first event disappears. When the assumption of conditional independence is made, the likelihood ratio for each item of information is independent of all other information.

The form of Bayes' theorem that applies when information is conditionally independent has certain important psychological implications. It suggests that, in a sequential task, it is necessary only to revise one's odds after each item of information, without having to remember the complete sequence of information. This is not true when conditional independence does not hold. In other words, if Eq. (3) is true, the memory load on the decision maker is considerably reduced. No matter how long the sequence of information, each event may be encoded as a likelihood ratio, and then forgotten. To test this prediction, a task was designed in which memory for individual events would become increasingly difficult, to see if effective decision-making was still possible under these conditions.

There is one particularly simple form of decision task that has been studied extensively in previous experiments in which Bayes' theorem leads to other implications for psychological theories. If information is binary, i.e., if there are only two possible events that can occur, the posterior odds is a function only of the frequencies of the two events. Furthermore, if $P(E_1|H_1) = P(E_2|H_2)$, only the difference between the two frequencies is relevant. If E is a sequence of events in which E_1 occurs f_1 times and E_2 occurs f_2 times, Eq. (1) leads to

$$\frac{P(H_1|E)}{P(H_2|E)} = \left[\frac{P(E_1|H_1)}{P(E_1|H_2)}\right]^{f_1-f_2} \frac{P(H_1)}{P(H_2)}. \tag{4}$$

Hence, a Bayesian theory might predict that the frequency information is all that is used by a subject in making his decisions. In fact, all the subject need do is keep track of which event occurs more often.

In previous studies of binary decision tasks, individual occurrences of the events were generally indistinguishable, making it difficult to study memory for individual events. In the studies described here, every occurrence of the events E_1 and E_2 was unique. The judgments and decisions concerned populations of words, for example, animal names or household objects. In the decision task, subjects were required to decide whether a randomly selected sequence of words came from a population that was predominantly animal names or predominantly household objects. The events E_1 and E_2 were the two word classes, and the information in any one sequence was conditionally independent. Performance in the decision task was compared with performance in recall and recognition memory tasks, as well as with performance in simple frequency judgment tasks.

All the tasks were trivially easy at the simplest level. However, several simultaneous sequences of information could be presented on each trial, so that subjects might observe up to five independent sequences that were occurring concurrently. In this way, a subject had to monitor several on-going sequences, keeping track of the individual events in a memory task, keeping multiple counts of some sort in the frequency tasks, and maintaining a current belief for each sequence in the decision task.

In one experiment, up to five independent, simultaneous sequences were monitored, each sequence consisting of either three or seven events. The results for the decision task are shown in Fig. 4. An optimal decision was defined as one that had a probability exceeding .5 of being correct, and was determined entirely by the event that occurred more often. It may

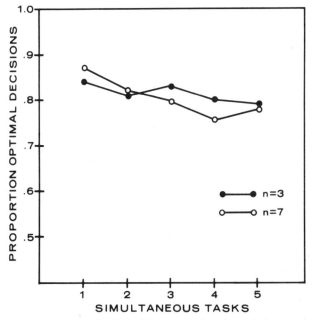

FIG. 4.   Proportion of optimal decisions as a function of the number of simultaneous sequences of information that were monitored.

be seen that there was only a slight decline in decision performance as the number of sequences to be monitored increased, and the longer sequences did not produce poorer performance than the shorter sequences. Bayesian likelihood ratio tests (Bayes' theorem used for statistical purposes) tended to support the null hypothesis of no difference in performance as a function of number of simultaneous tasks or length of sequence. It does appear that subjects were able to take advantage of the conditional independence of the information, in order to maintain the level of their performance when the amount of information became overwhelming.

Figure 5 shows what happened to other processes under the same conditions. The recognition memory task was actually a discrimination task; subjects had to be able to identify from which sequence an event had come. The data for the recognition task show that keeping track of individual events was indeed made increasingly difficult by increasing the amount of information. Recognition performance never did fall to chance level (which would have been a .5 probability of correct response). However, the variables that had little or no effect on performance in the decision task did serve to make recognition more difficult. If the subject had been forced to make his decisions at the end of a sequence on the basis of his ability to remember which information was associated with each sequence, there

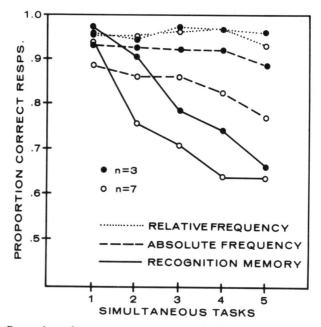

FIG. 5. Proportion of correct responses made in the recognition and frequency estimation tasks, as a function of the number of simultaneous sequences.

is no way that he could have performed at the level shown in Fig. 4 when processing more than three simultaneous sequences. The degree of confusion indicated in Fig. 5 would have produced far fewer optimal decisions than observed in Fig. 4.

In contrast, Fig. 5 shows that subjects were quite good at keeping track of frequencies. In the conditions labeled "relative frequency," subjects were required merely to indicate which type of event occurred most often in each sequence; this they could do almost flawlessly throughout. In the conditions labeled "absolute frequency," subjects had to know exactly how many events of one kind had occurred; performance here did decline somewhat as the amount of information increased. Tentatively, it was concluded that the decision process was related in some way to the relative frequency estimation process; both sets of results showed little or no decline as the amount of information increased. Ideally, of course, knowing the relative frequencies would have produced completely optimal decision performance. The difference between the proportion of correct relative frequency judgments and the proportion of optimal decisions indicates that decisions were not made on the basis of frequency estimates alone.

There are many ways in which one could study the relationship between the decision process and memory or frequency-estimation processes. As one more illustration of how it might be done, let me briefly describe the results of another experiment that reinforce the conclusions just reported. In the previous experiment, independent groups of subjects were used under the different task conditions. One might also ask subjects to perform two or more tasks simultaneously. Some care must be exercised in using such a procedure, but it does permit the testing of interesting hypotheses about the way in which subjects process information. In one such study, two groups of subjects were used. The primary task for one group was a standard decision task, while the other group was given a relative frequency-judgment task. On randomly selected trials, a secondary task was used; subjects were asked to recall any one item of information presented on that trial that belonged to a specified category. As before, multiple sequences were used to increase the amount of information to be processed.

There was one further difference in procedure from that employed in the experiment reported previously. In an attempt to make frequency judgment and decision performance more alike, subjects were required to pronounce each word aloud as it was presented. This procedure served two functions; it ensured some uniformity of attention to all of the information, and it effectively prevented subjects in the frequency task from keeping a verbal count of the number of events.

The results of this experiment are shown in Fig. 6. Note first that recall performance declined markedly as the number of simultaneous tasks in-

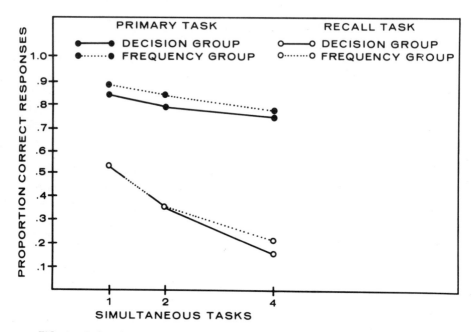

FIG. 6.   Proportion of optimal decisions or correct responses in the primary task, either decision-making or frequency judgment, together with proportion of correct recall responses in each task group.

creased, while there was a slight, non-significant decrease in performance for the decision and frequency tasks. These data confirm the conclusions reached from the last experiment. Second, note that recall was almost identical for the two primary tasks. Finally, the procedure of requiring the words to be pronounced made the frequency judgment and decision performance more alike than they were in the previous experiment. In other words, performance in the decision task seems to be rather like performance in a frequency-judgment task when subjects are not permitted to keep a verbal count, especially in terms of the ability to recall specific information. There was, however, a slight, but consistent, superiority of frequency judgment performance over decision performance, implying that the need to translate frequency information into decisions produces some errors in the decision task.

Some tentative conclusions can be reached from the results reported here. And it should be emphasized that these conclusions are tentative. In an opinion-revision task, subjects apparently keep track of relative frequencies without necessarily storing the irrelevant specific characteristics of the information. Some errors in frequency estimation can occur, since subjects typically do not maintain a verbal count of the events, as they try to do in a direct frequency-estimation task. In making a decision, the frequency information is translated into a choice among alternative hypotheses, introducing the possibility of further mistakes in the decision process.

It is not difficult to frame such a hypothesis within the terminology of Eq. (1). In the particular form of decision task studied here, Bayes' theorem generates Eq. (4), which states in algebraic terms essentially what has been postulated here in terms of psychological processes. If Bayes' theorem is to serve some function in the study of human judgment and inference, it must be one of this sort. Normative theories are useful to the extent that they suggest hypotheses about how a subject might perform a task, and to the extent that they suggest possible explanations for a failure by the subject to perform at the level predicted by the normative model. When Bayes' theorem is regarded in this light, it may turn out to be a valuable stimulus to psychological theories of inference.

ACKNOWLEDGMENTS

Assistance in conducting the studies reported here was provided by a number of people—Robert Chidel, Rosemary Schwartz, Nina Wham, and Steve Zang. The research was supported by Grants GB-28708X and GB-40313 from the National Science Foundation and by funds from the Graduate School of Southern Illinois University at Carbondale.

REFERENCES

Anderson, N. H. Integration theory and attitude change. *Psychological Review,* 1971, **78,** 171–206.

Bayes, T. An essay towards solving a problem in the doctrine of chances. *Philosophical Transactions of the Royal Society,* 1763, **53,** 370–418. [Edited version in *Biometrika,* 1958, **45,** 293–315.]

Beach, L. R., & Solak, F. Subjective judgments of acceptable error. *Organizational Behavior & Human Performance,* 1969, **4,** 242–251.

Becker, G. M. Decision making: Objective measures of subjective probability and utility. *Psychological Review,* 1962, **69,** 136–148.

Edwards, W. The prediction of decisions among bets. *Journal of Experimental Psychology,* 1955, **51,** 201–214.

Edwards, W., & Phillips, L. D. Emerging technologies for making decisions. In G. L. Bryan & M. W. Shelly (Eds.), *Human judgments and optimality.* New York: Wiley, 1964.

Jeffreys, H. *Theory of probability.* (3rd ed.) Oxford: Clarendon Press, 1961.

Peterson, C. R. & Beach, L. R. Man as an intuitive statistician. *Psychological Bulletin,* 1967, **68,** 29–46.

Peterson, C. R., Snapper, K. J., & Murphy, A. H. Credible interval temperature forecasts. *Bulletin of the American Meteorological Society,* 1972, **53,** 966–970.

Phillips, L. D. The "true probability" problem. *Acta Psychologica,* 1970, **34,** 254–264.

Pitz, G. F. On the processing of information: Probabilistic and otherwise. *Acta Psychologica,* 1970, **34,** 201–213.

Pitz, G. F. A structural theory of uncertain knowledge. In D. Wendt & C. Vlek (Eds.), *Utility probability and human decision making.* Dordrecht: Reidel, 1975.

Pitz, G. F. Simultaneous information integration in decisions concerning normal populations. *Organizational Behavior & Human Performance,* 1972, **8,** 325–339.

Pitz, G. F. Subjective probability distributions for imperfectly known quantities. In L. W. Gregg (Ed.), *Knowledge and cognition.* Hillsdale, New Jersey: Lawrence Erlbaum Assoc., 1974.

Pitz, G. F. & Reinhold, H. Payoff effects in sequential decision making. *Journal of Experimental Psychology,* 1968, **77,** 249–257.

Savage, L. J. *The foundations of statistics.* New York: Wiley, 1954.

Shanteau, J. Descriptive versus normative models of sequential inference judgment. *Journal of Experimental Psychology,* 1972, **93,** 63–68.

Smedslund, J. Circular relation between understanding and logic. *Scandinavian Journal of Psychology,* 1970, **11,** 217–219.

Stael von Holstein, C. A. S. Two techniques for the assessment of subjective probability distributions—an experimental study. *Acta Psychologica,* 1971, **35,** 478–494.

Stevens, S. S. On the psychophysical law. *Psychological Review,* 1957, **64,** 153–181.

Vlek, C. A. J. Coherence of human judgment in a limited probabilistic environment. *Organizational Behavior & Human Performance,* 1973, **9,** 460–481.

von Neumann, J., & Morgenstern, O. *Theory of games and economic behavior.* Princeton, New Jersey: Princeton Univ. Press, 1944.

von Winterfeldt, D., & Edwards, W. Costs and payoffs in perceptual research. Technical Rept. No. 011313-1-T, Engineering Psychology Laboratory, University of Michigan, 1973.

Wallsten, T. S. Conjoint-measurement framework for the study of probabilistic information processing. *Psychological Review,* 1972, **79,** 245–260.

PART III
MODELS OF SHORT-TERM MEMORY

Richard M. Shiffrin

Short-term memory was studied extensively by introspectionists in the late nineteenth and early twentieth centuries. Interest in human memory fell off, however, with the rise of behaviorism and the corresponding emphasis on animal learning. As part of the overall explosion of interest in human cognitive processes during the last 10–15 years, research on, and models of, short-term memory have grown at a phenomenal rate. Those not working directly in this area at the present time would as likely as not be overwhelmed by the confusion of findings, models, and terminology in this area. Viewing this state of affairs with some amusement, Edwin Martin arranged a symposium on short-term memory at the Midwestern Psychological Association meetings in 1973. Presentations were given by Robert A. Bjork, Richard M. Shiffrin, Fergus I. M. Craik, Dominic W. Massaro, and Bennett B. Murdock. Surprisingly, their views on short-term memory were actually far more congruent than previous writings may have indicated. Subsequent to that symposium it was agreed that it would be extremely valuable to point out these similarities in print, to cut through terminological and definitional differences and expose issues of real substance. The three papers printed here are the result. They were presented at the Indiana Theoretical and Cognitive Psychology Meetings in April, 1974. Each contribution gives a brief exposition of the authors' present views of short-term memory, and of the memory system as a whole. At the end of each presentation is a section devoted to comparisons among the three models. We hope this format will allow the readers to compare our views directly, and to perceive the similarities as well as the differences among the systems of memory.

8

SHORT-TERM STORAGE: THE ORDERED OUTPUT OF A CENTRAL PROCESSOR

Robert A. Bjork
University of Michigan

The concept of short-term memory (STM), in the relatively well-speci-fied form outlined in the influential papers by Waugh and Norman (1965) and Atkinson and Shiffrin (1968), has suffered considerable damage in the last several years. Recent empirical results and theoretical efforts have left none of the assumed characteristics of STM standing as initially formu-lated. It has been necessary to repair, remodel, and complicate the concept of STM in terms of encoding format, capacity, role of rehearsal, and so forth.

It is usually the case in psychology that such frequent required mainte-nance signals the end of the usefulness of a concept. However, to me, the notion that there exists in the human information-processor a separate short-term storage system distinct from both peripheral storage systems and longer-term storage systems seems never more viable. It is the overall pattern of empirical results that I find so convincing. Any number of re-sults—whether differences in retrieval or recognition latency for items pre-sumed to be in STM or LTM, differences in types of confusions and intru-sions, differences between immediate and delayed recall of end items in a list relative to earlier items, or whatever—have a straightforward inter-pretation in terms of the distinction between STM and LTM. With some effort, any one of those results can be interpreted without making an STM–LTM distinction, but accounting for all of those results without such a distinction results at best in an extraordinarily complex and convoluted characterization of memory. Even the compelling levels-of-processing framework outlined by Craik and Lockhart (1972), which at first glance seems inconsistent with the notion of a functionally distinct short-term store, is quite compatible with the assumption that such a store exists. Taken together, this chapter and the chapters by Shiffrin and by Craik and Jacoby in this volume constitute presumptive evidence for that assertion: All three assume both a levels-of-processing framework and the existence of a short-term system that is functionally distinct from LTM.

In the section that follows, I present a characterization of the human memory system and the role of STM within that system. In the second section, I discuss the representation of rehearsal processes, and in the final section, I compare the human memory system as I have characterized it with the systems proposed by Shiffrin and by Craik and Jacoby.

THE HUMAN MEMORY SYSTEM

Figure 1 diagrams some structures and processes that I consider to be essential constituents of the human memory system.

Components of the System

Input analysis.   When a verbal item is presented to the system, it is analyzed by a series of processing mechanisms. In general, as shown in Fig. 1, each successive analyzer operates on the output of the preceding

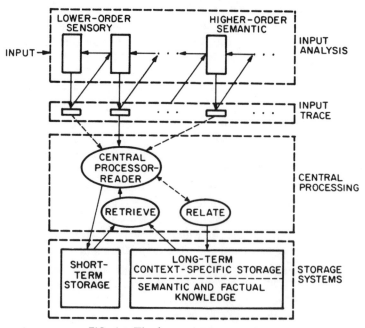

FIG. 1.   The human memory system.

analyzer, but I do not assume that the analysis is serial in any strict sense. The successive analyses overlap in time—higher-level analyzers start working on the incomplete products of lower-level analyzers before the lower-level analysis is complete—and the momentary state of a higher-level analyzer may, as I have attempted to show in Fig. 1, influence the momentary state of a lower-level analyzer. Thus, for example, if a letter string presented to the system at time t constitutes a common word, the meaningfulness of that input influences the input analysis by time $t + \Delta t$, where Δt is arbitrarily small.

In general, the output of any one analysis stage is determined by (a) the output of the preceding stage and (b) the momentary state of the analyzer, which is itself influenced by (1) the nature of recent inputs to that analyzer and (2) the momentary states of higher-level analyzers. The whole analysis process is relatively fixed at the beginning and becomes more variable as it proceeds. At the higher levels, the input analysis becomes more idiosyncratic and subject to variations in local context (i.e., to the nature of just-prior inputs to the system). It is also the case that higher-level analyzers are heavily influenced by the history of the system— that is, by the relatively permanent structure of semantic and factual knowledge. Thus, there is a kind of loop in the system from the long-term storage system back to the input analyzers that is not shown in Fig. 1.

There is nothing especially novel about my assumptions with respect to the input analysis of a verbal item; it is basically a levels-of-processing system. I assume, however, that the process is essentially automatic. If a verbal item is presented, the whole analysis proceeds whether the input is being attended to or not.

Input trace.   As a consequence of the input analysis, an input trace is left in the nervous system. The input trace subsumes what is usually referred to as *sensory storage*. It is the product of the overlapping stages of analysis, and it is formed during a period lasting in the hundreds of milliseconds. The various components of the input trace are highly susceptible to destructive interference from subsequent inputs to memory, but even without such interference, unattended components at all levels decay rapidly. On the average, lower-level components are lost more quickly than higher-level components because the degree of destructive interference from subsequent inputs is assumed to be an increasing function of similarity, and the lower-level components of successive inputs to memory are more likely to be similar than are the higher-level components.

Central processor.   The system assumes the existence of a central processor (or homunculus) that is central and critical to attention, storage, rehearsal, retrieval, and various other mnemonic activities. In general, the activities one might think of as "control processes" are under the control of the central processor. The central processor can attend to or retrieve aspects of the input trace, it can retrieve information from STM or LTM, and it can relate or associate items in constructive ways.

As a processor or handler, the central processor is a kind of bottleneck in the system; it is restricted to carrying out only one function in any given instant of time. In some nontrivial way, however, the central processor is sensitive to salience, pertinence, and so forth; as a monitor, the central processor is not serial in nature.

Storage systems.   Short-term storage (STS) is defined as the output of the central processor. That is, whenever something is handled by the central processor—whether that "something" is part of the input trace, an item retrieved from STS or LTS, or a newly constructed or integrated chunk based on a combination of pieces from STS or LTS—the output of that handling exists in a state that defines STS. When items are retrieved from STS or LTS and some relation or association based on semantic or factual knowledge is formed between those items, the structure so created amounts to a modification within or entry into LTS. Items are not, however, "transferred" from STS to LTS. In any act of storing items in LTS that were in STS, something new is added. That is, the items are not entered into LTS in their STS form; rather, those items as related or elaborated on the basis of long-term knowledge are entered into LTS. Also, immediately following any such act of storage in LTS, the items as modified exist in STS as well.

Within LTS, there is a distinction between context-specific information and context-independent knowledge. Thus, the knowledge that eggs, bacon, and orange juice are frequently eaten at breakfast, that Salt Lake City is the capitol of Utah, and that DOG denotes an animal with certain properties, is, in each case, context independent. On the other hand, remembering what one had for breakfast yesterday, what one did in Salt Lake City, and that DOG was one of a list of words studied an hour ago, are all context specific. This distinction corresponds, of course, to Tulving's (1972) distinction between *episodic* and *semantic* memory. It is not, fortunately, the burden of this chapter to specify how that distinction is represented in LTS. For what it is worth, however, I assume that the store of semantic and factual knowledge is modified whenever items within the context-specific long-term store are related to or interpreted in terms of information in the current store of semantic and factual knowledge.

Characteristics of Short-Term Memory

Format.   The short-term store has no particular format. The information stored in it may be acoustic, linguistic, visual, semantic, relational, or whatever depending on the activities of the central processor. In experimental settings, the format of information in STS will be determined primarily by the demands of the particular experimental task. Thus, given the nature of the responses required in typical memory experiments, those experiments will typically reveal that information in STS is stored in acoustic or linguistic form.

Forgetting. The short-term store is an "active" store; without reinstatement, items in STS are lost quickly—within a few seconds. Reinstatement consists of reprocessing by the central processor (i.e., rehearsal). Given no other demands on the central processor, such rehearsal is a compelling and habitual activity.

The mechanism by which items are lost from STS is similarity-dependent decay. The loss rate of an item in STS is independent of both the nature of that item and the number of other items in STS, but the loss rate is heavily influenced by the amount of similarity between the item in question and the other items in STS. Thus, even though loss rate is independent of number of items in STS, loss rate will tend to increase with number of items because, on the average, total amount of similarity will increase with number of items.

Capacity. The capacity of STS (the number of items that can, on the average, be maintained in or read out of STS without error) is determined by the interaction of the loss rate (independent of item type) and the rehearsal rate (a decreasing function of the complexity of the items in STS). Thus, in the present system, the fact that the number of chunks that can be maintained in or read out of STS decreases with chunk size (from letters to words to idioms, e.g., see Simon, 1974) is attributable to a decreasing rehearsal or central processing rate with increasing chunk size.

Order retention. As long as the number of items in STS does not exceed the capacity of STS, and the central processor is free to report or maintain those items, order information is retained automatically. That is, in contrast to the retrieval of episodic items from LTS, it is not necessary for the central processor, in maintaining or reporting a subcapacity set of items, to reconstruct the input order of those items. If, however, the central processor is distracted, order information is lost at least as rapidly as item information. As in the case of item information, the loss of order information is similarity sensitive.

Updating. Finally, when items are lost from STS they are completely lost in the sense that they provide no subsequent interference in the use of the STS system. Thus, the STS system is indefinitely updatable or reusable; it is, in that sense, proactive-interference-proof.

Some Comments on the System

The system as just outlined amounts to a kind of position statement. The system represents my current attempt to characterize short-term memory within the overall structure of memory in a way that makes peace with the results referred to at the start of this chapter. There remain, of course, certain results that are unfriendly if not hostile with respect to the present system.

The system as proposed is relatively unique in some ways, but it clearly shares some features with other systems that have been proposed, including the systems proposed by Craik and Jacoby and by Shiffrin in this volume. The present system has much in common with the system proposed in less explicit form by Posner and Warren (1972) in their article, "Traces concepts, and conscious constructions." The assumptions about the input process are quite close in the two systems, and Posner and Warren's "conscious constructions" correspond in a general way to the output of the central processor when it is operating in a RELATE mode. The notion of "concepts," however, as defined by Posner and Warren, seems to cut across functions viewed as separable in the present system.

In order to explicate the foregoing system in reasonably concise fashion, I avoided citing the results that influenced my assumptions with respect to the various structures and processes in Fig. 1. With respect to the input process, my characterization was influenced by the work of Posner and his co-workers (e.g., Posner, 1969; Posner & Boies, 1971; Posner, Boies, Eichelman, & Taylor, 1969), by Keele's (1972) work on the Stroop effect, and by a variety of work on visual processing (e.g., Bjork & Estes, 1973; Gardner, 1973; Reicher, 1969; Shiffrin & Gardner, 1972; Shiffrin & Geisler, 1973; Wheeler, 1970). The present system was formulated without knowledge of the elegant characterization of the reading process presented by La Berge and Samuels (1974), but I see the input process in the present system as quite compatible with their model, although the present system is mute with respect to the developmental processes treated in some detail by La Berge and Samuels.

As far as the characteristics of short-term memory are concerned, my assumptions about format were influenced by the work of Shulman (1970) and Massaro (1973), and my assumptions about forgetting and the role of similarity were influenced by the work of Ligon (1968), Reitman (1971, 1974), Shiffrin (1973), and Bjork and Healy (1974). In the next section, I discuss the research work that probably had the greatest influence on my overall characterization of STM within the human memory system.

THE ROLE OF REHEARSAL

Until recently, rehearsal was generally assumed (Atkinson & Shiffrin, 1968; Waugh & Norman, 1965) to have a dual function within the human memory system. Although it was generally realized that rehearsal was not a single activity, but a collection of activities, it was assumed that all of those activities both (*a*) maintained items in STM and (*b*) transferred those items to LTM. On the basis of a burst of recent research activity (Bjork & Jongeward, 1974; Craik & Watkins, 1973; Jacoby, 1973; Jacoby & Bartz, 1972; Mazuryk, 1974; Mazuryk & Lockhart, 1974; Meunier, Ritz, & Meunier, 1972; Woodward, Bjork, & Jongeward, 1973), however, it has become necessary to distinguish among different types of rehearsal.

Primary Rehearsal

One distinguishable type of rehearsal activity is the rote cycling or maintenance of items in STS, referred to as *maintenance rehearsal* by Craik and Watkins (1973) and as *primary rehearsal* by Woodward *et al.* (1973). Primary rehearsal appears to function primarily as a short-term holding operation; it has no consequences on long-term recall. Within the system in Fig. 1, primary rehearsal consists of a STS–retrieve–read–STS cycling of the items in STS. The process is independent of the LTS system; the items are simply maintained in their current form and are not interassociated or elaborated in any way.

The properties of primary rehearsal are illustrated quite clearly in Experiment III by Woodward *et al.* (1973). In each of four 36-word lists, subjects were cued after each word in turn whether to remember or to forget that word. The presentation of a given item (1 sec) was followed by a variable blank rehearsal period (0, 4, or 12 sec), at the end of which subjects were required, in response to a row of question marks presented for 1.5 sec, to recall the current word. Immediately subsequent to each such within-list test, there was a 1-sec cue to subjects to remember (R cue) or to forget (F cue) that word. After the R or F cue, the next word in the list was presented. In random sequence, half of the words in a list were R cued and half were F cued. At the end of each list there was an immediate recall test for the R words presented in that list, and at the end of the experiment there was a final recall test for all words presented during the experiment. After the final recall test, there was a final recognition test. The 144 words presented during the experiment were mixed together on two sheets of paper with an equal number of distractors, and subjects were asked to circle any words they remembered having seen during the experiment.

The experiment was designed to induce primary rehearsal of the current word during the rehearsal period following its presentation. Since the subject did not know, until the end of the rehearsal period, whether he was to remember the current word, it was not in his interest to do more than maintain the current word until the cue appeared. Any attempt to associate or integrate the current word with other R words in the list would be counterproductive since he might be cued to forget the current word.

In the top panel of Fig. 2, the probabilities of R-word recall and F-word intrusion during immediate recall are shown as a function of rehearsal time. Even though an increase in rehearsal time from 0 to 12 sec is enough to create order-of-magnitude improvements in recall in other situations (see, for example, the results of an experiment by Pollatsek reported in Bjork, 1970), the immediate recall of R words and intrusion of F words were independent of rehearsal time in the Woodward *et al.* experiment. The same result was obtained in the final recall of R words and F words.

In the bottom panel of Fig. 2, final recognition probabilities are shown for R words and F words as a function of rehearsal time. The picture in the bottom panel of Fig. 2 is very different from that in the top panel: Final recognition of both R words and F words increases systematically with rehearsal time. With a somewhat different procedure, Bjork and

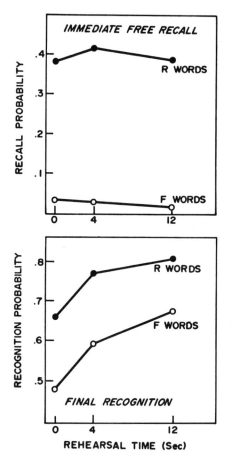

FIG. 2. Initial free recall and final recognition of to-be-remembered (R words) and to-be-forgotten (F words) as a function of rehearsal time. (After Woodward, Bjork, & Jongeward, 1973.)

Jongeward (1974) obtained a pattern of results identical to that in Fig. 2. That is, significant increases in recognition as a function of amount of primary rehearsal, but no effect of amount of primary rehearsal on recall.

Although the lack of any effects of primary rehearsal on long-term recall is consistent with the way in which I have characterized primary rehearsal in the present system, the increase in final recognition as a function of primary rehearsal obtained by Woodward *et al.* (1973) and Bjork and Jongeward (1974) poses something of a problem. Bjork and Jongeward, however, suggest an explanation of the recognition results that is at least semiplausible in terms of the present system. They propose that primary rehearsal of items in STS leads to associations between those items and the general situational context. In that sense, primary rehearsal does increase the strength of an item's representation in LTS, although no interassociation or elaboration of the items in STS are formed or stored in LTS during primary rehearsal. Since recall from LTS is mediated primarily by interassociations among items, primary rehearsal has litle or no effect on long-term recall. The recognition that a particular common word appeared during an experimental session is, on the other hand, a judgment of the word's association with the general situational context of the experiment. The question is not whether the word has been seen before—that is certainly the case—but whether the word appeared in the current context. Thus, long-term recognition should increase with amount of primary rehearsal.

Secondary Rehearsal

Another distinguishable type of rehearsal process, referred to as *elaborative rehearsal* by Craik and Watkins (1973) and as *secondary rehearsal* by Woodward *et al.* (1973), involves a variety of LTS-dependent activities by means of which items in STS are interassociated and elaborated. In terms of Fig. 1, secondary rehearsal consists of the following sequence: STS–retrieve, LTS–retrieve, relate, read–LTS (and STS). Thus, in contrast to primary rehearsal, secondary rehearsal both modifies the form of the items in STS and leads to the storage of the items as modified in LTS. From the standpoint of facilitating long-term recall, secondary rehearsal is a great deal more productive than is primary rehearsal. As a maintenance operation, however, secondary rehearsal is inefficient. It is slower than primary rehearsal, which means that items may be lost from STS while other items are being processed. Also, items in STS are not simply maintained by secondary rehearsal; they are modified and transformed in terms of item information and in terms of order information.

The differential properties of primary and secondary rehearsal are demonstrated clearly by the results of an experiment by Bjork and Jongeward (1974, Experiment II). On each of 20 trials in a modified Brown–Peterson design, subjects were asked to remember six common four-letter nouns. Each six-word string was presented for 4 sec, and the retention interval on each trial was a 20-sec unfilled interval. Prior to each trial, subjects were cued as to the way in which they were to rehearse the six words presented on that trial. On half the trials they were instructed to engage in primary rehearsal during the 20-sec retention interval, and on the remaining trials they were instructed to engage in secondary rehearsal during the retention interval. During several practice trials prior to the experiment, the difference between cycling items in rote fashion ("telephone strategy") and attempting to form associations, sentences, images, and so forth ("meaningful connections strategy") was explained in detail. At the end of each retention interval, there was a free-recall test for the six words presented on that trial. At the end of the experiment, without forewarning, one group of subjects was tested for their recall of all words presented during the experiment (final recall group), and another group of subjects was tested for their recognition of the words presented during the experiment (final recognition group). The final-recognition test was a yes–no task in which words from the experiment and a larger number of distractors were intermingled and presented one at a time.

In the left panel of Fig. 3, initial and final recall probabilities are shown as a function of processing strategy for the final recall group. In the right panel, initial recall and final recognition probabilities are shown for the final recognition group. In both panels, type of rehearsal clearly interacts with time of test. Primary rehearsal is better as a maintenance operation during the initial 20 sec following the presentation of a six-word string, but it is clearly inferior to secondary rehearsal in terms of facilitating long-term performance. A similar interaction is apparent in the results of experiments by Mazuryk and Lockhart (1974) and Mazuryk (1974).

Another analysis by Bjork and Jongeward (1974) illustrates that order information in STS tends to be maintained by primary rehearsal and lost as a natural consequence of secondary rehearsal. Bjork and Jongeward computed the proportion of trials on which the relative output order of the words that were recalled matched the input order of those words. Even though subjects were free to recall in any order, the overall proportion of primary-rehearsal trials on which the words were recalled in the correct relative order was .81. Given that all six words were recalled, the proportion was .93. On secondary-rehearsal trials, however, the corresponding proportions were .34 and .29. Thus, primary rehearsal is a fundamental maintenance operation not only in the sense that items are kept available in STS, but also in the sense that the ordering of those items is also

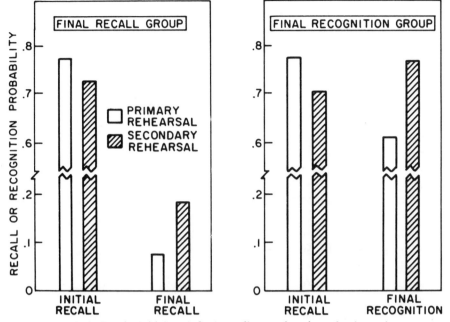

FIG. 3. Left Panel: Initial and final recall as a function of rehearsal strategy; Right Panel: Initial recall and final recognition as a function of rehearsal strategy. The false-alarm probability for new words on the final recognition task was .193. (After Bjork & Jongeward, 1974.)

preserved. On the other hand, secondary rehearsal elaborates, integrates, and rearranges the items in STS on the basis of idiosyncratic or not-so-idiosyncratic knowledge.

The differences between primary and secondary rehearsal are further illuminated by some research by Elmes and Bjork (1975). In several experiments, Elmes and Bjork employed a procedure similar to that employed by Bjork and Jongeward, except that five rather than six words were presented either once or twice on a given trial, and the retention intervals were both varied and filled with a distractor activity. As in the Bjork and Jongeward experiment, subjects were instructed to engage in either primary or secondary rehearsal at the time of each presentation. The recall proportions for once-presented words in Elmes and Bjork's Experiments I and II are shown in Fig. 4 as a function of rehearsal instruction and retention interval. The retention curves in Fig. 4 demonstrate again the increasing advantage of secondary rehearsal as recall is tested at increasing delays. Recall performance by the uncued control subjects in Experiment II fell, as one might expect, between the performance levels on primary and secondary trials for the cued subjects. For what it is worth, however, the details of the recall performance by control subjects indicate that they engaged almost exclusively in primary processing on first presentations, and

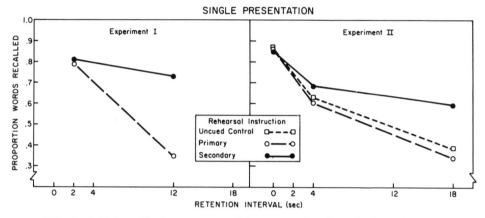

FIG. 4. Initial recall of once-presented items as a function of rehearsal strategy and retention interval. (After Elmes & Bjork, 1975.)

they engaged in a mixture of primary and secondary processing on second presentations.

Two additional analyses carried out by Elmes and Bjork, one of intrusions during initial recall and the other of clustering during final recall, provide support for the differential functions attributed in the above-cited experiments to primary and secondary rehearsal. During initial recall, the proportions of errors on primary-rehearsal trials that were acoustic or semantic intrusions were .34 and .03, respectively. The corresponding proportions on secondary-rehearsal trials were .19 and .16. Thus, in terms of those proportions, primary rehearsal resulted in about twice as many acoustic intrusions, but only about one-fifth as many semantic intrusions, as did secondary rehearsal. That pattern is consistent with the notion that primary rehearsal consists of a cycling of items in STS in a form suitable to the task, in this case acoustic, whereas secondary rehearsal consists of a semantic elaboration or interassociation of the items in STS. During final recall, the extent of clustering by input string was five times higher for strings given secondary rehearsal than it was for strings given primary rehearsal during input. Once again, that result is consistent with the idea that secondary rehearsal, in contrast to primary rehearsal, leads to storage in LTS of the items as elaborated and interrelated.

The Interaction of Primary and Secondary Rehearsal

To some extent, primary and secondary rehearsal can be viewed as having a symbiotic relationship. On the one hand, even if one's goal is long-term storage of the items being rehearsed, primary rehearsal provides the basis for subsequent secondary rehearsal. Since secondary rehearsal is relatively inefficient as a maintenance operation, interspersed periods of primary rehearsal are necessary to keep the current contents of STS available for additional secondary processing. Primary rehearsal is "primary" in the sense that it is a kind of re-presentation scheme by means of which a faithful copy of items is kept available in STS over the short term, either to be reported in that form or to be transferred in modified form to LTS. Secondary rehearsal, on the other hand, can both facilitate primary rehearsal by chunking separate items in STS and can, to some extent, remove the need for additional primary rehearsal by storing an adequate representation of the items in LTS.

DISCUSSION

Summary of the Present System

The present system is meant to characterize the principal components of the memory system of the adult human being. The system consists of (*a*) a set of highly sophisticated input mechanisms, the output of which is an input trace; (*b*) a single central processor that attends, reads, rehearses, relates, and so forth; and (*c*) two storage systems, a short-term store consisting of the output of the central processor, and a long-term store consisting of context-dependent episodic knowledge and context-independent semantic and factual knowledge.

The input process translates the nominal form of a verbal item as presented into a functional internal representation—the input trace. When a verbal item is seized by the input analyzers that underlie the input process, it is subjected to a series of overlapping levels of analysis that proceed from relatively fixed and primitive sensory analyses to more variable and idiosyncratic semantic analyses. With adult humans and common verbal materials the input process is automatic—that is, does not require attention. As a consequence of the input process, a multicomponent input trace is left in the nervous system, the components of which correspond to the different levels of analysis that are carried out. The notion of an input trace can be viewed as extending the notion of a sensory store to include higher-level as well as lower-level components. Although the input process is automatic, it is not deterministic; that is, the output of a given analyzer is a stochastic process determined by the momentary state of the analyzer, which is influenced by prior inputs to the system. Thus, the same nominal item presented to the same individual at different times may result in different input traces, especially in terms of the higher-level components.

Probably the most innovative feature of the present system is the overall dependence of the system on the activities of a single central processor. As a processor or handler of information, the central processor is limited to one function at a time; as a sensor or monitor, the central processor has no such limitation and is sensitive to salience, pertinence, and so forth. There is a sense in which the central processor drives the system. The output of the central processor defines STS, and although the input process is independent of the central processor, components of the input trace do not survive past the brief life of that trace unless read (entered into STS) by the central processor. The central processor is also responsible for the retrieval of information from STS and LTS, for the maintenance of information in STS, and for the storage of information in LTS. Items are maintained in STS via rehearsal, which consists of either a rote cycling of items in STS through the central processor (primary rehearsal) or a constructive, LTS-dependent activity by means of which items in STS are interassociated or chunked (secondary rehearsal). Storage in LTS is achieved when items retrieved from STS or LTS by the central processor are related or interassociated on the basis of semantic or factual knowledge. During secondary rehearsal, therefore, the items as chunked or interrelated are stored in LTS as well as maintained in STS. During primary rehearsal there is no such LTS storage, but the items being maintained in STS may become associated with the general situational context.

In the present system, STS is an active store; unless maintained via rehearsal, items in STS are lost quickly, within a relatively few seconds. Items in STS are lost via a decay process that is independent of item type, but is heavily influenced by amount of similarity among the items in STS. The capacity of STS is determined by the interaction of the loss rate of items in STS (independent of item type) and the rate at which those items can be rehearsed (a decreasing function of item size or complexity). As long as the number of items in STS do not exceed its maintenance capacity, order information as well as item information is preserved in STS.

Comparison with the Craik and Jacoby and Shiffrin Systems

Although there are important differences among the systems proposed in this symposium, their overall convergence is more striking than are their points of divergence. That convergence is especially remarkable since the three systems *do* diverge in substantial ways from systems proposed in the past—with the possible exception of the proposal by Posner and Warren (1972)—and since we each felt that we were staking out important new ground in our proposals. After the fact, there is one sense in which the convergence of the three systems is not so surprising: To some extent, we have all been influenced by the same empirical results, and we have interpreted those results in somewhat similar ways. Whether we have been led or misled remains to be seen.

In the remainder of this section, I comment on the similarities and differences among the three systems, and criticize certain aspects of each of the systems.

Input processes.   The input process is characterized in much the same way in each of the three systems. The process is assumed in each case to proceed from relatively fixed lower-level analyses to more variable higher-level analyses. All three systems assume that the process is essentially automatic, although Craik and Jacoby assert that attention is required for unfamiliar analyses.

The formal similarities in the three characterizations of the input process are not as apparent as they might be because there are substantial differences among the systems in terminology and emphasis. In my own system, the stress is on the input process as an active analysis, the product of which is an input trace: Input analyzers stand poised and ready to dissect verbal inputs. Shiffrin assumes something more like a multilevel template-matching process. Every possible coding or feature of an input exists in the long-term store, and upon presentation, a subset of those codes or features lights up automatically, without any active analysis being assumed. Craik and Jacoby assume a process that seems in emphasis to fall midway between my characterization and Shiffrin's characterization. To some extent, I find the template-matching aspect of Shiffrin's system implausible. Whereas it is not difficult for me to imagine that the visual receptors could, for example, achieve an encoding of any possible visual input, however novel, in terms of low-level features, it seems unlikely to me that every possible low-level feature of an item—every line, angle, curve, shading, figure–ground contrast, and so forth—exists in LTS waiting to be activated.

Central processing.   The notion of a central processor is fundamental to each of the three systems, but the systems differ in the degree to which any such processor or homunculus is brought out into the open. In my own system an explicit central processor is proposed as a kind of executive consciousness that controls and governs the system; without the involvement of the central processor, nothing happens in the system beyond the formation of input traces. In making the overall operation of human memory dependent on a limited-capacity consciousness or processor, I see myself as supporting the efforts of Mandler (1974, 1975), and of Posner and his co-workers (e.g., Posner & Klein, 1973), to rescue the concept of consciousness from the "oubliettes of behaviorism" (Mandler, 1975).

Although some kind of central processor is implicit in the systems of Craik and Jacoby and Shiffrin, they are much less explicit about its existence or properties. In Craik and Jacoby's system, the central processor has much the same functions as it does in my system, but there seems always to be an implicit executive or operator. Thus, for example, in statements such as "The processor is deployed within the existing cognitive structures" and "Once conscious attention has been removed from an item . . ." there is an implicit agent that does the deploying or removing. In Shiffrin's system, the central processor lurks in the background. He says, for example, "The most important function of STS . . . is that of active control of thinking, problem solving, and general memorial processes." Since STS in Shiffrin's system is a storage system—that is, a set of activated features in LTS—it cannot, by itself, control anything. Thus, the statement is clearly not meant to be taken at face value; rather, an implicit conscious agent is being assumed. Although I think it would be at least partly unfair, I think Mandler (1975) might view the Craik and Jacoby and Shiffrin papers (and possibly my own as well) as evidence for his assertion that "to speak freely of the need for a concept of consciousness still ties the tongues of not a few cognitive psychologists."

There are, I think, some advantages in assuming an explicit central executive. Not only does one avoid excessive use of the passive voice, one also avoids attributing control processes to repositories or buffers and, more important, one tends to think of processes such as attention, rehearsal, and retrieval as having certain common properties because they are governed by the same central processor. Thus, as Mandler (1974) points out, the similar restrictions on immediate memory span and absolute judgment that puzzled George Miller (1956) might both reflect the limitations of a single central processor. What I find unsatisfying at this point about my own characterization of the central processor is that I am so vague about the mechanisms involved. It is one matter to attribute explicit properties to the central processor—that it operates in serial as a processor and in parallel as a monitor, for example—but it is quite another to come up with a detailed mechanism that has those properties.

The nature of STS.   On the surface, it might appear that Craik and Jacoby, Shiffrin, and myself have very different ideas about the nature of STS. Certainly, Shiffrin and myself use the term "STS" in very different ways and Craik and Jacoby avoid the term altogether. In terms of formal properties, however, I see the systems as quite similar. There is a reasonably close correspondence between STS, "working memory," and "items selected for rehearsal" in my system, Craik and Jacoby's system, and Shiffrin's system, respectively. What Shiffrin refers to as STS corresponds more closely in its properties to the input trace in my system than it does to STS in my system.

Despite these definitional differences, each system assumes an STS with much the same properties. In each case, STS is an active store from which items are lost rapidly unless maintained by rehearsal, and the contents of

STS are unlimited in format. Our notions about the capacity of STS are also roughly similar in that the number of items that can be maintained or reported is assumed to be a function of the limitations of a central processor, although I assume that the capacity of STS is determined by the interaction of loss rate and rehearsal rate for the items in STS. It is also the case in all three systems, almost by definition, that items in STS can be retrieved rapidly and reliably.

There are, however, several differences between our characterizations of STS.

1. I make certain strong assumptions about the retention of order information in STS, whereas Craik and Jacoby and Shiffrin do not comment on that problem.

2. Shiffrin assumes that what he calls STS "has at least the structure of LTS, in which it is embedded." I presume that should also be the case for what I call STS, that is, for any subset of his STS that is selected for maintenance or rehearsal. A possible problem with that view is that STS capacity for words seems little affected by variables such as word frequency, concreteness–abstractness, semantic similarity, or even, in the case of bilingual or trilingual individuals, whether the words are presented in one, two, or three languages (for a review of those findings, see Craik, 1971).

3. Craik and Jacoby propose a "resolving power" interpretation of the limits on STS capacity. The idea is that conscious attention can be characterized as a kind of field analogous to a visual field: items in the center of the field are well attended or discriminated, whereas items nearer the pheriphery of the attentional field are not well discriminated. The resolving-power notion seems to me to have considerable potential, but it seems somewhat inconsistent with Craik and Jacoby's later assertion that an item is lost from STS in all-or-none fashion when attention is diverted from that item. They do say, however, that it may be necessary to "soften" that all-or-none assumption.

Forgetting from STS.   In all three systems, items in STS or working memory are lost quickly unless maintained in STS via conscious attention or rehearsal. I assume that the mechanism of loss is similarity-dependent decay. Shiffrin assumes that the loss mechanism is similarity-dependent interference. Those two mechanisms may not be differentiable. Craik and Jacoby attribute forgetting from working memory solely to diversion of attention, without assuming that similarity plays a role. In their system, however, items lost from working memory may be retrievable via backward scanning or reconstruction of recent episodic memory. Short-term forgetting phenomena are assumed, in Craik and Jacoby's system, to reflect several different mechanisms.

The nature of LTS.   Although there are some substantial differences in terminology, I do not think there are important differences among the three systems in the characterization of LTS. In all three systems there is a distinction between context-dependent or episodic memory and context-independent or semantic memory. Storage in or modification of LTS also seems to be viewed in much the same way. There are some differences in the extent to which retrieval mechanisms are specified; I comment on those differences in what follows.

The role of rehearsal.   In all three systems there is a distinction between rehearsal as a rote maintenance process (primary rehearsal) and rehearsal as a constructive coding process (secondary rehearasl). Only the latter is assumed to interassociate items in STS and to transfer or store the items thereby in LTS. The fact that long-term recall is independent of amount of primary rehearsal is consistent with the notion that primary rehearsal maintains items in STS without transferring those items to LTS, but the Woodward *et al.* (1973) and Bjork and Jongeward (1974) finding that long-term recognition does increase as a function of primary rehearsal poses a problem for that notion. As possible explanations of the recognition results, Shiffrin proposes that primary rehearsal does transfer low-level codes to LTS (codes that would not support recall but would support recognition), and I propose that items given primary rehearsal are associated in long-term episodic memory with the general situational context (which facilitates long-term recognition, but has no appreciable effect on long-term recall). Craik and Jacoby do not attempt to explain the recognition findings.

Retrieval.   It is a weakness of my own system that I have so little to say about retrieval from STS and LTS. Both Craik and Jacoby and Shiffrin have much more to offer in the way of explicit proposals about retrieval processes. Craik and Jacoby's dual-process representation of retrieval from episodic memory is particularly innovative and promising. I do agree with Shiffrin, however, that the overlap between the context in which an item was stored and the context in which retrieval of that item is attempted should be a critical factor in the reconstructive process proposed by Craik and Jacoby. I also think that the extent to which the backward-scan mechanism will produce systematic recency effects should be a function of the extent to which items or events as stored constitute a well-ordered temporal series. If items are presented too close together in time, or if the functional input position of an item is smeared over time via interassociation of successive items, the effects of recency should be attenuated (for more on that argument, see Bjork & Whitten, 1974).

Some Residual Common Problems

At this point, I am probably more impressed than I should be with the progress represented by the present papers. To end on a realistic note, I want to list a few important problems that remain relatively untouched in the proposals by Craik and Jacoby, Shiffrin, and myself.

1. The retention of order information. None of us has much to say in the way of providing specific mechanisms by means of which order information is retained or lost. Estes's (1972) model stands more or less by itself in the literature as an attempt to face up to that problem.

2. The representation of context. Each of the chapters in this book cites the importance of context in the overall operation of human memory, but mechanisms are lacking. To say that we know an item was presented in a certain context because it is associated with that context, or is stored together with information about that context, or is tagged in memory with a context label, amounts, without further specification, to stating a tautology.

3. The mechanisms by which items and sets of items are differentiated in memory. The difference in the recall of to-be-remembered and to-be-forgotten items in the Woodward *et al.* results in Fig. 2 is only one of many possible illustrations of the remarkable ability of subjects to differentiate sets of items in memory. Such set differentiation is fundamental to the executive control of rehearsal, to search processes such as those embodied in the Sternberg task and related tasks, and to the interaction and interference among items in memory. Beyond saying that subjects are remarkable, however, we have little to say about the possible mechanisms involved.

ACKNOWLEDGMENTS

The preparation of this report and author's research reported herein were supported by the Advanced Research Projects Agency and the Air Force Office of Scientific Research, respectively under Contract Nos. AF44-620-72-C-0019 and F44620-72-C-0038 with the Human Performance Center, Department of Psychology, University of Michigan. The author is now at the University of California, Los Angeles.

REFERENCES

Atkinson, R. C., & Shiffrin, R. M. Human memory: A proposed system and its control processes. In K. W. Spence & J. T. Spence (Eds.), *The psychology of learning and motivation,* Vol. 2. New York: Academic Press, 1968.

Bjork, E. L., & Estes, W. K. Letter identification in relation to linguistic context and masking conditions. *Memory and Cognition,* 1973, **1**, 217–223.

Bjork, E. L., & Healy, A. F. Short-term order and item retention. *Journal of Verbal Learning & Verbal Behavior,* 1974, **13**, 80–97.

Bjork, R. A. Repetition and rehearsal mechanisms in models of memory. In D. A. Norman (Ed.), *Models of human memory*. New York: Academic Press, 1970.

Bjork, R. A., & Jongeward, R. H. Jr. Rehearsal and mere rehearsal. (Paper submitted for publication, 1974).

Bjork, R. A., & Whitten, W. B. Recency-sensitive retrieval processes in long-term free recall. *Cognitive Psychology*, 1974, **6**, 173–189.

Craik, F. I. M. Primary memory. *British Medical Bulletin*, 1971, **27**, 232–236.

Craik, F. I. M., & Lockhart, R. S. Levels of processing: A framework for memory research. *Journal of Verbal Learning & Verbal Behavior*, 1972, **11**, 671–684.

Craik, F. I. M., & Watkins, M. J. The role of rehearsal in short-term memory. *Journal of Verbal Learning & Verbal Behavior*, 1973, **12**, 599–607.

Elmes, D. G., & Bjork, R. A. The interaction of encoding and rehearsal processes in the recall of repeated and nonrepeated items. *Journal of Verbal Learning & Verbal Behavior*, 1975, **14**, 30–42.

Estes, W. K. An associative basis for coding and organization in memory. In A. W. Melton & E. Martin (Eds.), *Coding processes in human memory*. Washington, D.C.: Winston, 1972.

Gardner, G. T. Evidence for independent parallel channels in tachistoscopic perception. *Cognitive Psychology*, 1973, **4**, 130–155.

Jacoby, L. L. Encoding processes, rehearsal, and recall requirements. *Journal of Verbal Learning & Verbal Behavior*, 1973, **12**, 302–310.

Jacoby, L. L., & Bartz, W. A. Rehearsal and transfer to LTM. *Journal of Verbal Learning & Verbal Behavior*, 1972, **11**, 561–565.

Keele, S. W. Attention demands of memory retrieval. *Journal of Experimental Psychology*, 1972, **93**, 245–248.

La Berge, D., & Samuels, S. J. Toward a theory of automatic information processing in reading. *Cognitive Psychology*, 1974, **6**, 293–323.

Ligon, E. The effects of similarity on very-short-term memory under conditions of maximal information processing demands. Tech. Rept. No. 8, Human Performance Center, University of Michigan, 1968.

Mandler, G. Memory storage and retrieval: Some limits on the reach of attention and consciousness. In P. M. A. Rabbitt & S. Dornic (Eds.), *Attention and performance—V*. New York: Academic Press, 1974.

Mandler, G. Consciousness: Respectable, useful, and probably necessary. In R. L. Solso (Ed.), *Information Processing and Cognition: The Loyola Symposium*. Hillsdale, New Jersey: Lawrence Erlbaum Assoc., 1975.

Massaro, D. W. The dimensions of short-term memory. Paper presented at a symposium on the concept of short-term memory, Meetings of the Midwestern Psychological Association, Chicago, Illinois, May, 1973.

Mazuryk, G. F. Positive recency in final free recall. *Journal of Experimental Psychology*, 1974, **103**, 812–814.

Mazuryk, G. F., & Lockhart, R. S. Negative recency and levels of processing in free recall. *Canadian Journal of Psychology*, 1974, **28**, 114–123.

Meunier, G. F., Ritz, D., & Meunier, J. A. Rehearsal of individual items in short-term memory. *Journal of Experimental Psychology*, 1972, **95**, 465–467.

Miller, G. A. The magic number seven, plus or minus two: Some limits on our capacity for processing information. *Psychological Review*, 1956, **63**, 81–97.

Posner, M. I. Abstraction and the process of recognition. In G. H. Bower & J. T. Spence (Eds.), *The psychology of learning and motivation*. Vol. 3. New York: Academic Press, 1969.

Posner, M. I., & Boies, S. J. Components of attention. *Psychological Review,* 1971, **78,** 391–405.

Posner, M. I., Boies, S. J., Eichelman, W. H., & Taylor, R. L. Retention of visual and name codes of single letters. *Journal of Experimental Psychology Monograph,* 1969, **79**(No. 1, Part 2).

Posner, M. I., & Klein, R. M. On the functions of consciousness. In S. Kornblum (Ed.), *Attention and performance—IV.* New York: Academic Press, 1973.

Posner, M. I., & Warren, R. E. Traces, concepts, and conscious constructions. In A. W. Melton & E. Martin (Eds.), *Coding processes in human memory.* Washington, D.C.: Winston, 1972.

Reicher, G. M. Perceptual recognition as a function of the meaningfulness of the material. *Journal of Experimental Psychology,* 1969, **81,** 275–280.

Reitman, J. S. Mechanisms of forgetting in short-term memory. *Cognitive Psychology,* 1971, **2,** 185–195.

Reitman, J. S. Without surreptitious rehearsal, information in short-term memory decays. *Journal of Verbal Learning & Verbal Behavior,* 1974, **13,** 365–377.

Shiffrin, R. M. Information persistence in short-term memory. *Journal of Experimental Psychology,* 1973, **100,** 39–49.

Shiffrin, R. M., & Gardner, G. T. Visual processing capacity and attentional control. *Journal of Experimental Psychology,* 1972, **93,** 72–82.

Shiffrin, R. M., & Geisler, W. S. Visual recognition in a theory of information processing. In R. Solso (Ed.), *The Loyola Symposium: Contemporary viewpoints in cognitive psychology.* Washington, D.C.: Winston, 1973.

Shulman, H. G. Encoding and retention of semantic and phonemic information in short-term memory. *Journal of Verbal Learning & Verbal Behavior,* 1970, **9,** 499–508.

Simon, H. A. How big is a chunk? *Science,* 1974, **183,** 482–488.

Tulving, E. Episodic and semantic memory. In E. Tulving & W. Donaldson (Eds.), *Organization of memory.* New York: Academic Press, 1972.

Waugh, N. C., & Norman, D. A. Primary memory. *Psychological Review,* 1965, **72,** 89–104.

Wheeler, D. D. Processes in word recognition. *Cognitive Psychology,* 1970, **1,** 59–85.

Woodward, A. E., Jr., Bjork, R. A., & Jongeward, R. H., Jr. Recall and recognition as a function of primary rehearsal. *Journal of Verbal Learning & Verbal Behavior,* 1973, **12,** 608–617.

9

A PROCESS VIEW
OF SHORT-TERM RETENTION

Fergus I. M. Craik
Larry L. Jacoby[1]
Erindale College, University of Toronto

In this chapter we question the notion that the phenomena of recent memory are best attributed to one short-term or primary memory mechanism. Instead, we want to suggest that the various characteristic features of short-term retention may be due to several different features of a general memory system. Other workers have also pointed out difficulties for the notion that all short-term effects in memory arise from a single mechanism or process; for example, Bjork and Whitten (1972) and Tzeng (1973) have demonstrated recency effects that are not wiped out by interpolated activity. More explicitly, Baddeley and Hitch (1974) have suggested that short-term memory effects illustrated by "span" techniques may be rather different from recency effects in free recall. They develop the view that span phenomena reflect the limitations of a central processor (working memory) while the recency effect may be attributable to a retrieval strategy which utilizes recency cues (cf. Tulving, 1968). Lockhart, Craik, and Jacoby (1975) put forward some suggestions on the workings of a general memory system, and it is in this framework that we will consider the phenomena of short-term retention.

As a starting point, take Tulving's (1972) distinction between semantic and episodic memory. Our interpretation of these terms is that semantic memory is that part of the system concerned with storing general knowledge about the world; common features from many past events are

---

[1] On leave from Iowa State University.

combined to provide general laws and rules. These rules, in turn, are used to guide and interpret subsequent patterns of stimulation. Thus, as well as being a storehouse of generalized knowledge, semantic memory is seen as the pattern-recognition system whose function is to interpret incoming stimuli and prescribe the best course of action on the basis of past experience. Episodic memory, on the other hand, is the system in which the records of specific events and episodes are stored. Thus, questions like *What is the capital of France?* address semantic memory whereas *What did you eat for lunch yesterday?* is a question for episodic memory. Although Tulving points up the possible independence of these two systems, we would like to stress their very close *interdependence*—indeed it seems likely that the semantic–episodic distinction actually refers to aspects of one system rather than two distinct systems, but for the moment the heuristic and conceptual advantages of regarding them as separate, outweigh arguments for a unitary system. Since, in this chapter, the perceptual and interpretive aspects of semantic memory are stressed rather than the mnemonic aspects, the more neutral term "cognitive structures" will be used to refer to this part of the system.

If the notion of cognitive structures is extended to involve all levels of perceptual analysis and not just higher-level cognitive activities, then the levels of processing ideas suggested by Craik and Lockhart (1972) can be incorporated into this part of the system. It was argued that incoming stimuli are subjected to a series of analyses, starting with "shallow" sensory analyses and proceeding to "deeper" analyses of a more complex, abstract, and semantic nature. These ideas were modified somewhat by Lockhart, Craik, and Jacoby (1975). The general notion of depth of processing was still retained, but the original idea that processing involves a necessary and inevitable series of stages was largely abandoned. We still believe that some *domains* of processing to use Sutherland's (1972) term, must necessarily precede others (e.g., some sensory processing must precede semantic analysis) but further processing within a domain may be better characterized as a lateral "spread" of encoding rather than as a hierarchically organized series of levels. In any event, when a stimulus enters the system, a series of analyses is performed, and it is proposed that the products of these analyses both form the basis for conscious perception of the stimulus, and also constitute the memory trace of the stimulus in episodic memory.

In this system, the ease of carrying out a particular analysis is determined both by the "depth" of that analysis and by the compatibility of the stimulus with the analyzing structures. Thus, both shallow sensory analyses and deeper analyses that have received much practice, will be carried out easily. Such analyses require little conscious attention to be carried out effectively.

On the other hand, unfamiliar stimuli requiring deep semantic analysis cannot be processed "automatically" and do require conscious attention. Thus, the processes of attention are seen as regulating the analyses performed on the input—processing will be apparently "preattentive" or "automatic" when little processing is required (e.g., detection of a tone) and when the stimulus is more complex but is highly familiar (e.g., the evocation of a word's name and some aspects of its meaning by its printed form). The more complex and unfamiliar the processing, the more attention must be devoted to the processes of analysis.

The products of the analyzing operations carried out on a stimulus form the conscious percept evoked by the stimulus and they also provide one source of short-term memory phenomena. That is, the products of current operations are still in mind, still in conscious awareness—following James (1890), Waugh and Norman (1965) and others, we refer to this phenomenon as "primary memory." In this sense, an encoded item is still "in short-term memory" while we continue to pay attention to some aspects of the item. The notion that short-term memory has affinities with continued attention and awareness has also been suggested by Norman (1969), Atkinson and Shiffrin (1971) and by Anderson (1972). However, we also want to suggest that some phenomena of recent memory still occur after the item has been dropped from primary memory—specifically, that retrieval of recent events is particularly good for two or more reasons. Some speculations about these retrieval mechanisms are presented later. One further point about primary memory is that the type of coding, the nature of the material in mind, will depend on the nature of the features attended to. That is, rather than viewing primary memory as a structure in which items are placed, this type of memory is seen as the activation of some part of the perceptual analyzing system by the processes of conscious attention. These attentive processes are themselves neutral in character, but take on the attributes of the structures in which they are deployed. Finally, it is suggested that the contents of primary memory also form the latest addition to the episodic memory system—we are still aware of the current episode—but as soon as a further perceptual event occurs, the last event is pushed out of mind and "down the line" of episodic memory. This formulation removes the necessity for the notion of transfer to long-term memory; by the present view, perceptual encoding is sufficient to form the episodic memory trace—no further processes are necessary. Perhaps the best evidence that can be cited in support of the view that perceptual encoding is sufficient for trace formation is evidence from incidental learning experiments. Several studies have shown that performance under incidental conditions can be quite as good as performance in an intentional learning situation (Craik, 1973; Hyde & Jenkins, 1969, 1973).

Episodic memory is seen as a temporally ordered series of traces; our view is quite similar to Murdock's (1974) "conveyor-belt" model. Once an item has left primary memory (the proximal end of episodic memory) it must be retrieved and brought back into consciousness before some relevant decision can be made or some action performed. Jacoby (1974) postulated two mechanisms of retrieval from episodic memory. First, recent items can be retrieved by means of a search or scanning process in which the retrieval information is used to discriminate the target item from other items in recent memory. The search process proceeds backward from the present and becomes rapidly less efficient as increasingly more items intervene between presentation and test. Since the retrieval information is not used to provide access to the trace in any sense, but is used merely to select the target items from other items, the nature of the retrieval information (semantic, acoustic, etc.) has little effect on the forgetting rate—that is, the drop in effectiveness with increasing delay or a greater number of intervening items.

With very long delays between the presentation of an event and its attempted retrieval, it is quite implausible that the subject searches through all intervening items. In this second case, Jacoby suggested that the subject uses the retrieval information as a basis for reconstructing, as nearly as possible, the original perceptual encoding of the event. The reconstructive activities involve the cognitive structures, as did the initial encoding, and are guided and constrained both by the structure of semantic memory and by feedback from the episodic trace itself. This sounds rather mystical, but the basic idea is quite simple: when retrieval information is presented (either as a cue for recall, or the item itself for recognition) the system attempts to achieve a perceptual encoding of the type specified by the retrieval information. Formation of this percept is guided by processing rules in the cognitive structures, and also by feelings of partial recognition as the developing percept approximates the structure of the episodic trace. This type of retrieval is thus seen as "guided reconstruction" and in this case the nature of the retrieval information is highly important: deeper, semantic information is usually much more effective in the process of reconstruction, and such information will specify a particular episode more precisely. That is, shallower phonemic or structural features may be shared by many events, whereas deeper semantic patterns are generally more unique and distinctive.

Some evidence for these two retrieval strategies was also provided by Jacoby (1974). He presented each of two groups of subjects with a continuous list of 80 words. For one group, the list contained pairs of rhyming words at spacings of 0, 3, 6, and 12 intervening items, and the subject's task was simply to decide for each word whether a rhyming word had occurred previously in the list. The second group of subjects had a similar task on their 80-word list except they were looking for the presence of pairs of words from the same semantic category. The results of this part of the experiment are shown in the upper part of Fig. 1. The figure shows that in both cases detection of the paired word decreased somewhat as the spacing between words increased, but that there was no difference in the rate of decline between semantic and rhyme judgments. Jacoby suggested that subjects were using the scanning strategy to search for related words and that acoustic information was as effective for selection as semantic information. In an unexpected second phase of the experiment, subjects were given the first member of each pair of words and were asked to recall the second member. The results are also shown in Fig. 1 and it is seen that acoustic information is now much less effective than semantic information as an aid to retrieval. In this case, with a much longer delay between presentation and test, the scanning strategy is ineffective and the reconstructive strategy must be used. Now the richer encoding, and more powerful retrieval processes, associated with semantic information give rise to superior memory performance.

Jacoby points out that apparent discrepancies in past experiments can be resolved if the distinction between scanning and reconstruction is accepted. Although many studies have shown large benefits of semantic retrieval information over acoustic information (e.g., Craik, 1973; Hyde & Jenkins, 1969) other experiments have shown little or no difference

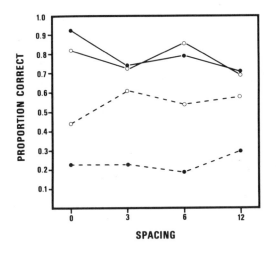

FIG. 1.   Performance on a detection task (top two crves) and on a recall task (bottom two curves) for semantic and rhyme groups: open circles, semantic; closed circles, rhyme. (Data from Jacoby, 1974.)

between the two types of information (e.g., Bregman, 1968; Shulman, 1970). It is suggested that, whereas reconstructive activities dominated retrieval in the former set of studies, subjects tended to use a scanning strategy in the latter set, perhaps because of the generally shorter lags between presentation and test. Other studies that fit a backward search model are the reaction-time experiments by Murdock and Anderson (1973), although in this case, the lags can be quite long. Finally, it should be pointed out that Jacoby's distinction between two retrieval strategies bears many resemblances to Tulving's (1968) distinction between two types of retrieval cues in memory. The difference between the notions lies principally in the fact that Jacoby's retrieval strategies are not equated with any particular types of retrieval information—they are different modes of cue utilization—whereas Tulving's distinction is largely between two kinds of cue, temporal–phonemic on the one hand and semantic on the other.

To summarize, when a stimulus enters the system it is first processed more or less elaborately in the perceptual–cognitive system or "semantic memory." The subject is consciously aware of the products of these processing operations, and the resulting encoding simultaneously forms the latest addition to episodic memory. After further perceptual events have intervened, the original stimulus must be retrieved from episodic memory if it is to reenter consciousness. If the event was recent, it may be retrieved by means of a backward scanning process, otherwise the retrieval information is used to reconstruct the initial encoding.

It is suggested that the phenomena of recent memory may be tentatively attributed to three aspects of this general memory system. The first aspect is primary memory, described here as the products of current perceptual and cognitive operations. Items "in primary memory" are still in conscious awareness and are obviously more easily retrieved than items presented some time ago. It also seems likely that the characteristic of limited capacity is due to this part of the system (the notion of capacity is examined further later). The second source of recency is the backward scanning process. It is postulated that this retrieval strategy becomes rapidly less efficient as intervening events accumulate, thus giving rise to a further type of short-term forgetting. Finally, there may also be recency effects associated with the reconstructive retrieval strategy. Two possibilities are (a) that recently activated patterns of encoding in the cognitive structures can be relatively easily reactivated, provided little time has elapsed or few further events have intervened; and (b) that the reconstructive processes in the cognitive structures obtain more effective feedback and guidance from relatively recent episodes.

In the next section, some classic characteristics of short-term retention are described in terms of the present model. In the final section, some experiments are briefly reported and their compatibility with the present scheme examined.

CLASSIC FEATURES OF SHORT-TERM RETENTION

Four central issues for short-term memory research will be discussed and reinterpreted in the light of the ideas just outlined. These issues are capacity, coding, short-term forgetting, and the notion of transfer from short-term to long-term store.

Capacity

In the present scheme, primary memory reflects the activity of analyzing operations in the perceptual system. This activity may be thought of as one function of a limited-capacity processor that is deployed within the cognitive structures. The limited number of operations activated by the processor are then phenomenologically "in mind." By this view, memory span is simply the number of items for which activation can be maintained. The fact that span is affected by the nature of the material—sentence span is longer than digit span or word span—can be handled either by postulating that with deeper, more meaningful strings of items, the processor deals with superordinate descriptors of feature bundles (Miller's "chunks"); or by postulating that meaningful strings can more easily be maintained by the reconstructive processes in semantic memory, since they conform to learned rules and regulations.

Thus, the phenomenon of limited capacity is a function of the limited-capacity processor operating within the cognitive structures. The number of items held in this way will depend on the depth at which the processor is operating—more items can apparently be held at deeper levels, since the reconstructive processes can utilize learned rules.

A somewhat different way of looking at the phenomenon of limited capacity is that the limit is in terms of discriminability or resolving power rather than in terms of the number of items held. Thus, rather than the metaphor of a limited volume which can hold a fixed number of items, the alternative metaphor is a perceptual one, likening those items in consciousness to items in the visual field. Items in the center of the field are well perceived and discriminated from each other; items in the periphery are perceptually present but are not well discriminated, and items beyond peripheral vision are not present at all. A description of capacity effects in terms of discriminability has also been suggested by Kinsbourne and Wood (1975). The discriminability view has the attraction that Miller's (1956) observations on the similarities between memory span and absolute perceptual judgments may not be coincidental after all.

Coding

Many short-term memory studies have been concerned with the coding issue—that is, with the nature of the short-term trace. Although much initial work pointed to an acoustic code for verbal items held in short-term memory (Baddeley, 1966; Conrad, 1964), later studies have postulated articulatory (Hintzman, 1967), visual (Kroll, Parks, Parkinson, Bieber, & Johnson, 1970), and semantic codes (Shulman, 1970).

In the present scheme, the coding issue is largely bypassed, since the nature of the code is a function of the type of operations currently active. Put another way, primary memory encoding depends on those features of the item which are being attended to or rehearsed. Whereas it seems likely that *any* salient feature may be used to hold the item, it is also reasonable that the name of a verbal item would provide a compact "handle" by which the word can be retained. The position suggested, then, is that while short-term encoding can involve any set of features which are activated or attended to, verbal items may usually be held in terms of their phonemic features.

Forgetting

Short-term forgetting is the function of several different processes. First, once a new perceptual event occurs, the previous event is no longer attended to and is dropped from conscious awareness or primary memory. This element of short-term forgetting has thus an all-or-none flavor—the item is either attended to or not attended to. It seems reasonable, however, to soften the description and suggest that when some new event occurs, some critical features of a few previous events can still be maintained— especially if the subject is trying to retain them, as in a memory test. If the subject's attention was totally diverted to some other event, however, the initial item would presumably be dropped from primary memory.

A second source of short-term forgetting is the drop in efficiency of the episodic scanning process as the event becomes less recent—empirical findings attributed to this source include the effect of spacing in Jacoby's (1974) data shown by the top two curves in Fig. 1; also the results of studies by Shulman (1970) and Bregman (1968). Further data relevant to this aspect of forgetting are presented in the following section. It is also tempting to include under this heading Murdock and Anderson's (1973) result of a linear increase in recognition latency with increasing lag, although this necessitates a backward scanning process which can operate effectively through at least 200 intervening items.

The third source of short-term forgetting is the declining effectiveness of the reconstructive processes as the event becomes remote. The sort of empirical findings which may be speculatively attributed to this source are the reports of relatively long-term recency by Bjork and Whitten (1972) and Tzeng (1973). Both studies found evidence that recent groups of items were better recalled than less recent items, even although an irrelevant task was interpolated between presentation and recall. Such recency effects are apparently relatively stable as opposed to the very fragile recency obtained in immediate free-recall tasks (Glanzer & Cunitz, 1966). Similar long-term recency effects have been found in cases where subjects are unexpectedly asked to recall all the words from a series of preceding lists. It is consistently found that words from recent *lists* are recalled better than words from early lists, although many further presentations and tests have intervened (Murdock, 1972).

In general, then, short-term forgetting is seen as multiply determined and not as the function of one store or process. It may be noted that decay plays little part in these suggested mechanisms—forgetting is generally seen as an active process involving displacement and interference, although the postulated drop in effectiveness of the reconstructive processes might be viewed as a type of autonomous decay.

Transfer to Long-Term Store

The notion of transfer from one store to the next was especially important in the models of Waugh and Norman (1965) and Atkinson and Shiffrin (1968). In the present scheme, the formation of a rich, elaborate, deep encoding in the perceptual–cognitive system is also the formation of a strong memory trace in episodic memory. Since the proximal end of episodic memory is conceptualized as the perceptual present, the trace does not need to be transferred to any other system, it is already in the episodic memory system. Thus, the notion of transfer becomes redundant.

Craik and Lockhart (1972) distinguished between two types of rehearsal: maintenance and elaborative rehearsal. The first involves reactivation of analyses that have already been carried out, whereas the second involves further, deeper processing. Although elaborative processing improves memory performance, it is best viewed as further cognitive activity rather than as transfer of the material to a different memory store.

SOME ILLUSTRATIVE EXPERIMENTS

Empirical evidence from three areas will now be reviewed briefly. The data come largely from recent experiments performed in Toronto and they illustrate the effects of diversion of attention, the effects of rehearsal, and the distinction between the two postulated modes of retrieval: scanning and reconstruction.

The Effects of Diversion of Attention

In a previous paper (Craik, 1973) it was predicted that total diversion of attention from an item should lead to complete short-term forgetting of the item. This prediction was based on the notion that primary memory was equivalent to conscious experience—once attention was removed from the item it had, by definition, left primary memory. However, there is now evidence that diversion of attention does not have such a dramatic all-or-none effect. In fact, both Reitman (1971) and Shiffrin (1973) have argued that diversion of attention by itself causes no short-term forgetting. In their studies, subjects held short lists of letters or words in memory over intervals of 15–40 sec. In one condition, subjects attempted to detect faint tonal signals during the retention interval, and the finding was that this signal-detection task (which presumably required the subject's attention) caused virtually no forgetting of the memory items. There was some forgetting however (about 35%) in a parallel study where subjects detected the syllable "toh" in a mixed series of "dohs" and "tohs" (Reitman, 1971). While Shiffrin (this volume) still stands by his statements that diversion of attention is not by itself sufficient to cause short-term forgetting, a further study by Reitman (1974) has shown that when all subjects who show signs of surreptitious rehearsal were excluded from the data analysis, the remaining subjects showed 34% memory loss in one experiment and 12% loss in the second. When the interpolated task was verbal, as opposed to tonal signal detection, there was a substantial further loss. Shiffrin explains Reitman's latest results in terms of intralist interference; it is not clear, however, why no evidence of such interference was found in Shiffrin's (1973) own experiments in which five verbal items also formed the memory load. An alternative explanation is that diversion of attention from items in consciousness or primary memory, causes some loss, but not total forgetting. The items still have an excellent chance of being retrieved from recent episodic memory. An interpolated task that involves similar events to the memory items will reduce the efficiency of retrieval and give rise to more forgetting.

Two further studies can be cited in support of the position that diversion of attention causes some forgetting, although not so much as when the interpolated task resembles the memory items. Watkins, Watkins, Craik, and Mazuryk (1973) found about 50% forgetting of verbal items when subjects performed very demanding nonverbal tracking or shadowing tasks during the retention interval. Again, however, forgetting was less than that usually found with a verbal interpolated task. Also, Anderson and Craik (1974) reported a free-recall study in which the recency effect for visually presented words, was reduced by a choice reaction-time task performed concurrently with list presentation.

All these findings may be subsumed under a simple description of forgetting from primary memory. Two main factors are implicated: the first is the degree to which the distractor task diverts attention from the memory items and thus prevents even minimal rehearsal; the second is the similarity between the distractor and memory tasks. Similarity may have its effect by reducing the discriminability of memory items from other recent events and thus reducing the effectiveness of the scanning process; similarity may also be detrimental to the reconstructive strategy in that reconstructed features are now shared by many recent episodic events and precise guidance of the reconstruction is less possible. An experiment by Deutsch (1970) nicely illustrates the negative effects of distractor similarity. She found that when tones formed the material to be remembered, a further series of interpolated tones caused more forgetting than an interpolated series of numbers.

The Effects of Rehearsal

In the models proposed by Waugh and Norman (1965) and Atkinson and Shiffrin (1968), rehearsal had a dual role in short-term retention. First, the items were maintained in the short-term store or rehearsal buffer and, second, this rehearsal activity also had the effect of transferring the material to long-term storage where it was laid down in a more permanent form. The results of several later experiments make it clear, however, that the maintenance function of rehearsal can be separated from its trace-strenghtening function. These studies show that further short-term rehearsal or longer residence of an item in short-term store, is not by itself sufficient to improve long-term retention.

In one such study, Jacoby (1973) presented five-word lists which different groups of subjects recalled either immediately, or following a 15-sec period of overt rehearsal. Following presentation and recall of several such lists, the subjects were given a final free-recall test in which they were asked to recall all previous words. Final recall performance was no better for the second group of subjects, despite the fact that they had rehearsed the words more often. Craik and Watkins (1973) reported a similar experiment in which the last four words of a 12-word list were recalled immediately after presentation or were given a 20-sec period of overt rehearsal. Again, it was found that final-recall performance for the last four words was not improved by the extra rehearsal period. Using a somewhat different paradigm, Woodward, Bjork, and Jongeward (1973) also conclude that prolonged residence in the short-term store does not necessarily lead to better long-term retention.

On the basis of these studies, it is concluded that "rehearsal" must be broken down into at least two component processes. To the extent that subjects merely maintain activity at one level of analysis—that is, repeat encoding operations already accomplished—rehearsal will maintain the items in mind but will not lead to improved memory performance. Alternatively, if the subject uses the rehearsal period to perform further, more elaborate analyses then better retention will result. This distinction between the maintenance and elaborative aspects of rehearsal (primary and secondary rehearsal) is also made by Bjork in this volume. However, secondary or elaborative rehearsal is not seen as "transferring" the item to a different storage system—more simply, elaborative rehearsal involves the formation of a richer, more unique encoding of the item. This richer trace facilitates the reconstructive processes and thus enhances long-term retention.

An experiment by Mazuryk (1974) illustrates the differences between primary and secondary rehearsal processes. Subjects were presented with 14-word lists for immediate free recall. The first ten words of each list were silently learned in all cases, but the last four words were studied in one of three ways: by silent learning, by overt rehearsal, or by generating verbal associates to each list word. The immediate free recall phase was followed by a final free recall for all lists. Figure 2 shows that the "associate" condition was somewhat detrimental to immediate recall, for the last four items, while Fig. 3 shows that association yielded *superior* recall of these items in the final test. This study illustrates a positive effect of primary, maintenance rehearsal—it is a more efficient method of holding verbal items for a short time, although subsequent long-term performance is poor. Presumably, in short-term retention, more items can be held in mind if only their shallow phonemic features are processed and attended to.

The Distinction between Scanning and Reconstruction

It was suggested earlier in this chapter that after an item is dropped from conscious awareness, it can still be retrieved efficiently for some short time. Furthermore, it was suggested that very recent events may often be retrieved by means of a backward scanning or search process that uses retrieval information to select the target item. For remote events, this retrieval process is inefficient and a second, reconstructive process is involved in such cases. It was postulated that the nature of the encoded trace (phonemic, semantic, etc.) had little effect on the scanning process, whereas such encoding differences had large effects on reconstruction. The empirical justification for these ideas comes from studies by Bregman (1968), Shulman (1970), and Jacoby's (1974) experiment described earlier.

One further study by the present authors will be reported in support of the distinction between scanning and reconstruction. The experiment was originally conceived as one study in a series exploring the effects of

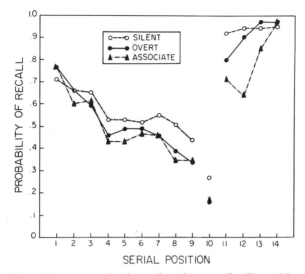

FIG. 2. Serial position curves for immediate free recall. (From Mazuryk, 1974.)

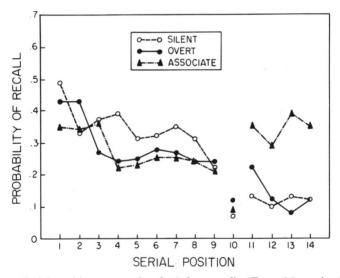

FIG. 3. Serial position curves for final free recall. (From Mazuryk, 1974.)

different encoding operations on subsequent memory performance and was
designed to look at the effects of lag between encoding and recognition.
Encoding was manipulated by asking subjects different types of questions
about subsequently presented target words. "Shallow" encoding was induced by asking *Is the word in capital letters?* A deeper level was induced
by asking *Does the word rhyme with* _____? and a semantic encoding

was encouraged by asking *Is the word a member of the following category?*
A long series of words was presented, each was preceded by an encoding
question to which the subject answered yes or no. Also within the one
long series, interspersed with the encoding questions, were recognition tests
for words presented earlier in the series. Half of the recognition words
were "new" distractor items; the old items were presented at lags of 0,
1, 3, 6, 12, and 24, where "lag" refers ro the number of intervening encoding and recognition trials. On the basis of previous studies in the series
it was expected that the deeper semantic questions would lead to better
recognition, but Fig. 4 shows that no such effect was found—recognition
performance declines with lag, but there is no difference between the encoding questions or whether they necessitated a yes or no response. After
10 subjects had been tested in the experiment, it was decided to see
whether the expected "levels" differences would reemerge in a final free-
recall test, given subsequent to the long encoding and recognition series.
The idea was that final recall performance must depend on reconstruction,
since the events had occurred some time previously, and semantic encoding
should benefit the reconstructive process. Thus, Fig. 4 shows the results
for 20 subjects on the initial recognition test and final recall performance
for the last 10 subjects. In the recall phase, the typical "levels of processing" result reappears (Craik, 1973) even although there is no trace of
such differences in the recognition phase. This extremely interesting result
should be treated with some caution, as attempts to replicate the finding
have yielded inconsistent and noisy data—it is possible that subjects in
the experiment reported here treated the study rather casually or became

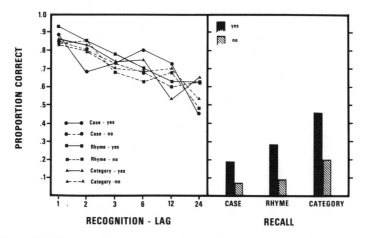

FIG. 4.   Initial recognition (left panel) and final free recall (right panel) in a
"levels-of-processing" task.

bored by the rather tedious procedure. In any event, under these conditions, subjects show no differences between semantic, phonemic, and structural encoding during one phase of the experiment, but such differences do appear in a later phase. The data provide persuasive evidence for the existence of two retrieval processes in recent memory, the first of which (scanning) uses retrieval information to select the target item, whereas the second process uses the retrieval information as the basis for reconstruction of the original event. Deeper level, semantic encodings are beneficial to the second process but not to the first.

CONCLUSIONS

Summary of the Ideas Put Forward

The main point made in the paper is that short-term memory should no longer be thought of as a single mechanism or process, but rather that there are a number of characteristic effects associated with short-term retention and these effects may be due to several different underlying processes. Baddeley and Hitch (1974) have also suggested that more than one process gives rise to short-term memory effects; our views have obvious affinities with their suggestion.

We have tried to document the position that three main processes underlie the phenomena of recent memory: a limited capacity central processor; retrieval by means of a backward serial scan, and a second method of retrieval in which the item's initial encoding is reconstructed. Our view of the central processor resembles the notion described by Broadbent (1958) and developed by Moray (1967) and Posner and Warren (1972)—processing is deployed within the existing cognitive structures, where it emergizes a limited number of perceptual or cognitive operations. Products of the active operations are phenomenologically "in mind" and are immediately translatable into overt responses. The precise representation of an item in the processor depends on the amount of analysis or "depth of encoding" the stimulus has been subjected to. The items or elements activated by the processor may be grouped and manipulated in novel ways—in this sense the items are described as being "in primary memory" and the processor may be viewed as a heuristic problem-solving device. The formation of a percept or "conscious construction" (Posner & Warren, 1972) in the cognitive structures is also seen, by the present view, as forming the latest addition to episodic memory.

Once conscious attention has been removed from an item, it must be retrieved from episodic memory before it can be matched with a further stimulus or given as an overt response. It is suggested that recent items can be retrieved by means of a serial search process which proceeds back into episodic memory and which uses retrieval information to select the desired item. The efficiency of the search process is impaired for remote items and for items embedded in very similar events. In the second method of retrieval, an encoding of the original item is reconstructed in the cognitive structures. Reconstruction is guided by the retrieval information provided by the environment, by habitual routines in the cognitive structures, and by feedback from the episodic trace itself. In this sense the reconstructive processes resemble a servomechanism. Further constructive efforts are guided by the memory trace so that the new encoding "homes in" on an approximate reconstruction of the original event. Recent events are easier to reconstruct than remote events since the operations underlying their representations are still primed in the cognitive structures and feedback from the episodic trace is more precise. To these two suggestions, a third may be added (Shiffrin, this volume); recent episodes will share the same contextual features as those currently energized by the processor, thus reconstruction of recent events is further aided.

Many traditional ways of speaking about short-term memory are at least partly invalidated if the present set of views is accepted. To talk of an item being "*in* short-term store" has relevance only to those items activated by the processor, not to items retrieved from episodic memory. Similarly (as Baddeley and Hitch point out) "capacity" notions are relevant only to operations involving the central processor, and not to the retrieval processes. Finally, neither coding nor forgetting can be attributed to a single structure or mechanism—both are multiply determined. On the other hand, we do not believe that the system is totally flexible and that behavior merely reflects the subject's current strategy. Further explorations must document the limitations imposed by mental structures and assess the freedom of mental operations to work within these limitations.

Comparisons with the Chapters by Bjork and Shiffrin

Although the viewpoint of the present paper is somewhat different to that adopted by either Bjork or Shiffrin, there is a substantial degree of overlap in the basic concepts. First, there is general agreement that perceptual analysis proceeds from shallow sensory analyses to deeper cognitive analyses and that short-term storage essentially involves continuing processing, or activity of operations in the permanent cognitive structures (long-term or "semantic" memory). The energizing of operations is carried out by a limited-capacity central processor which is also involved in the processes of attention, rehearsal, and retrieval (Bjork). In his paper, Shiffrin is less general about activation of long-term structures or processes, but the basic notion seems the same. All three papers agree that the active contents of the short-term store include processes induced by the present environment and also processes contributed by the organism from past learning. There is agreement that short-term storage is an active process.

Although this contribution provided no evidence on the mechanism of attention, we feel reluctant to endorse the rather automatic view of encoding put forward by both Bjork and Shiffrin. Both papers espouse a "late selection" view of attention (Deutsch & Deutsch, 1963; Norman, 1969) in which all inputs are fully analyzed but only a few are then selected for conscious awareness. It is not clear what "fully analyzed" means here. Does it imply that stories, images, and past associations are all evoked and in some sense present in the system when a series of unrelated words is presented at a rate of two words per second? That seems very unlikely. We prefer a view based on Treisman's (1969) model of attention in which shallow sensory analyses are carried out relatively easily and require very little attention; deeper cognitive analyses—especially unfamiliar, novel analyses—progressively require attention for their successful completion. Thus, while simple or well-practiced analyses can be carried out as well when attention is deployed elsewhere, the apparent "automaticity" is only relative. Even here there may be no disagreement between the papers, at an empirical level at least, since Shiffrin allows that the subject has control over the later stages of encoding.

We are in full agreement with Bjork that the qualitative nature of short-term encoding will reflect the type of operations energized (or elements activated) by the central processor. Shiffrin's view does not seem radically different. There is a growing consensus also on the roles of rehearsal. Both Bjork's paper and this chapter explicitly distinguish between the maintenance aspects (primary rehearsal) and the elaborative aspects (secondary rehearsal) of the process. Shiffrin also distinguishes between *rehearsal* of shallow (e.g., phonemic) information and higher-order coding; it seems that he too is willing to attribute two rather different roles to rehearsal. At a more empirical level, we are all agreed that longer residence in short-term store does not necessarily strengthen the item's long-term representation. Shiffrin uses the term "transfer" to describe the formation of a long-term trace, but it is not the short-term items which are transferred; rather the notion of transfer refers to the formation of a new association between items already present in long-term store. By our view, the encoding operations carried out during the item's initial presentation are sufficient to establish the trace.

Bjork's paper deals largely with encoding and storage problems. Shiffrin tackles questions of forgetting and retrieval—it is perhaps here that agreement is least and that most future effort should be expended. Shiffrin's view is that short-term forgetting is a function of interference by similarity; this notion is also a part of our scheme, in that similarity reduces the effectiveness of the scanning retrieval process by reducing discriminability, and also reduces the effectiveness of the reconstructive process since the retrieval information provided by cues does not specify an episodic trace uniquely.

Thus, although there are differences in emphasis and description between the three papers, there is an impressive degree of agreement too.

CONCLUDING COMMENTS

Is the distinction between short- and long-term memory still a useful one? If STM and LTM are conceptualized as two distinct mechanisms we are inclined to answer "no." The answer is "yes" however, if the question is asking whether there is something qualitatively different about items retrieved recently after presentation. Furthermore, since the whole functioning of the perceptual–memory system in some sense revolves around those operations that are currently active—those items in conscious awareness— we believe that a fuller understanding of the phenomena of recent memory may provide the key to a fuller understanding of cognitive functioning more generally.

ACKNOWLEDGMENTS

This research was supported by Grant A8261 from the National Research Council of Canada to F. I. M. Craik.

REFERENCES

Anderson, C. M. B., & Craik, F. I. M. The effect of a concurrent task on recall from primary memory. *Journal of Verbal Learning & Verbal Behavior,* 1974, **13,** 107–112.

Anderson, J. R. FRAN: A simulation model of free recall. In G. H. Bower (Ed.), *The psychology of learning and motivation,* Vol. V. New York: Academic Press, 1972.

Atkinson, R. C., & Shiffrin, R. M. Human memory: A proposed system and its control processes. In K. W. Spence & J. T. Spence (Eds.), *The psychology of learning and motivation,* Vol. II. New York: Academic Press, 1968.

Atkinson, R. C., & Shiffrin, R. M. The control of short-term memory. *Scientific American,* 1971, **225,** 82.

Baddeley, A. D. Short-term memory for word sequences as a function of acoustic, semantic, and formal similarity. *Quarterly Journal of Experimental Psychology,* 1966, **18,** 362–365.

Baddeley, A. D., & Hitch, G. Working memory. In G. M. Bower (Ed.), *The psychology of learning and motivation,* Vol. VIII. New York: Academic Press, 1974. Pp. 47–89.

Bjork, R. A., & Whitten, W. B. Recency-sensitive retrieval processes in long-term free recall. Paper presented at the meetings of the Psychonomic Society, St. Louis, Missouri, 1972.

Bregman, A. S. Forgetting curves with semantic, phonetic, graphic, and contiguity cues. *Journal of Experimental Psychology,* 1968, **78,** 539–546.

Broadbent, D. E. *Perception and communication.* New York: Pergamon Press, 1958.

Conrad, R. Acoustic confusions in immediate memory. *British Journal of Psychology,* 1964, **55,** 75–84.

Craik, F. I. M. A "levels-of-analysis" view of memory. In P. Pliner, L. Krames, & T. M. Alloway (Eds.), *Communication and affect: Language and thought.* New York: Academic Press, 1973.

Craik, F. I. M., & Lockhart, R. S. Levels of processing: A framework for memory research. *Journal of Verbal Learning & Verbal Behavior,* 1972, **11,** 671–684.

Craik, F. I. M., & Watkins, M. J. The role of rehearsal in short-term memory. *Journal of Verbal Learning & Verbal Behavior,* 1973, **12,** 599–607.

Deutsch, D. Tones and numbers: Specificity of interference in immediate memory. *Science,* 1970, **168,** 1604–1605.

Deutsch, J. A., & Deutsch, D. Attention: Some theoretical considerations. *Psychological Review,* 1963, **70,** 80–90.

Glanzer, M., & Cunitz, A. R. Two storage mechanisms in free recall. *Journal of Verbal Learning & Verbal Behavior,* 1966, **5,** 351–360.

Hintzman, D. L. Articulatory coding in short-term memory. *Journal of Verbal Learning & Verbal Behavior,* 1967, **6,** 312–316.

Hyde, T. S., & Jenkins, J. J. Differential effects of incidental tasks on the organization of recall of a list of highly associated words. *Journal of Experimental Pscyhology,* 1969, **82,** 472–491.

Hyde, T. S., & Jenkins, J. J. Recall for words as a function of semantic, graphic, and syntactic orienting tasks. *Journal of Verbal Learning & Verbal Behavior,* 1973, **12,** 471–480.

Jacoby, L. L. Encoding processes, rehearsal, and recall requirements. *Journal of Verbal Learning & Verbal Behavior,* 1973, **12,** 302–310.

Jacoby, L. L. The role of mental contiguity in memory: Registration and retrieval effects. *Journal of Verbal Learning and Verbal Behavior,* 1974, **13,** 483–496.

James, W. *The principles of psychology.* New York, Holt, 1890.

Kinsbourne, M., & Wood, F. Short-term memory processes and the amnesic syndome. In J. A. Deutsch (Ed.), *Short-term memory.* New York: Academic Press, 1975.

Kroll, N. E. A., Parks, T., Parkinson, S. R., Bieber, S. L., & Johnson, A. L. Short-term memory while shadowing: Recall of visually and of aurally presented letters. *Journal of Experimental Psychology,* 1970, **85,** 220–224.

Lockhart, R. S., Craik, F. I. M., & Jacoby, L. L. Depth of processing in recognition and recall: Some aspects of a general memory system. In J. Brown (Ed.), *Recognition and recall,* London: Wiley, 1975.

Mazuryk, G. F. Positive recency in final free recall. *Journal of Experimental Psychology,* 1974, **103,** 812–814.

Miller, G. A. The magical number seven, plus or minus two: Some limits on our capacity for processing information. *Psychological Review,* 1956, **63,** 81–97.

Moray, N. Where is capacity limited? A survey and a model. In A. Sanders (Ed.), *Attention and performance.* Amsterdam: North-Holland Publ., 1967.

Murdock, B. B., Jr. Short-term memory. In G. H. Bower (Ed.), *The psychology of learning and motivation,* Vol. V. New York: Academic Press, 1972. Pp. 67–127.

Murdock, B. B., Jr. *Human memory: Theory and data.* Hillsdale, New Jersey: Lawrence Erlbaum Associates, 1974.

Murdock, B. B., Jr., & Anderson, R. Retrieval of item information: Direct access or search? Paper presented at the Psychonomic Society Meeting, St. Louis, Missouri, 1973.

Norman, D. A. *Memory and attention.* New York: Wiley, 1969.

Posner, M. I., & Warren, R. E. Traces, concepts, and conscious constructions. In A. W. Melton & E. Martin (Eds.), *Coding processes in human memory.* Washington, D.C.: Winston, 1972.

Reitman, J. S. Mechanisms of forgetting in short-term memory. *Cognitive Psychology,* 1971, **2,** 185–195.

Reitman, J. S. Without surreptitious rehearsal, information in short-term memory decays. *Journal of Verbal Learning & Verbal Behavior,* 1974, **13,** 365–377.

Shiffrin, R. M. Information persistence in short-term memory. *Journal of Experimental Psychology,* 1973, **100,** 39–49.

Shulman, H. G. Encoding and retention of semantic and phonemic information in short-term memory. *Journal of Verbal Learning & Verbal Behavior,* 1970, **9,** 499–508.

Sutherland, N. S. Object recognition. In E. C. Carterette & M. P. Friedman (Eds.), *Handbook of perception,* Vol. III. New York: Academic Press, 1972.

Treisman, A. Strategies and models of selective attention. *Psychological Review,* 1969, **76,** 282–299.

Tulving, E. Theoretical issues in free recall. In T. R. Dixon & D. L. Horton (Eds.), *Verbal behavior and general behavior theory.* Englewood Cliffs, New Jersey: Prentice-Hall, 1968.

Tulving, E. Episodic and semantic memory. In E. Tulving & W. Donaldson (Eds.), *Organization of memory.* New York: Academic Press, 1972.

Tzeng, O. J. L. Positive recency effect in a delayed free recall. *Journal of Verbal Learning and Verbal Behavior,* 1973, **12,** 436–439.

Watkins, M. J., Watkins, O. C., Craik, F. I. M., & Mazuryk, G. Effect of nonverbal distraction on short-term storage. *Journal of Experimental Psychology,* 1973, **101,** 296–300.

Waugh, N. C., & Norman, D. A. Primary memory. *Psychological Review,* 1965, **72,** 89–104.

Woodward, A. E., Jr., Bjork, R. A., & Jongeward, R. H., Jr. Recall and recognition as a function of primary rehearsal. *Journal of Verbal Learning & Verbal Behavior,* 1973, **12,** 608–617.

10

SHORT-TERM STORE:
THE BASIS FOR A MEMORY SYSTEM

Richard M. Shiffrin
Indiana University

This contribution aims to present in brief but unified form my current model of short-term memory along with some pertinent data. This model differs in a number of significant ways from that presented in 1968 by Atkinson and Shiffrin and the changes in the model will be justified. Detailed consideration will be given to six of the most basic issues involving short-term store:

1. The role of sensory memory and stages of processing.
2. Selective attention.
3. Retrieval from short-term store.
4. Short-term capacity and forgetting.
5. Transfer from short- to long-term store.
6. Transfer from long- to short-term store (i.e., retrieval) and long-term forgetting.

The general memory system is depicted in Fig. 1. The system consists of just two memory structures, a temporary structure, called short-term store (or STS) and a permanent repository, called long-term store (or LTS). Sensory information enters the system and is encoded in a series of stages. At first, this encoding is automatic, but the subject has control over the encoding at later stages. As various features are encoded from the sensory input they are at once entered into short-term store, where they can serve as a basis for additional encoding. What is meant by encoding? Features are presumed to be present, but normally inactive in long-term store. Encoding consists of contacting one of these features in LTS and activating it. Thus, in Fig. 1, the sensory registers lead directly to LTS. The activation of a feature in LTS is equivalent to the placing of this item in STS. Hence, the picture in Fig. 1 is somewhat misleading, because it shows STS as separate from LTS. It would be a closer analogy to depict LTS as a collection of wires with STS consisting of those wires that happen to be carrying current at any given moment. Figure 2 attempts to depict this view. This figure shows a simulation of STS and LTS at a given time after presentation of a simple visual stimulus—a word. The early stages of processing are concerned with simple physical attributes: contrasts, dots, line segments, angles, open spaces. Later stages involve higher-order codes like the names of letters and the name of the word, both visual and verbal. Still higher stages are concerned with linguistic and semantic correlates of the word and the previous occurrences of the word in particular contexts. Short-term store is depicted by the solid lines in this figure.

We make a general assumption that the earliest stages of processing tend to be lost from STS first. By lost, we mean the reversion of a currently active feature to a stable inactive mode in LTS. That the simpler sorts of sensory information are lost quickly from STS is well documented. In visual processing, note the work of Sperling (1960) on the visual icon, and Posner (1969) on visual and verbal levels of coding; in auditory processing, note the work of Wickelgren (1966), Massaro (1972), Crowder

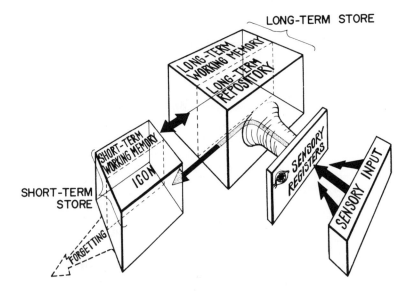

FIG. 1.   A framework for human information processing.

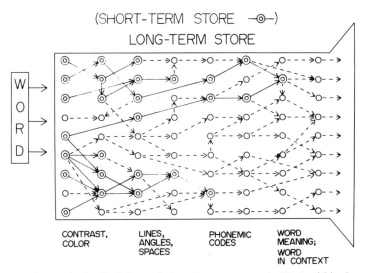

FIG. 2. An analogic depiction of short-term store embedded within long-term store. Hypothetical stages of feature abstraction are indicated shortly following visual presentation of a word.

and Morton (1969), Deutsch (1970), and work in speech perception (Pisoni, 1973); in the tactile area, note the work of Sullivan and Turvey (1972). What is the cause of loss from STS? It is assumed that interference by similar activity causes a loss occurring over time, but this issue will be discussed later in great detail. Now let us return to Fig. 1.

In the system proposed here, selective attention is relegated entirely to the action of control processes in STS following the completion of the automatic stages of sensory processing—that is, there is no gating or filtering or attenuating of sensory information, either between or within modalities. I will discuss the evidence for this assumption later. The basic conclusion is that sensory information is dumped into STS in parallel from all sensory sources, with almost no subject control applying before very high levels of processing are reached. Most of this information dumped into STS will be lost very quickly so that the subject must select certain important components for rehearsal, coding, and decision making. This selective process within STS is assumed to be the locus of selective attention.

The most important function of STS, and certainly the most commonly accepted function, is that of active control of thinking, problem solving, and general memorial processes. Since these control processes have been discussed in detail in previous papers, in this chapter I mention just two:

rehearsal and coding. Rehearsal may be defined as activity primarily designed to maintain traces in STS (and only secondarily to cause transfer to LTS), whereas coding may be defined as activity primarily designed to store information effectively in LTS (and only secondarily to maintain information in STS). The maintenance function of rehearsal is universally accepted, but the active agent in LTS transfer is still in debate. In any event, we assume that all storage occurs in combination with the context in short-term store at the moment of storage. This context is at least as important as that information the subject may have been intending to store.

Retrieval from LTS (to STS) is assumed in this system to be governed both by probe information placed in STS by the subject and transient information, like context, which also happens to be present. This probe information tends (perhaps automatically) to activate associated information in LTS and thereby enter it in STS. It is important to note that LTS retrieval will be governed both by particular retrieval cues and context actively generated by the subject, and also by background context which happens to be present in STS at the moment of retrieval. One important component of long-term forgetting will be governed by this fact. Efficient retrieval will result when the transient context in STS at the moment of test has not changed much from that which was present during storage. However, retrieval may often fail when the retrieval context has changed considerably from that during storage (e.g., when the test is much delayed).

Any characterization of a memory system must carefully define the capacity of STS. In the present system the capacity is defined by the forgetting axiom already mentioned: interference based on similarity. The result is that STS may contain a great deal of information at any given moment, but most of this information will be lost from STS virtually at once (within half a second, say). Relatively little information will manage to remain in STS for significant periods of time, and most of the information that does remain will do so through active control processes like rehearsal imposed by the subject. This stochastic view of STS is most important because it allows for a tremendous capacity for STS at any given moment, and yet, can explain the great difficulty in maintaining simple materials for lengthy periods (i.e., the magic number seven plus or minus two). That is, I am proposing that STS has a large momentary capacity but a small maintenance capacity.

Finally, I assume that STS is highly organized: that it has at least the structure of LTS, in which it is embedded, and that this structure may be utilized for directed retrieval. Thus it may be necessary to scan serially a set of random digits in STS in a Sternberg scanning task, but it must be possible to go directly to the verbal rather than visual or tactile area of STS if it is verbal information that is desired.

THE ROLE OF SENSORY REGISTERS,
OR SENSORY ICONS

Atkinson and Shiffrin (1968), Crowder and Morton (1969), Massaro (1972), Sperling (1960), and many others have argued for, and presented data indicating, the existence of a sensory memory store of high accuracy, fairly large capacity, and very short duration. Atkinson and Shiffrin (1968) argued for a system in which there are sensory icons in each modality. It was pointed out there that the evidence for icons was almost entirely centered in the visual modality. Since that time, evidence for iconic storage has been developed in audiory and tactile modalities. Despite this the sensory icons have now been incorporated into a unitary, generalized STS. Why? There are at least five reasons.

First are the arguments of parsimony—it is difficult enough to deal with a two-stage system without adding a third stage.

Second is the development of forgetting models for STS which can explain the very fast loss of low-level sensory information, even if this information is simply part of STS. The similarity-interference mechanism predicts fast decay because there is always a large flow of simple sensory information into STS at low levels of analysis. Of course, our models of forgetting from STS are still in a formative stage. If data should be found indicating different forgetting mechanisms governing the loss of sensory information on the one hand, and, say, verbal materials on the other hand, then the distinction between sensory icons and a longer lasting STS could be reconsidered.

Third is the finding that attention processes do not operate so as to filter information at low levels of processing. That is, one purpose of the icon was the brief maintenance of large amounts of information from which attentive processes can select portions for transmittal to STS. We have collected evidence that filtering does not occur, however; that all processed information is dumped directly into STS. This eliminates one of the reasons for a separate icon.

Fourth are a series of findings regarding rehearsal in modalities other than the auditory–verbal–linguistic. The icon in the visual system studied by Sperling and others seemed qualitatively different from the short-term auditory system in part because the many auditory–verbal rehearsal effects were not found in visual tachistoscopic situations. The reason for this lies in the visual modality, and not in the structure of an icon. That is, complex visual materials are simply difficult to rehearse, even with slow presentation rates (see Shaffer & Shiffrin, 1972). In addition, there is evidence that simpler visual materials can be rehearsed, though with great difficulty (La-Berge, 1973; Posner, 1969; Sternberg, 1969).

The final, and possibly most important, reason for incorporating the icon into a generalized STS are the discoveries of many levels of processing within each modality. An icon is a plausible construct if it is a unitary store with unitary rules. Recent developments, however, have exposed varied processing levels, each with its own characteristics (such as decay rates, susceptibility to masking, etc.). This is illustrated by the different auditory levels of analysis studied by, say, Crowder and Morton (1969), Duifhuis (1973), and Massaro (1972). Posner (1969), Shiffrin and Geisler (1973), Sperling (1960), Turvey (1973), and others have examined several levels in visual processing. Thus, I propose that there is a continuum of processing levels in STS, the higher levels representing more sophisticated coding, and generally exhibiting slower decay. In the light of present evidence it would seem purely arbitrary to choose one of these levels as a dividing point between two distinct structural features of the memory system.

One final point concerning levels of processing needs consideration. In the present system, STS is defined as a store of information that is at least potentially available to the subject for decision making. That is, information not obviously available to the subject at a given point in time would still be considered part of the contents of STS if the subject could be made to perceive that information following sufficient practice, feedback, or aids, such as post-stimulus cueing. As a corollary of this position, information that is never available to the subject will not be considered as part of STS. Thus, if a backward mask obliterates all information in a preceding stimulus, then any processing stages that had been completed before the backward mask took effect would not be considered part of the contents of STS. Turvey (1973) has presented evidence along these lines suggesting that a good deal of "peripheral" visual processing may occur but an appropriate backward mask may still be effective, owing to interference at a more "central" locus in the system. To the extent that this information from the target stimulus cannot be made available to the subject, in the present model, such information is considered to be outside of, and prior to, the STS system. A different way of saying this would be to point out that the physiological locus of STS may well be central (say, in the cortex) rather than peripheral (in the transmission lines). Information which is abstracted in the periphery (say the retina), but which does not reach the central locus (perhaps due to masking), will not be considered part of STS. In nonmasking situations this distinction is not crucial, since peripherally abstracted information will normally be transmitted in some form to the central locus, and hence be available.

Finally, note that Craik and Lockhart (1972) and Bjork are also concerned with levels of processing, but in a somewhat different sense. They are concerned with different levels of coding operations, which lead to differential retrieval from LTS at test. We will take up coding later.

THE LOCUS OF SELECTIVE ATTENTION

Suppose information is entering the sensory system along n channels simultaneously, where "channels" refers to physical sensory locations (like ears or eyes), or to readily discernible sensory characteristics of the stimuli (like frequency or color). Does the subject have internal control over the amount of information processed in a given channel and entered into STS? In particular, does processing in one channel occur at the expense of processing in others? The techniques that I have been using seem to answer this question negatively (see Shiffrin, 1974). In one paradigm, information is presented on n channels either simultaneously or successively. In the successive condition the subject is told to pay attention to the successive channels in a specified order at specified intervals—masking is controlled by presenting information on all channels during each interval. The subject makes some well-defined decision regarding the information input on the specified channels. When great care is taken to ensure that short-term forgetting will not be a significant factor in either condition, a clear-cut finding occurs. Performance in the simultaneous condition, where attention must be allocated to all channels at once, is identical to performance in the successive condition, in which all the attention may be directed to only one channel at a given time. This finding has been verified in more than a dozen experiments, within the auditory, tactile, and visual modalities taken separately and within all these modalities taken together. (See Gardner, 1973; Shiffrin, Craig, & Cohen, 1973; Shiffrin & Gardner, 1972; Shiffrin, Gardner, & Allmeyer, 1973; Shiffrin & Geisler, 1973; Shiffrin, Pisoni, & Castaneda-Mendez, 1973; Shiffrin & Grantham, 1974.) As a result of these studies, it can be concluded that selective attention does not occur during perceptual processing; that information from all channels is dumped together into STS. Once information has entered STS, selective mechanisms occur. First, short-term retrieval mechanisms scan the contents of STS and select certain of the information present for examination. Then, rehearsal and coding processes are used to prevent the loss of this part of the flood of information arriving, while most of the information is allowed to decay and to become lost. I suggest that selective attention best be viewed as selective accentuation for just this reason.

RETRIEVAL FROM SHORT-TERM STORE

In the previous section I argued that selective attention is a phenomenon of STS; that after sensory input arrives in STS most of it is forgotten quickly, so that a search of STS must be carried out as fast as possible. I argued that attentional failures corresponded to failures in the STS search process. Consider a simple example. The subject views a field of 15 briefly presented letters; he is asked to report the vowel that is present. In a control condition the subject is told in advance to consider only the letters in four indicated spatial locations (one of which contains the vowel). Suppose his performance is higher in the control condition. This may be described as a selective attention effect—the subject's attentional capacity is overloaded by the presence of a large number of letters. But what is the cause of the performance shift? One factor is the limitation of the short-term retrieval process. Suppose that all the letters are encoded equivalently and placed in STS where they begin to decay. If the subject has a spatial cue, he may retrieve and consider the letters in the indicated positions first, before they are lost from STS. Without a spatial cue, he may retrieve and consider letters at random in various spatial locations, stopping when no more letters remain because they have been forgotten from STS. Sometime the forgotten letters will occupy the four positions used in the control condition and hence the experimental condition will show lower performance.

The equating of attentional deficits with limitations on retrieval from STS allows a number of predictions to be made. In cases where short-term retrieval must proceed serially, as indicated by the work of Atkinson, Holmgren, and Juola (1969), Sternberg (1969), etc., then "attentional" deficits should appear whenever short-term maintenance capacity is exceeded and rapid STS forgetting occurs. However, in cases where parallel, independent processing of the elements of STS can occur, as in the work by Egeth, Jonides, and Wall (1972), Gardner (1973), Jonides and Gleitman (1972), then attentional deficits will not be seen.

At this point we are now led to the basic question: What are the types of STS retrieval modes, and when is each used? Consider first the procedure in which a small set of items is maintained by the subject in STS and then a single-item probe is presented to be matched against the memory set. Sternberg (e.g., 1969) has examined this situation when the memory set consists of a homogeneous group of randomly chosen items. He finds that a serial, exhaustive search process adequately describes the results. Many factors, however, can change the scanning process in such a situation. If the memory set is an ordered subset of the total pool, then analogue scanning processes appear to come into play (DeRosa & Morin, 1970). If the memory set consists of two distinct subgroups, then the subject appears to search first within one subgroup, then through the other only if necessary (Naus, Glucksberg, & Ornstein, 1972). If the subject becomes highly practiced at searching for one or more unchanging targets, then a new search process begins to appear (Simpson, 1972). See Shiffrin and Schneider (1974) for details.

Second, we may consider procedures in which a single target is presented first and then a field of visual items presented for test. Data by Atkinson,

Holmgren, and Juola (1969) appear to indicate a serial exhaustive search when the target and field consist of random selections from a homogeneous set of items. However, visual STS search appears to become parallel when the target and field are from different sets (i.e., numbers and letters—see Jonides & Gleitman, 1972).

At the present time development of a general model of STS retrieval, a model which will define the types of scanning possible and which will define the situations in which each occur, is just beginning. Most of the work to date has used reaction times to formulate models, but a breakthrough in this area probably requires a joint consideration of accuracy and latency data from the same experiment. One reasonably successful attempt of this sort is the visual recognition model of Shiffrin and Geisler (1973) which combines a variety of STS retrieval assumptions with a perceptual model to predict both accuracy and latency data.

SHORT-TERM STORE CAPACITY AND FORGETTING

It is usual to contrast interference models of loss with models proposing that time is the cause of loss. Of course no one argues that time is the causative agent, merely that decay will occur in the absence of any apparent, experimentally controlled, variables. A pure time-decay theory assumes that loss will be governed by a process that occurs uniformly in time, unaffected by input of other material. Numerous studies, however, have shown that the amount of (if not the character of) intervening material is much the greater determiner of short-term loss (see Reitman, 1971, and Shiffrin, 1973, for brief reviews). Therefore, "time decay" theory proposes that intervening activity acts indirectly to govern decay. The theory supposes that decay is normally very rapid except when delayed by attentive processes like rehearsal. Intervening material tends to prevent rehearsal of previous items, thereby allowing them to decay. Indeed, I have occasionally argued in this way in previous papers. Since the maintenance effect of rehearsal upon short-term traces is universally accepted, it is no easy matter to distinguish between a "time decay plus rehearsal" model and an interference model.

What then is an interference theory?[1] Such a model assumes that loss is governed by the occurrence of specifiable and experimentally controllable

---

[1] Interference is meant here in the same sense as displacement, though we must note that both forward and backward displacement are possible, in general. Furthermore, in this paper we are concerned only with loss occurring during a retention interval. Additional loss may occur during the process of recall and the act of output. We do not consider such output loss in this paper, though it may be governed by interference mechanisms similar to those described in the text.

variables. A pure interference theory might say that loss occurs instantaneously, at the moments when new inputs are presented. Such a model has at least as many difficulties as the pure time-decay theory. For example, how does it deal with the case of multiple inputs simultaneously presented? Sperling (1960) carried out such an experiment and observed forgetting taking place over time. When we speak of interference theory as a model for short-term forgetting, then, we refer to the following model: short-term forgetting will not occur unless short-term capacity is exceeded; when capacity is exceeded then loss will occur stochastically, over observable periods of time.

There are a number of sources of evidence supporting such an interference model. Consider the studies by Reitman (1971) and Shiffrin (1973) in which a demanding task requiring signal detection of tones in white noise causes no STS forgetting of verbal material for periods of at least 40 sec in length. The design of Shiffrin's experiment is shown in Fig. 3 and the results in Fig. 4. Attempts were made to determine whether rehearsal was being used during the signal-detection period in these studies. Indications in both studies tended to support the hypothesis that the subjects were allotting their major part of their attention to the signal-detection task rather than to the verbal material. In addition Reitman showed that detection of even minimally verbal material rather than tones did cause STS loss. It seems likely that the attention demands of these verbal and tonal detection tasks are equal. Thus, it appears plausible that interference and not time is a cause of short-term loss.

At first glance, some of the data seem at odds with this view. Watkins, Watkins, Craik, and Mazuryk (1973) utilized nominally nonverbal tasks as intervening activity and still found some loss of verbal information. It

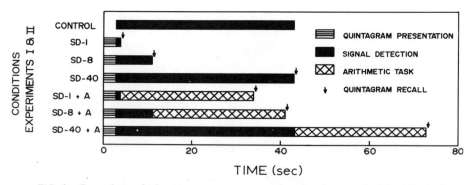

FIG 3. Procedure of short-term memory experiment using varying durations of auditory signal detection as an intervening task. The sequence and timing of events on a single trial are depicted for each condition. The last three conditions utilize an additional intervening arithmetic task prior to test. (After Shiffrin, 1973.)

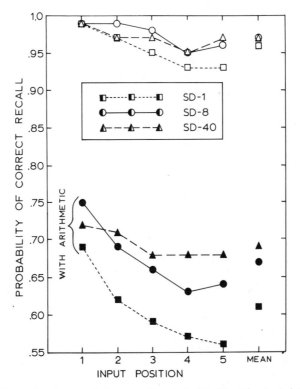

FIG. 4.   Data showing recall for experiment depicted in Fig. 3. A letter is scored as correctly recalled only if it is recalled in the correct serial input position. (After Shiffrin, 1973.)

is possible that the loss occurred because the subjects tended to think verbally about the nonverbal task they were attempting. Signal detection may be a uniquely suitable task for preventing subjects' thinking about the task they are carrying out. Alternatively, loss could have occurred because the load on short-term store already exceeded capacity. In any event, this evidence has led Craik to argue for a dual process in which both interference and also time in the absence of attention cause loss. I suggest that this dual view can be condensed into the interference view with no loss of power. The key is the reasonable hypothesis that in almost all situations there is enough other similar information in STS simultaneously with the information in question to cause loss of that information, even if no additional information is entered. The loss will be caused by mutual interference among the related information simultaneously present. In almost all cases, therefore, cessation of attention will appear to lead to loss, even though interference is the agent.

This hypothesis of mutual interference among items simultaneously present in STS can explain recent results by Reitman (1974). The study was similar to one that Reitman carried out in 1971 but utilized five rather than three words to be remembered. We may suppose that five words exceeds short-term capacity, and hence, mutual interference among these five words may be expected to occur. Over time, then, some forgetting of these words should appear, unless the subject maintains these words by rehearsal processes. This is just the pattern of results found by Reitman. What are the conditions in which items in STS will interfere with each other and cause loss? I suspect that, in the absence of rehearsal, loss will be prevented only when the separate items are coded by the subject into an effective single unit.

To test this hypothesis James R. Cook and I have carried out an experiment, using an auditory signal detection task, in which the subject was instructed not to try to remember or to encode the letters presented. The design is shown in Fig. 5. All conditions utilized 35–40 sec of auditory signal-detection. During this period five letters were presented visually. The subject said each letter aloud as it appeared but otherwise was instructed to "put it out of his mind." These instructions were used to eliminate the

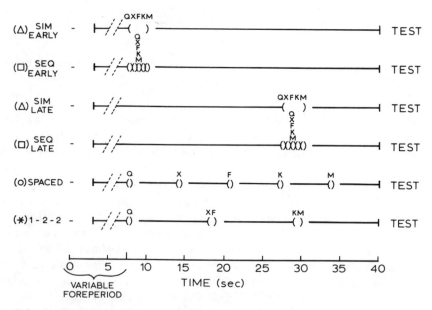

FIG. 5.   Procedure of short-term memory experiment in which letters are presented at various times during a primary task of auditory signal detection. The sequence of events and timing are shown for each of the six conditions. SIM implies simultaneous presentation of all five letters for 2.5 sec. SEQ implies sequential presentation of the letters for .5 sec each.

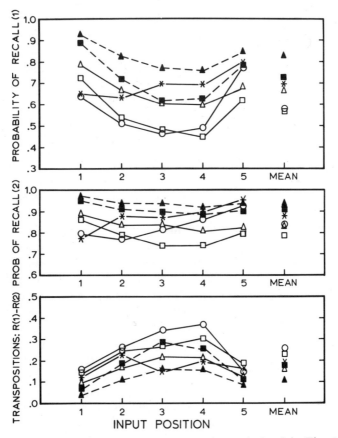

FIG. 6. Data from short-term memory experiment depicted in Fig. 5. Top: A letter is scored as correct only if recalled in correct serial position. Middle: A letter is scored as correct if recalled in any serial position. Bottom: Difference between top two panels; indicates transpositions, or tendency for an item to shift out of correct temporal position. (Symbols are indicated in Fig. 5.)

possibility that subjects would encode the five letters into a single unit. The six conditions varied the manner and timing in which the letters appeared. The simultaneous (SIM) conditions presented the five letters spatially adjacent and simultaneously for 2.5 sec. The sequential (SEQ) conditions presented the letters successively in time, spatially superimposed, for .5 sec each. The "early" and "late" and "spaced" and "1–2–2" conditions should need no explanation beyond that given in Fig. 5. Subjects always gave five letters at test. The results are shown in Fig. 6. The top panel gives serial position curves when a response is scored as correct only if it is output in correct serial position. The second panel gives the data when a response is scored correct if it appears anywhere in the response protocol. The bottom panel gives the difference between the two methods of scoring which may be interpreted as the tendency for items to shift out of correct temporal order.

Space limitations preclude detailed discussion of this experiment here. A few points are particularly relevant to the present discussion, however. First, the change in instructions clearly resulted in considerable forgetting as compared with Fig. 4. Five letters clearly exceed short-term capacity under these instructions. Second, a comparison of the "early" with the "late" conditions shows forgetting of about .15–.20 in recall probability during an extra 20-sec delay before test. Thus the effects of a short-term store overload are certainly far from instantaneous. When capacity is exceeded the subsequent loss occurs over a considerably extended period of time.

In summary, then, we argue for the parsimonious view that interference governed by similarity is the mechanism underlying STS loss, the loss itself taking place over time. Even if this hypothesis is accepted we are still far from a model for short-term capacity and forgetting. In the next few years I expect we will see the development of models of STS capacity and loss of such complexity that the questions of current interest will be superceded and irrelevant. Promising first steps toward such a model seem to have been taken by Estes (1972). He proposes a stochastic perturbation model in which items in an organized reverbatory hierarchy first tend to move out of correct temporal position and then become lost. Indeed, some of the data from the experiment depicted in Fig. 5 and 6 appear to support the Estes model. For example, the "spaced" condition, in which items will not be encoded into a strong temporal circuit, shows the greatest tendency for items to move out of correct temporal position (the bottom panel). Furthermore, the 1–2–2 condition shows an interesting pattern of errors. The two separated groups of two letters tend to transpose with each other, but correct temporal order tends to be maintained within each group of two letters. Whether or not a model similar to that of Estes develops, remains to be seen. In any event we can expect shortly the development of models of high sophistication and complexity.

TRANSFER FROM SHORT-TERM STORE
TO LONG-TERM STORE

What do we mean by transfer from STS to LTS? We mean by this the formation in permanent memory of information not previously present there. In particular, this will consist of the association (in a new relationship) of information structures already in LTS. A minimal requirement for this new associative structure will be the simultaneous presence in STS of the separate elements to be associated or related. Other necessary requirements will be discussed in what follows. Thus, transfer to LTS does not imply the removal of the transferred information from STS, nor the placing of new "subunits" in LTS that do not already exist in either LTS or STS. Rather, transfer means the formation of new associations in LTS between information structures not previously associated there, usually in conjunction with current context in STS.

It appears to be generally accepted that the type and level of coding operation given to a set of information will be a crucial determiner of the later retrievability of that information (e.g., see chapters by Craik and Jacoby and Bjork in this volume). However, independent of the level of coding operation taking place, what is the mechanism which actually causes the transfer to LTS? If PGS-3 is coded as *three little pigs, three little pigs* may be rehearsed in STS. But how is this code transferred to permanent storage? Atkinson and Shiffrin (1968) suggested that the amount transferred may be a function of something like the integration of STS trace strength over the time spent in STS. In many cases, this function might be closely related to the number of rehearsals given the code in question.

The strongest evidence against this "automatic storage" view was found in studies on signal detection as an interfering task (Shiffrin, 1973). No loss of a five letter quintagram was found, regardless of whether 1, 8, or 40 sec of signal detection was utilized as an intervening task. In some conditions the signal detection was followed with arithmetic to eliminate STS recall. The surprising result is shown in the lower panel of Fig. 4. Whether an item had remained in STS for 1, 8, or 40 sec during signal detection did not appreciably affect storage in LTS, as measured by recall (especially for the 8- and 40-sec conditions). This leaves little question that time of residence of a trace in STS has little to do with transfer to LTS. Transfer to LTS did occur, however, when subjects were forced in other conditions to rehearse overtly the verbal material during the signal-detection period.

The finding that rehearsal engenders storage suggests that rehearsal of a code is the active agent in transfer. However, Craik and Bjork have carried out experiments indicating that rehearsal alone does not necessarily lead to enhanced retrieval, at least when measured by recall tasks (see Craik & Watkins, 1973; and the first two chapters of this volume). The resolution of these apparently discrepant findings may lie in the nature of the code being rehearsed. In my experiment the subjects were told to rehearse the actual "high-level" codes which they had learned to use to facilitate LTS retrieval. In Craik's and Bjork's situations the subjects may have rehearsed a "low-level" phonemic code which was of little use for later retrieval. It is possible that the phonemic code was stored well in memory, and that a different sort of memory test would have shown this to be the case. Indeed, Bjork has found such facilitation when he utilizes a final-recognition test, supporting the view that rehearsal is the active agent in transfer of codes to LTS.

To summarize these considerations, we can conclude that transfer to LTS is highly unrelated to the time of residence of a trace in STS. The type of coding operation given to an item is an important determiner of later retrievability but the mechanism governing the storage of the code is still unspecified. Some evidence suggests that rehearsal-like operations, whether maintenance rehearsal or coding rehearsal, are involved in completing the transfer from STS to LTS.

Before leaving the subject of transfer from STS to LTS, we might take note of the constraints upon long-term organization imposed by the short-term system. Since the long-term structure must first appear in STS, the capacity of STS will place restrictions on the resultant structure. Mandler (1967) for example has argued strongly for grouping in LTS based upon a tree structure with a maximum of five items or concepts per node. If the formation of a node depends upon the simultaneous and extended representation of the contents of that node in STS, then the maintenance capacity of STS provides a natural rationale for the proposed limitations on long-term structures.

RETRIEVAL FROM LONG-TERM STORE AND LONG-TERM FORGETTING

At first, it seems out of place to discuss LTS retrieval and forgetting in a chapter on short-term store. Indeed, this discussion will be kept quite short. However, important links to short-term functioning exist. First, the LTS retrieval probe must be placed by the subject in STS, and an important part of this probe may be the current general context present in STS. Second, the information found in LTS is transferred to STS and then mixes with the probe information already present. Both of these assumptions may have important implications for long-term forgetting, and I will review these implications briefly.

First, consider the list-length effect in free recall, which is illustrated by typical data in Fig. 7. The longer a presented list, the less well any word in that list is recalled (prior to the recency part of the curve which is due to STS retrieval). What is the cause of this effect? It is a retrieval rather than a storage effect, and it is not due to any simple form of retroactive interference (see Shiffrin, 1970b). Shiffrin (1970a) presented a model in which retrieval cues based on immediate context were placed in STS in order to access words from the most recent list seen. I proposed there that the list-length effect occurred because the subject stopped his search

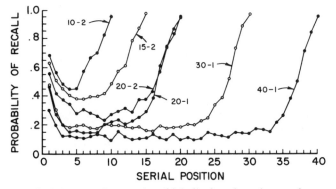

FIG. 7. Typical free-recall data in which list-length and seconds per word are varied. (After Murdock, 1962.)

of LTS before retrieval was complete. However, no truly satisfactory explanation was developed in that paper for the subject's decision to stop searching LTS. Thus I proposed (Shiffrin, 1970c) that the subject stopped his LTS search on account of a difficulty arising during the course of retrieval. The argument runs as follows: The tendency for any item in LTS to be retrieved will be governed by the strength of the association between that item and the probe information in STS. When any item happens to be retrieved, it is placed in STS in the context of the probe information. The resultant complex of information will, in turn, be stored in LTS. Hence, the associative strength bonding the retrieved item to the probe information will increase. Then at the next retrieval attempt, there will be an increased tendency to recall the item already recalled. After a number of retrieval attempts have occurred, there will be such a strong tendency to retrieve items already recalled that the subject will cease attempting to retrieve further items from LTS. Indeed, further retrieval at that point will be largely useless unless the subject can effectively change the probe information in STS. Evidence supporting this view was obtained by Roediger (1973), Rundus (1973), Slamecka (1968, 1969), and Smith (1971). In the Slamecka experiments, it was found that giving at test some of the items from a free-recall list, supposedly as retrieval aids, actually inhibits recall of the remaining items.

The second point I wish to consider is the role of general context in STS as a factor in long-term forgetting. Suppose that context in STS tends to be stored with items at the time of study. Suppose that this context gradually changes over time and that the subject incorporates the current context in STS as part of his retrieval probe at the moment of test. Then the subject's ability to retrieve will depend on the similarity of the context at test to that at the time of study. To the extent that the context has changed, retrieval will fail and forgeting will be seen. An excellent example of this phenomenon is also seen in free recall. The list-length effect in free recall is seen when an immediate test is given, because the retrieval probe consists of context cues similar to those involved during storage. These cues enable the subject to separate the most recent list from previous lists in the session. In a number of studies, however, we have given end-of-session tests for all words from the entire session. During this end-of-session test, the context is very different from that which obtained during the storage of the earlier lists. Hence the subject will be using retrieval cues that will not discriminate the various lists from each other. Thus, we would not expect the list-length effect to appear. Figure 8 shows some relevant data. It gives the first five points from serial position curves for long and short lists, when tested within session or at end of session. It can be seen that the list-length effect is no longer obtained at session end.

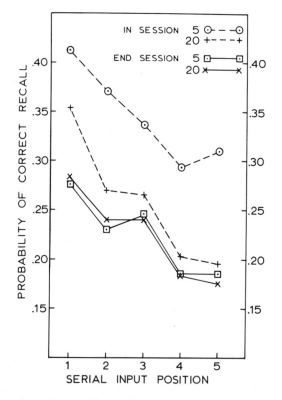

FIG. 8. Data from free-recall experiment varying list length (5 or 20 words), and utilizing arithmetic following list presentation and preceding free recall. Probability of correct recall is shown for the first five serial positions of the 5- and 20-word lists. An additional free-recall test for all words from all 24 lists was given at end of session; these results are also shown.

Note that my view of context as a cue providing temporary access to LTS can be identified with the concept of "episodic" memory discussed by Tulving (1972) and by Craik and Jacoby in this volume. In Fig. 1 long-term store is divided by a dotted line into long-term working memory and a permanent repository. This division is indicated to reflect the difference between information stored in such a way that retrieval will depend upon temporarily available context, and information stored in such ways that retrieval will occur even when appropriate local context cues are not available. Of course, we imply no hard and fast division here—some "temporary" context cues could well last for years. We wish to emphasize, moreover, that much long-term forgetting, even of "semantically" stored information, may occur as a result of contextual changes in the retrieval probe.

One consequence of this "contextual" view is that it can handle and predict the data presented in the Craik and Jacoby chapter. For example, coding by phonemic or semantic methods might make little difference if retrieval was primarily dependent upon temporal–contextual cues. On the other hand, a delayed test might force the subjects to switch to a semantic retrieval mode and a recall difference will appear. Indeed, this explanation is similar to that presented by Craik and Jacoby. My working memory and their episodic memory are quite similar, save that I do not impose any conditions of strict temporal ordering, and I prefer to incorporate the working memory within LTS. Finally, note that the contextual model can predict the results of Bjork and Whitten (1974) in which an immediate long-term test shows primacy and recency effects that a more delayed test does not show.

SUMMARY

In this presentation I have developed the concept of STS as the control center for active cognitive functioning. Sensory icons are placed within STS as active available sets of information. Short-term store is considered to be the beneficiary of the results of a series of processing stages, each activating features or information which then serve as the bases for further processing. Attention is shown to be a result of the rehearsal, coding, retrieval, and forgetting properties of STS, rather than a property of the perceptual stages of encoding. A variety of retrieval mechanisms are ascribed to STS and selective attention is described as a concomitant of these: Failures of attention are equated with failures to retrieve information before forgetting occurs. Short-term capacity and forgetting are modeled as the result of a stochastic process: A great deal of information can be maintained for short periods of time, or a much smaller set of information for longer periods of time. Loss from STS is ascribed to interference by similar information as a root cause, but the loss itself was shown to occur stochastically, over time. Storage in LTS, or transfer from STS to LTS, is shown to be relatively independent of the time of residence of a trace within STS. It is argued that rehearsal and coding operations are the active agents in the transfer process: Heavy weight is given to the level of the information being rehearsed or coded. Finally, the role of STS in long-term memory and forgetting is discussed. Contextual information in STS is given great importance as a retrieval cue, and it is shown how context could provide a basis for "episodic" memory. Data are presented indicating how long-term forgetting might be associated with changes in the availability of contextual cues.

COMPARISON WITH THE CHAPTERS BY BJORK AND CRAIK AND JACOBY

In this section, I will compare the models within the six major topic areas presented above. The comparisons will naturally emphasize points of disagreement, but in no way is this meant to downplay the overall consensus of agreement of these models.

Sensory Memory and Stages of Processing

My view seems to coincide most closely with that of Craik and Jacoby. Bjork specifically defines STS to exclude sensory input that is not handled by the central processor. Thus the great majority of sensory input will never reach STS (by definition). Nevertheless, Bjork's forgetting axiom for sensory information is similar both to mine, and to his own forgetting axioms for STS. My view is to treat all activated input that is potentially available as part of the contents of STS. Craik and Jacoby seem to agree with this "activation" view but further propose that all these contents are "phenomologically in 'mind,' " which carries an attentional import. I prefer not to identify "consciousness" with all the contents of STS, only with a subset of that information. However, these differences appear ones of definition rather than substance. There do not appear to be any important differential predictions derivable from these views.

Selective Attention

All three contributions seem to agree about the automaticity of peripheral encoding, and the placement of selective attention within the bounds of short-term store. Craik attempts to establish a separate position, but states Treisman's (1969) views in a manner with which both I (and I suspect Bjork) would have trouble taking issue. Beyond this, the only remaining difference appears to be my greater specification of the souce of selective attention in short-term retrieval, capacity and forgetting processes.

Retrieval from Short-Term Store

Bjork does not discuss this issue in any detail. Craik and Jacoby also seem to bypass discussion of the mechanisms of retrieval within their central processor. They do propose a backward serial scan through the contents of episodic memory, which I would consder a matter of retrieval from *long-term store* using contextual cues. For a variety of reasons, I doubt that "episodic" memory is accessed by an item-to-item serial backward scan. Perhaps such an assumption could explain greater difficulty for finding older items, or for items embedded in similar context, but a simple direct retrieval model based on contextual retrieval cues would make the same predictions without requiring scanning of all intervening events. I also suspect such a backward serial scheme would have difficulties with prediction of response latencies, and refer the reader to Shiffrin (1968, 1970a) for a fuller discussion of this point.

Short-Term Capacity and Forgetting

Bjork defines capacity in terms of an interaction between rehearsal rate and autonomous loss rate. I agree that the interaction of forgetting with rehearsal is crucial. The question remains: How is capacity determined in the absence of rehearsal, say, in the face of sensory information overloads? Of course, Bjork limits his STS to the *output* of the central processor, which might eliminate the need to consider sensory information and its decay. In any event he defines capacity in terms of forgetting (as I do), and differs only in the proposed cause of that forgetting. Craik and Jacoby also consider rehearsal, or attention, crucial to the capacity of the central processor. In addition, they seem to adopt forgetting axioms more in line with those proposed in this paper. However, the capacity defined by both Bjork and Craik and Jacoby is what I have called "maintenance capacity": the amount of information which can be maintained (indefinitely) in STS, if desired. This capacity estimate will be relatively small. I prefer a more general stochastic model of STS capacity, defined in terms of the forgetting axioms. One can then talk about "momentary capacity" which may be very large for short periods of time (as in visual-display experiments).

There are some differences in our treatments of short-term forgetting. Bjork emphasizes decay governed by similarity; Craik and Jacoby in their discussion of forgetting from the central processor emphasize the role of diversion of attention. I agree that forgetting will not be seen unless attention is diverted from an item, but maintain that forgetting following attention diversion will be based upon interference mechanisms. In practice, these three positions are not as divergent as they seem, since I hold that a capacity overload will cause forgetting to occur over time while attention is diverted. At the moment, I do not see how Bjork's similarity–decay model differs from my similarity–interference model. Nor does Craik and Jacoby's view appear very different. One possible differential prediction is based on the effect of load when attention is diverted. Interference models would expect greater rates of loss under greater load, whereas simple decay models (not dependent upon similarity) would not. I hope to test this prediction soon.

Transfer from Short-Term Store to Long-Term Store

Craik and Jacoby attack the very idea of "transfer." In one sense, this attack may be misleading. Clearly something is learned—an association between information not previously associated or related in that way. The learning of this association is what is meant by transfer to LTS. However, Craik and Jacoby raise the question of transfer in a more meaningful fashion. Is the "transfer" to LTS equivalent to the placement of an item in STS in the first place? Is no additional step necessary? There is at least one piece of evidence arguing strongly against this view. LaBerge (1973) carried out a study showing perceptual, long-term learning (of a visual form) over a series of days. However, early in training, before long-term learning had taken place, a form could appear to be learned, if the subject was shown it prior to a particular trial and was thereby able to maintain it in short-term store. The reader is referred to the LaBerge article for details.

A second question at issue concerns the mechanism governing long-term storage. Although we all agree that increased time of residence in STS does not necessarily lead to increased storage, we differ somewhat on the role of maintenance rehearsal and coding rehearsal. I argue that rehearsal is an active agent in transfer, but maintenance rehearsal transfers low-level codes, whereas coding rehearsal transfers higher level codes. Craik and Jacoby, on the other hand, ascribe no storage effect to maintenance rehearsal, and Bjork takes an intermediate position. The crucial evidence here seems to be Bjork's finding that increased maintenance rehearsal does lead to increased storage if testing is carried out with recognition rather than recall tests.

Retrieval from Long-Term Store and Long-Term Forgetting

All of us seem to agree on a division of information in LTS into two major groupings: semantic knowledge and contextual or episodic knowledge. Also, we all agree on the contextual basis of the episodic information, although Craik and Jacoby make some strong assumptions about the temporal order of storing episodic information, and also about the temporal order of retrieval of this information. I am unwilling to make such strong assumptions at the present time. Furthermore, they describe two retrieval modes: episodic *scanning* and semantic *reconstruction*. I would rather describe the differences in retrieving from these stores in terms of the type of information utilized in probing memory. This probe information is assumed to be primarily contextual when retrieving episodic information and primarily semantic or conceptual otherwise.

General Comparisons

Bjork makes a strong assumption that a serially acting (but not serially perceiving), very limited, homunculus operates his system. Bjork argues that the serial limitation occurs at output rather than input, but some results on subjects' abilities to do several tasks and produce several outputs at once seem to call this assumption into question (see Shaffer, 1973, 1974, and Peterson, 1969). Finally, Bjork has yet to specify what "one function" means for central processing. On the other hand, what alternative approaches are there to Bjork's serial homunculus? Neither Craik and Jacoby nor I have made any detailed alternative proposals.

Craik and Jacoby several times reject the concept of "STM" and "LTM" as two distinct mechanisms, but I think this reflects a certain confusion between effects and hypothetical stores and processes. Certainly, there is no simple rule distributing observed effects to short- and long-term stores. But the complexity of the system has never been in doubt. I would argue, as does Bjork, that the hypothetical stores of "STS" and "LTS" still provide a very plausible and quite effective approach to memory phenomena.

Finally, I should like to point out what should be obvious by now: The three systems described so far in this volume are remarkably similar. This similarity is all the more surprising, since each system is quite complex and detailed. Of course there are now, and always will be, differences in these systems. Yet the similarities testify to the beginnings of a certain maturity in the recently revived study of short-term memory.

ACKNOWLEDGMENTS

The work in this presentation was supported by PHS Grant 12717-07.

REFERENCES

Atkinson, R. C., Holmgren, J. E., & Juola, J. F. Processing time influenced by the number of elements in a visual display. *Perception & Psychophysics*, 1969, **6,** 321–326.

Atkinson, R. C., & Shiffrin, R. M. Human memory: A proposed system and its control processes. In K. W. Spence & J. T. Spence (Eds.), *Advances in the psychology of learning and motivation research and theory*. Vol. II. New York: Academic Press, 1968.

Bjork, R. A., & Whitten, W. B. Recency-sensitive retrieval processes in long-term free recall. *Cognitive Psychology*, 1974, **6**, 173–189.

Craik, F. I. M., & Lockhart, R. S. Levels of processing: A framework for memory research. *Journal of Verbal Learning & Verbal Behavior*, 1972, **11**, 671–684.

Craik, F. I. M., & Watkins, M. J. The role of rehearsal in short-term memory. *Journal of Verbal Learning & Verbal Behavior*, 1973, **12**, 599–607.

Crowder, R. G., & Morton, J. Precategorical acoustic storage (PAS). *Perception & Psychophysics*, 1969, **5**, 365–373.

DeRosa, D. V., & Morin, R. E. Recognition reaction time for digits in consecutive and nonconsecutive memorized sets. *Journal of Experimental Psychology*, 1970, **83**, 472–479.

Deutsch, D. Tones and numbers: Specificity of interference in immediate memory. *Science*, 1970, **168**, 1604–1605.

Duifhuis, H. Consequences of peripheral frequency selectivity for nonsimultaneous masking. *Journal of the Acoustical Society of America*, 1973, **54**, 1471–1488.

Egeth, H., Jonides, J., & Wall, S. Parallel processing of multielement displays. *Cognitive Psychology*, 1972, **3**, 674–698.

Estes, W. K. An associative basis for coding and organization in memory. In A. W. Melton & E. Martin (Eds.), *Coding processes in human memory*. Washington, D.C.: Winston, 1972.

Gardner, G. T. Evidence for independent parallel channels in tachistoscopic perception. *Cognitive Psychology*, 1973, **4**, 130–155.

Jonides, J., & Gleitman, H. A conceptual category effect in visual search: 0 as letter or as digit. *Perception & Psychophysics*, 1972, **12**, 457–460.

LaBerge, D. Identification of two components of the time to switch attention: A test of a serial and a parallel model of attention. In S. Kornblum (Ed.), *Attention and Performance—IV*. New York: Academic Press, 1973.

Mandler, G. Organization and memory. In K. W. Spence & J. T. Spence (Eds.), *The psychology of learning and motivation: Advances in research and theory*. New York: Academic Press, 1967.

Massaro, D. W. Perperceptual images, processing time, and perceptual units in auditory perception. *Psychological Review*, 1972, **79**, 124–145.

Murdock, B. B., Jr. The serial position effect of free recall. *Journal of Experimental Psychology*, 1962, **64**, 482–488.

Naus, M. J., Glucksberg, S., & Ornstein, P. A. Taxonomic word categories and memory search. *Cognitive Psychology*, 1972, **3**, 643–654.

Peterson, L. R. Concurrent verbal activity. *Psychological Review*, 1969, **76**, 376–386.

Pisoni, D. B. Auditory and phonetic memory codes in the discrimination of consonants and vowels. *Perception & Psychophysics*, 1973, **13**, 253–260.

Posner, M. I. Abstraction and the process of recognition. In G. H. Bower & J. T. Spence (Eds.), *The psychology of learning and motivation*. New York: Academic Press, 1969.

Reitman, J. S. Mechanisms of forgetting in short-term memory. *Cognitive Psychology*, 1971, **2**, 185–195.

Reitman, J. S. Without surreptitious rehearsal, information in short-term memory decays. *Journal of Verbal Learning & Verbal Behavior*, 1974, **13**, 365–377.

Roediger, H. L. Inhibition in recall from cueing with recall targets. *Journal of Verbal Learning & Verbal Behavior,* 1973, **12,** 100–113.

Rundus, D. Negative effects of using list items as recall cues. *Journal of Verbal Learning & Verbal Behavior,* 1973, **12,** 43–50.

Shaffer, L. H. Latency mechanisms in transcription. In S. Kornblum (Ed.), *Attention and performance—IV.* New York: Academic Press, 1973.

Shaffer, L. H. Multiple attention in continuous verbal tasks. In P. M. A. Rabbitt & S. Dornic (Eds.), *Attention and performance—V.* New York: Academic Press, 1974.

Shaffer, W. O. & Shiffrin, R. M. Rehearsal and storage of visual information. *Journal of Experimental Psychology,* 1972, **92,** 292–296.

Shiffrin, R. M. Search and retrieval processes in long-term memory. Tech. Rept. 137, Institute for Mathematical Studies in the Social Sciences, Stanford University, 1968. Doctoral dissertation.

Shiffrin, R. M. Memory search. In D. A. Norman (Ed.), *Models of human memory.* New York: Academic Press, 1970, 374–447. (a)

Shiffrin, R. M. Forgetting: Trace erosion or retrieval failure? *Science,* 1970, **168,** 1601–1603. (b)

Shiffrin, R. M. Models for retrieval in free recall. Paper presented at the Mathematical Psychology meetings, Miami, Florda, 1970. (c)

Shiffrin, R. M. Information persistence in short-term memory. *Journal of Experimental Psychology,* 1973, **100,** 39–49.

Shiffrin, R. M. The locus and role of attention in memory systems. In P. M. A. Rabbitt & S. Dornic (Eds.), *Attention and performance—V.* New York: Academic Press, 1974.

Shiffrin, R. M., Craig, J. C., & Cohen, U. On the degree of attention and capacity limitations in tactile processing. *Perception & Psychophysics,* 1973, **13,** 328–336.

Shiffrin, R. M., & Gardner, G. T. Visual processing capacity and attentional control. *Journal of Experimental Psychology,* 1972, **93,** 72–82.

Shiffrin, R. M., Gardner, G. T., & Allmeyer, D. H. On the degree of attention and capacity limitation in visual processing. *Perception & Psychophysics,* 1973, **14,** 231–236.

Shiffrin, R. M. & Geisler, W. S. Visual recognition in a theory of information processing. In R. Solso (Ed.), *The Loyola Symposium: Contemporary viewpoints in cognitive psychology.* Washington, D.C.: Winston, 1973.

Shiffrin, R. M., & Grantham, D. W. Can attention be allocated to sensory modalities? *Perception & Psychophysics,* 1974, **15,** 460–474.

Shiffrin, R. M., Pisoni, D. B., & Castaneda-Mendez, K. Is attention shared between the ears? *Cognitive Psychology,* 1974, **6,** 190–215.

Shiffrin, R. M., & Schneider, W. An expectancy model for memory scanning. *Memory & Cognition* 1974, **2,** 616–628.

Simpson, P. J. High-speed memory scanning: Stability and generality. *Journal of Experimental Psychology,* 1972, **96,** 239–246.

Slamecka, N. J. An examination of trace storage in free recall. *Journal of Experimental Psychology,* 1968, **76,** 504–513.

Slamecka, N. J. Testing for associative storage in multitrial free recall. *Journal of Experimental Psychology,* 1969, **81,** 557–560.

Smith, A. D. Output interference and organized recall from long-term memory. *Journal of Verbal Learning & Verbal Behavior,* 1971, **10,** 400–408.

Sperling, G. The information available in brief visual presentations. *Psychological Monographs,* 1960, **74.**

Sternberg, S. Memory scanning: Mental processes revealed by reaction time experiments. *American Scientist,* 1969, **47,** 421–457.

Sullivan, E. V., & Turvey, M. T. Short-term retention of tactile stimulation. *Quarterly Journal of Experimental Psychology,* 1972, **24,** 253–261.

Treisman, A. Strategies and models of selective attention. *Psychological Review,* 1969, **76,** 282–299.

Tulving, E. Episodic and semantic memory. In E. Tulving & W. Donaldson (Eds.), *Organization of memory.* New York: Academic Press, 1972.

Turvey, M. T. On peripheral and central processes in vision: Inferences from an information processing analysis of masking with patterned stimuli. *Psychological Review,* 1973, **80,** 1–52.

Watkins, M. J., Watkins, O. C., Craik, F. I. M., & Mazuryk, G. Effect of nonverbal distraction on short-term storage. *Journal of Experimental Psychology,* 1973, **101,** 296–300.

Wickelgren, W. A. Phonemic similarity and interference in short-term memory for single letters. *Journal of Experimental Psychology,* 1966, **71,** 396–404.

PART IV
COGNITIVE STRUCTURES

Frank Restle

One attractive feature of recent cognitive psychology is that it deals with familiar psychological processes and asks questions that one could explain to his mother-in-law. This is indeed a refreshing change from the esoterica of learning theory. The research in these three chapters is about how a person understands a paragraph and how he answers questions about it. The reader may find it a useful exercise to introspect while reading, and see the characteristics of his own process of comprehension and the nature of his own resulting cognitive structure.

This work builds upon the whole framework of modern cognitive psychology, and especially psycholinguistics and computer-based models of cognitive processing. However, a crucial step in arriving at the present stage was to break away from the mold of formalism, which thinks in terms of the literal form of the language, and move out into the informal but inevitable problem of "meaning." Bransford and Franks and their colleagues broke away by showing that their subjects often would falsely recognize a statement that had not literally been given, if that statement could readily be inferred from what was given. Memory was not for words, not even for propositions, and the content of a sentence is assimilated to existing cognitive structures.

In his chapter, Scott Paris shows that young children are no more literal than their parents, and often wrongly recognize inferences as if they had been given. Children, like adults, go for the meaning and discard the words. They even recognize sentences as familiar when they had received the information in pictorial form—a clear and extreme case of discarding the means of communication. Paris then extends the point by asking children for various kinds of inferences, such as semantic entailments, presuppositions, etc., and finds that they do very well with such questions. The process of inference is part of memory, and comprehension itself is an active, constructive process. A special significance of these studies, using young children, is that they demonstrate that the "constructive" processes demonstrated by Bransford and Franks are not special accomplishments of sophisticated college students, but do, in fact, tap the wellsprings of linguistic accomplishment.

In conclusion, Paris clearly states that the constructive process of comprehension both elaborates the incoming information by assimilating it to the reader's whole body of knowledge, but also compresses it by eliminating redundancies.

If comprehension changes the information given into a cognitive structure, we may ask the nature of the cognitive structure. Potts, in his chapter, shows that a paragraph of comparisons like *The fish is smarter than the frog,* which will give rise to an ordering, is recoded into a list or rank ordering. The top item in the list is especially well known to be above all others, and the bottom item is special for some subjects. In general, subjects are fast at picking the better of two items if they fall far apart on the scale. Potts also reports some new experiments on true assimilation, pouring new wine into old bottles, and shows how judgments result from a restructured blend of old semantic knowledge and new, arbitrary information. At the end of Potts' chapter, the reader should feel acquainted with the inner workings of at least one cognitive structure, the linear ordering.

The third chapter by Restle brings Potts' methods to bear on several different cognitive structures. The old idea of cognitive balance is analyzed, and the possibility is raised that it is mainly the basis for classifying a set into categories. "Balance" is definitely shown to be a property of the whole set, not just of triads.

A new topic is the narrative, in which studies show that memory is organized more by threads of narrative than as a perfect temporal sequence. This study of the dual narrative throws some light on how two linear orderings of events in time can be coordinated. Finally, in a study using an organizational tree, Restle and Swaine show how cognitive structuring may be affected by the questions anticipated.

The progression of the studies is from demonstration that cognitive structures exist, to delineating one such structure in detail, to extending the result to other more complex structures.

A key concept throughout the three chapters is that of inference. An inference is knowledge that cannot be obtained by mere literal recall. The fact that subjects answer on the basis of inference more readily than on the basis of literal memory, in some cases, is the foundation of the Bransford–Franks findings and their extension by Paris. Paris says that in order to infer, a person must both remember the facts and then compute from them. Potts argues that since inferences may be made faster than the component facts can be regurgitated, inference cannot be a two-stage process. From a formalist position, be it psycholinguistic or logical in source, inference must be two stage; but if subjects build and use nonpropositional cognitive structures, then inferences are not functionally different from literal retrievals. The investigation of cognitive structures is, therefore, closely related to the study of inferring and to logical thinking generally.

11
INTEGRATION AND INFERENCE IN CHILDREN'S COMPREHENSION AND MEMORY

Scott G. Paris
Purdue University

The concern of the present studies, as well as much of contemporary cognitive psychology, is the characterization of knowledge and the psychological acts of knowing. The renewed interest in these formidable problems has been prompted by many factors, including characterizations of language competence (Chomsky, 1957, 1965; Katz & Fodor, 1963), new findings about the structure of human memory (Anderson & Bower, 1973; Collins & Quillian, 1972; Rumelhart, Lindsay, & Norman, 1972), and studies of computer simulation of natural language relationships (Carroll & Freedle, 1972; Schank, 1972; Winograd, 1972). Oftentimes, the issue has been the characterization of competence, the knowledge possessed by people of their language and their world. Yet, competence cannot be unrelated to performance, and it was recognized that what is known must be specified in accordance with the psychological process of knowing. Clear examples of this are the current emphases on contextual theories of meaning (Bransford & McCarrell, 1975; Olsen, 1970; Perfetti, 1972), the necessity of incorporating psychological indices of reference into structural characterizations of language (McCawley, 1968), and the concern for intentional, social, and communicative aspects of speech acts (Austin, 1970; Schlesinger, 1971; Searle, 1969).

The contributing role of the organism as an intermediate agent is stressed in these approaches that emphasize the constructive aspects of cognitive processes (Bransford & Franks, 1972; Cofer, 1973; Garner, 1966). The acts of perceiving and remembering are not static states of accumulation

223

and retrieval of experience, but rather are activities determined by the cognitive operations applied to that experience by a subject. The conceptual nature of perception has been advocated by Weimer (1973) in his emphasis on "the conceptual primary of the abstract" and has been noted by Hebb, Titchener, Gibson, and Kant among others. Bruner (1973) said:

> . . . all perception is generic, in the sense that whatever is perceived is placed in and achieves its meaning from a class of percepts with which it is grouped. To be sure, in each thing we encounter there is an aspect of uniqueness, but the uniqueness inheres in deviation from the class to which an object is assigned [p. 8].

The categorical and generative aspects of perception have been demonstrated in research on concept identification (Bruner, 1973), speech perception (Liberman, 1970; Pisoni, 1973), and comprehension of anomalous pictures and sentences (Bransford & McCarrell, 1975). The central tenet of this approach is that psychological meaning of events is not immanent within the external stimuli but instead is created by the individual in the context of that experience.

Memory is also influenced by the cognitive strategies and organization of the subject. It is not a reified entity isolated from cognition, but rather, is a world-view of the person that reflects the individual's metamemorial plans, specific mnemonic strategies, determinants of attention, and conceptual knowledge structure. Piaget and Inhelder (1973) emphasized that the acts of remembering and what is remembered are functions of the child's operative intelligence. The constructive nature of memory and its dependence upon the individual's representational knowledge of the world was also stressed by Smirnov and Zinchenko (1969) who said, "Memory, being a reflective process by nature, from the very beginning of its development functions to orient the individual in the context of its existence and to regulate his activity on the basis of previous experience [p. 453]." Thus, we can regard perceiving and remembering as unified cognitive activities which are imputed on the environment by the subject in moment-to-moment acts of understanding.

BEYOND THE INFORMATION GIVEN

The heading to this section is borrowed from Bartlett (1932) and Bruner (1973) and it succinctly states the primary act of comprehension. The constructive nature of comprehension requires that the subject go beyond the explicit information in order to perceive, understand, and remember the achieved significance of the constructed meaning. Craik and Lockhart (1972) have argued that there are many levels of representation and there are various degrees to which one can go beyond the given information. "Deeper" or more complete processing of information leads to enhanced memory. Although we do not yet know in detail the various levels of processing nor their differences in required strategies or knowledge structures, we do know that a variety of experimental manipulations, such as tacit structuring of the stimuli or explicit instructions, can facilitate memory. When a subject unitizes, chunks, clusters, elaborates, provides continuation, or images the information, enhanced memory usually results. Why? The common mechanism of these various manipulations is that subjects must provide additional information and cues to the available stimuli. The application of processing effort is crucial and we may label the act "analysis by synthesis" (Neisser, 1967), "effort after meaning" (Bartlett, 1932), "assimilation" (Piaget), or the "click of comprehension" (Brown, 1958). The product of the activity, the qualitative nature of the self-generated embellishments, is also important for memory because it is an idiosyncratic construction that reflects the individual's cognitive structuring of environmental relationships and permits assimilation of the new information to his schemata. A developmental, epistemological analysis must describe the strategies applied by the child in the effort toward understanding as well as the nature and quality of the mediational activity (Brown, 1975; Flavell, 1970).

SEMANTIC INTEGRATION

The popularity of the constructivist position is partly due to the results derived from research on how adults remember sentences. In a variety of studies it has been shown that adults do not remember individual sentences or words, but rather, they abstract semantic relationships from the context described and integrate these relationships in memory (Barclay, 1973; Bransford & Franks, 1971; Bransford, Barclay, & Franks, 1972; Cofer, 1973; Fillenbaum, 1966; Johnson, Bransford, & Solomon, 1973; Kintsch & Monk, 1972; Potts, 1972; Sachs, 1967). The subject's goal of comprehension and memory is the apprehension of the ideas expressed by the sentences and the particular linguistic utterance is only the vehicle used to help the subject construct meaning. This is congruent with Piaget's notions of the primacy of thought over language and reflects the view of Soviet researchers that material related to the goal of cognitive activity is remembered better than material that functions as a means of expression (Smirnov & Zinchenko, 1969). Language maps onto the cognitive schemata of the subject according to the individual's strategies of comprehension and structural knowledge. These strategies can be deliberate, induced, or spontaneous but the act of comprehending usually involves making inferences from the explicit information which in turn are incorporated into

semantically integrated memory representations.[1] It is precisely these processes of inference and integration that we chose to investigate in children's
comprehension and memory.

PROBLEM

Our first study was motivated by the question, *How do children remember sentences?* Presumably, what subjects remember reflects, to a large degree, how they understand the material (Jenkins, 1971). The semantic
integration research with adults indicates that adults (*a*) spontaneously
produce inferred relations within and between sentence constituents and
(*b*) integrate the explicit and implicit information into holistic memory
representations. There has been little research with children's sentence
memory of a corresponding nature, and we were interested in investigating
children's spontaneous strategies of comprehension. Do children go beyond
the given information when trying to understand and remember sentences?
Do children spontaneously construct implied inferential relations, like
adults, or do they attend to and rehearse lexical and syntactic constituents?

SEMANTIC INTEGRATION IN CHILDREN'S MEMORY

We chose to investigate children's semantic integration in a recognition
memory paradigm. The task consisted of the oral presentation of several
brief paragraphs to children who were instructed to remember the sentences they were hearing and repeating. The three sentences of each paragraph were contextually related, the first two were premise statements and
the third sentence was a filler. An example is:

(*1*) *The bird is in the cage.*   (Premise)
(*2*) *The cage is under the table.*   (Premise)
(*3*) *The bird is yellow.*   (Filler)

The premise sentences permitted the subject to infer an intersentence relationship, e.g., *The bird is under the table.*

This true inferential relationship was the critical item in the recognition
memory test because different hypotheses about sentence memory posit
different predictions. Any conception of memory that relies on rote repetition of the sentences or syntactic interpretation of sentences would predict
that subjects should readily recognize a true–inference sentence as a new

---

[1] Except for the assertion that derived meaning is not equivalent to a storehouse
of separate images or word strings, the issue of the form of this mental representation will be avoided in this chapter in favor of a concentration on the generative
operations of comprehension.

item. However, if subjects abstract and construct the semantic relationships among events in the sentences and integrate them in memory, then true inferences, which are consistent with the situational description, should be incorrectly recognized as old items.

In our first study (Paris & Carter, 1973), we presented seven stories similar to the example given previously, to second- and fifth-grade children. After a brief interpolated task, subjects were presented four different sentences pertaining to each story in a recognition memory test and instructed to indicate which sentences were exactly like the acquisition sentences. Two sentences were semantically true, an old true premise and a new true inference; two other sentences, which were both new items, were semantically false, one a premise and one an inference (i.e., the nouns were the same as true premises and inferences but the prepositions were false relations). For example, the recognition sentences for the previous story were:

(4) *The bird is in the cage.*   (True Premise)
(5) *The cage is over the table.*   (False Premise)
(6) *The bird is under the table.*   (True Inference)
(7) *The bird is on top of the table.*   (False Inference)

The results of this study are shown in Fig. 1. Children in both grades consistently recognized true inferences as old items. Indeed, the probability of responding "old" to true premises and true inferences did not differ significantly, which suggests that children integrated the semantic relationships among sentences and stored these general, abstracted descriptions rather than specific words or sentences.

Of course, a high rate of false alarms on true inferences (i.e., responding "old" to these new items) could mean that subjects were confused or had generally poor memory for the sentences. This does not appear to be the case, though, for several reasons. First, the children readily rejected false inferences, although the true and false inference recognition items shared the same syntactic structure and many of the same words—the only difference was in the relational term such as a locative preposition (e.g., on—under). Second, the children who responded to true inferences as "old" were those who remembered the premise information. The conditional probability of responding "old" to a true inference, given that the true premise of the same story had been recognized correctly, was .78, indicating a strong relationship between the information conveyed by sentence constituents and the contextually derived meaning of the total message. Although the implied information derived by the subject is contingent upon the meaning of the premise information, the actual memory representation may be relatively unconstrained by specific lexical and syntactic factors. A third bit of evidence that true inference errors are the result of semantic

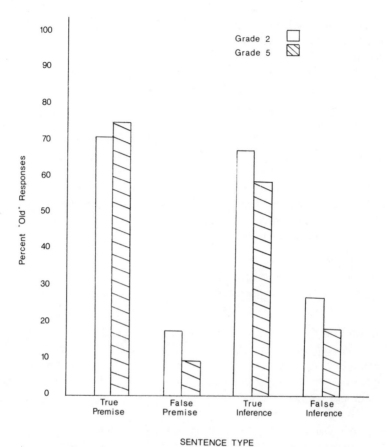

SENTENCE TYPE

FIG. 1.   Percentage of "old" responses on recognition test sentences.

strategies of comprehension is derived from subjects' certainty scores. Children were asked to evaluate their recognition responses on a three-point certainty scale and subjects consistently responded "old" to true inferences with a great deal of confidence. Of all the correctly identified sentences, true-inference items were recognized as "new" with the *lowest* certainty, whereas among the incorrectly recognized items they were identified as "old" (e.g., errors) with the *highest* degree of confidence.

The principal finding of this study is that children, like adults (Bransford, Barclay, & Franks, 1972), could not discriminate old from new sentences which shared consistent meaning. This conclusion should not be overgeneralized, but when the sentences are not grossly different in length, vocabulary, or construction, when they are not overlearned, and when the sentences are contextually or thematically related, children appear to be unable to discriminate old and new sentences that are congruent with their semantically integrated memory representations. This result is inconsistent with the assertion that comprehension and memory of sentences can be described by word associations or interpretation of syntactic features. Although lexical and syntactic factors influence understanding, an adequate account of how children remember sentences must attempt to characterize the generation of the semantic context that the sentences describe.

Semantic integration was originally offered as an alternative view of language processing (Barclay, 1973, Bransford, Barclay, & Franks, 1972; Bransford & Franks, 1971; Potts, 1972), yet it need not be limited to verbal processing. Most studies concerned with memory for pictorial stimuli have employed lists of unrelated pictures and found that children and adults are quite proficient at recognizing large numbers of pictures. We were interested in the way children would remember a series of related pictures. If integration and inference of explicit and implicit relationships reflect strategies of comprehension, one would expect semantic integration with pictorial stimuli as well.

Paris and Mahoney (1974) investigated semantic integration of sentences and pictures in a similar recognition memory paradigm. We generated stories, each composed of two premises and a filler item, which could be portrayed either in discrete sentence or picture triads. All relationships were spatial orientations; right–left, above–below, in front of–behind, and higher–lower. The four test stories, with initial and terminal filler stories, were presented to three groups of second- and fourth-grade children. One group was exposed to sentences in both the acquisition and recognition memory phases (verbal–verbal), one group was exposed to pictures in both phases (picture–picture), and one group saw pictures in acquisition but was tested with sentences during the recognition test (picture–verbal). (There was no verbal–picture group because the filler sentences were superficially true about the recognition pictures.)

The recognition test for each group included several other items in addition to the four described previously. The verbal–verbal and picture–verbal groups received eight recognition sentences per story; the four original recognition items described already and four propositionally similar items which were semantic transformations of the original four sentences. For example, if an original item was *A is to the right of B,* the new propositionally similar item was *B is to the left of A.* These items were included in order to determine children's ability to abstract propositional meaning from semantically transformed sentences, a process previously demonstrated by adults (Bransford *et al.,* 1972; Kintsch & Monk, 1972).

The children's responses to the original four types of recognition items are shown in Table 1. Again, it can be seen that children responded to

TABLE 1
Percentage of "Old" Responses on Original Recognition Items

	Groups					
	Verbal acquisition Verbal recognition		Picture acquisition Verbal recognition		Picture acquisition Picture recognition	
			Grade			
Recognition item	2	4	2	4	2	4
Premise						
True	72.9	66.7	85.4	79.2	83.3	87.5
False	45.8	35.4	41.7	37.5	37.5	33.3
Inference						
True	72.9	62.5	62.5	75.0	89.6	66.7
False	50.0	29.2	37.5	29.2	45.8	27.1

true-inference recognition items as similar to acquisition sentences and pictures. Subjects responded consistently that true premises and true inferences were old items, whereas they discriminated false items as new. Semantic integration occurred for sentences as before but also for picture–picture and picture–verbal groups, indicating that integration and inference occurred in memory regardless of the stimulus and test mode of the material. Again, the conditional probabilities and certainty judgments concerning true inference responses indicated that children made the false positive responses with confidence and knowledge of the premise information.

On the propositionally similar recognition items, subjects in the verbal–verbal and picture–verbal groups performed near chance levels. They did not recognize semantically transformed true premises and true inferences as identical with original items, in general, although fourth-graders, particularly in the picture–verbal condition, responded to true premises and true inferences as old items 83 and 65% of the time, respectively. Unlike adults, children were apparently constrained by the words and syntax in the verbal–verbal condition and did not equate old and new items solely on the basis of meaning.

The finding that children do not remember individual pictures but rather the abstracted relationships among related pictures suggests that semantic integration is not limited to a verbal processing strategy. Although covert labeling may have occurred, visual or imaginal cues also play a role in achieving integrated comprehension. The role of visual cues in this task is similar to a verbal processing strategy. It is not a passive storage of individual elements, but rather a dynamic process of constructing relationships among elements and deriving a contextual representation (Reese, 1970). Indeed, in a study that demonstrated semantic integration by mildly retarded children (mental ages ranged from 5 to 8), we found that imagery instructions enhanced integration and the false alarms to true-inference items (Paris, Mahoney, & Buckhalt, 1974). We have also observed that imagery instructions facilitate semantic integration in nonretarded children as well, and it appears that imaginal cues do not achieve independent representation in memory, but instead, serve as additional cues to promote the construction of a contextual memory representation.

These tasks yield strong support for the postulation of an active strategy of children's comprehension which includes expanding explicit information through inferential operations and integrating these constructed relationships. Constructive elaboration may be viewed as enhancing access to the information, whereas integration may be viewed as a process to achieve efficiency and parsimony of storage. Although the operations of encoding and storage may be viewed as conceptually discrete, they are often temporally and structurally interdependent.

The task used in these studies has several limitations and shortcomings. The boundary conditions for semantic integration have not been delineated, but, in general,

1. The stimulus material must share contextual or thematic relatedness.
2. The presentation must preclude the rote memorization of the stimuli, by time of exposure or difficulty of the material.
3. The recognition test items must not be grossly different from the acquisition items in terms of vocabulary or syntactic style.

The recognition memory task employed in these studies may be insensitive to developmental changes in semantic integration because all errors, including the false alarms, should decrease with age. Yet, the index of integration is the false-alarm rate to true inferences and integration may reasonably be expected to improve with age. In the studies previously described, older children committed fewer errors on most items of the recognition test than younger subjects. This does not necessarily imply that older children integrated less; the finding could be due to increased memory capacity, higher incidence of deliberate mnemonic strategies, better understanding of the task requirements, and familiarity with similar tasks in school. For these reasons, we decided to assess children's understanding of sentences with other tasks, albeit still memory measures.

CHILDREN'S COMPREHENSION OF PROSE

We were concerned with going beyond the demonstration of such inferential behavior by children to inquire about the differences among types of inferences and the developmental progression of these abilities. Much of the research has involved only transitive inferences and we know that the ability to make such inferences when required increases from ages 5 to 18 with parallel improvements in remembering the premise information (Bryant & Trabasso, 1971) and integrating the premise information (Glick & Wapner, 1968). There are, however, many kinds of inferences that one can draw from sentences, and some of these may be more crucial to understanding than others. For example, we might ask if children understand the logical presuppositions and consequences of sentences. Intuitively, these inferences reflect a great deal of elaborative work by the subject in order to make the sentences contextually plausible. If this is true, one might expect that initial comprehension of such inferences would enhance the individual's memory for the meaning of the sentences.

In addition to our concern for comprehension of other linguistic inferences and their subsequent effects on memory, we were interested in developmental differences in comprehension. Our previously discussed studies did not reveal age-related improvement in semantic integration as measured by the recognition memory paradigm. Barclay and Reid (1974) observed that children integrated actors into truncated passive sentences in a free-recall task, yet there were no age-related differences in the integrative ability. We decided that the simplest way to determine if children of different ages apprehend different information from prose was to ask them directly.

We devised six paragraphs, ranging from seven to nine sentences in length, which contained various types of semantic information, read them aloud to children, and interrogated them for their understanding of words and relationships in the passages (Paris & Upton, 1974). We were concerned specifically with children's comprehension of different kinds of inferences and chose four linguistic inferences to study. The first two we labeled contextual inferences because they required the amalgamation of information from several sentences. These were: *presuppositions,* the pre-existing conditions necessary to make a sentence or paragraph true; and *inferred consequences,* the probable conclusion of a series of statements or conditions. The other two inferences were termed lexical inferences because the inferential relationship was dependent upon a single word. These included *semantic entailment;* an object is a subset of a larger class; and *implied instruments;* a verb implies a particular instrument to accomplish the action.

Six paragraphs were read to individual subjects, 12 children each from kindergarten through grade 5. Immediately after listening to a paragraph, subjects were asked eight yes–no questions concerning the story. Four of these questions interrogated the inferential relationships described above. We also asked four questions regarding verbatim information in order to provide a base line comparison for inferences as well as to prevent subjects from biasing their processing of subsequent paragraphs. The verbatim items included *prenominal adjectives,* such as big, new, and red and *locative prepositions,* such as in, over, and under. The eight questions were balanced for verbatim and inferential items as well as truth–falsity within each item category. The orders of paragraphs and questions were randomized for every subject. The following passage is an example of a story and the questions asked of subjects:

> Linda was playing with her new doll in front of her big red house. Suddenly she heard a strange sound coming from under the porch. It was the flapping of wings. Linda wanted to help so much, but she did not know what to do. She ran inside the house and grabbed a shoe box from the closet. Then Linda looked inside her desk until she found eight sheets of yellow paper. She cut up the paper into little pieces and put them in the bottom of the box. Linda gently picked up the helpless creature and took it with her. Her teacher knew what to do.

Question type	Answer	
Adjective	Yes	1. Was Linda's doll new?
Adjective	No	2. Did Linda grab a match box?
		3. Was the strange sound coming from
Preposition	Yes	under the porch?
Preposition	No	4. Was Linda playing behind her house?
Presupposition	Yes	5. Did Linda like to take care of animals?
		6. Did Linda take what she found to the
Consequence	No	police station?
Entailment	No	7. Did Linda find a frog?
Instrument	Yes	8. Did Linda use a pair of scissors?

The mean percentages of correct responses for verbatim and inferential questions for each grade level are shown in Fig. 2. Performance improved monotonically across grades, showing the sensitivity of this task to differences between children's comprehension and memory in successive grades. Inferential questions were answered correctly more often than verbatim

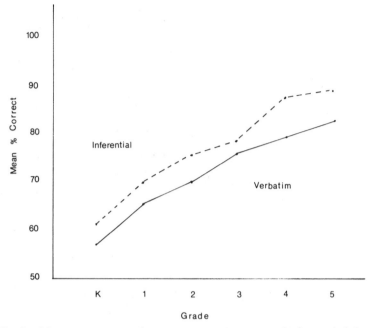

FIG. 2. Mean percentage of correct responses on verbatim and inferential. questions by grades.

questions and both the grade and question type factors yielded highly significant F ratios ($p < .01$). We also treated our stimulus materials as random factors and computed the appropriate quasi-F ratios which yielded significant grade and question × story effects. A response bias is often observed in young children and, indeed, our kindergarten subjects responded affirmatively to 72% of the questions while fifth-graders responded affirmatively only 48% of the time. Since a signal-detection analysis takes response bias into account, we calculated d's for the data points in Fig. 2 and found that both effects could not be attributed to response bias (see Fig. 3).

The categories of questions are broken down further in Fig. 4, where it can be seen that lexical inferences (i.e., semantic entailments and implied instruments) were much easier to process than other items, possibly because they involved operations on nouns and verbs. However, it should be noted that there was age-related improvement on the *same* items within all categories. We do not want to emphasize absolute comparisons among categories on this task, rather, we want to ask if there is developmental improvement for the operations of inference and the spontaneous process-

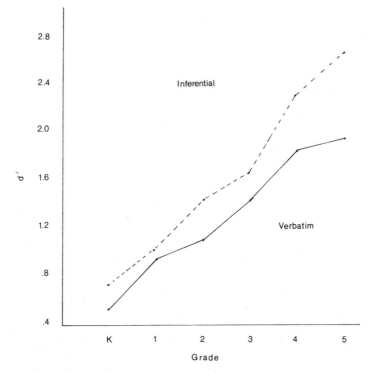

FIG. 3.   Values of d for verbatim and inferential questions by grades.

ing of implicit information above and beyond developmental increases in memory span.

In order to answer this question, we assumed that a correct answer to a verbatim question involves memory for a bit of information, whereas a correct answer to an inferential question involves remembering the information plus the product of an inferential operation. Both kinds of questions, verbatim and inferential, involve comprehension of attributes and relationships but the operations necessary to understand the different kinds of information may be different. In essence, we can regard the developmental improvement on questions of verbatim information as evidence for changes in something like memory "capacity" and inquire whether the developmental improvement on inferential questions simply parallels this curve or changes at a different rate. If the ability to comprehend inferences does not parallel a memory-capacity curve, then it suggests that different cognitive operations underlie inferential understanding. (It should be noted that the strength of this analysis is diminished by the nature of the task which does not permit direct comparisons between retention of the premise information from which an inference is made and the inference itself.)

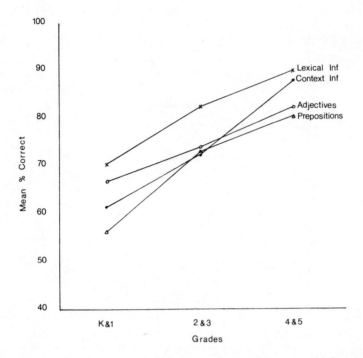

FIG. 4. Mean percentage of correct responses for question categories by grades.

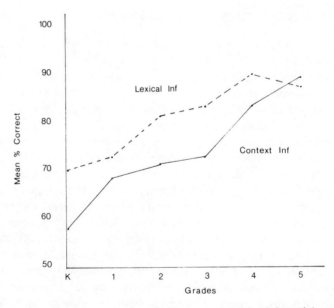

FIG. 5. Adjusted mean percentage of correct responses for inferential questions.

236

We separated the effects of memory improvement from the inferential operations by computing an analysis of covariance and partialing out the effects of verbatim items. When we did this, our adjusted scores, shown in Fig. 5, still revealed significant developmental improvement in the inferential operations. As in other figures, the more difficult contextual inferences accounted for the majority of the improvement. This effect is not a matter of response bias (as shown in the d's) and the greater comprehension and memory for contextual inferences with age appears to reflect more than increased memory span. The results of this study suggest that children from 6 to 11 years of age increase the amount of both explicit and implicit information that they comprehend from paragraphs. Even when we take into account the variability due to paragraphs, items, and response bias, there is an increased proficiency with age of spontaneously performing inferential operations on linguistic material.

One might argue that the covariance analysis in the preceding study overestimated the development of inferencing because the covariate was memory for verbatim adjectives and prepositions. Perhaps these words were less salient or more difficult to remember than the nouns and verbs embodied in contextual inferences. We therefore revised our questions to include noun and verb categories, eliminated two stories (for brevity), and did the experiment again with 16 subjects from each of three grades: kindergarten, second, and fourth. We added one other variation by requiring subjects to free recall as much of the paragraphs as possible. The recall period followed a 10-min interpolated memory game after all the paragraphs had been presented. The purpose of the free recall was to investigate the relationship between initial comprehension of the stories (with minimal time constraints on memory) and children's later memory for the ideas expressed in the stories. If the elaborative activity of inference is critical for memory, then one would expect a strong relationship between understanding inferences and later recall of the passages.

The results of the interrogated recall were similar to the previous study. As shown in Table 2, performance improved at successive grades, although the main difference was between the two youngest groups. As expected, the noun and verb categories of questions were answered correctly more often than preposition and adjective questions, and there were no differences between inferential and verbatim items as in the previous study. Our concern, though, was not in comparisons among item categories but in the developmental differences in the operations of inference. We computed an analysis of covariance with correct responses to noun and verb questions as the covariate. The adjusted mean percentage of correct responses (after noun and verb performance on the same stories was partialed out) for the inferential items are shown in Table 3. Both types of inferences showed

TABLE 2
Mean Percentage of Correct Responses
by Question Categories

	Grade		
Question category	K	2	4
Adjectives and prepositions	61.7	78.9	76.6
Nouns and verbs	72.7	83.6	80.5
Contextual inferences	60.2	78.1	80.5
Lexical inferences	77.3	89.8	87.5

TABLE 3
Adjusted Mean Percentage of Correct Responses for
Contextual and Lexical Inference Questions

	Grade			
Questions	K	2	4	Quasi-F
Contextual inferences	60.6	77.8	80.4	$p < .05$
Lexical inferences	78.3	89.1	87.3	$p < .05$

steady improvement over grades and both effects yielded significant quasi-F ratios ($p < .05$). As in the previous study, children in the grades sampled showed consistent improvement with age in their ability to comprehend inferential relations.

The free-recall data were analyzed for each subject's total number of idea units recalled from each story. These units were identified a priori and included explicit propositions from the sentences as well as inferential relations. Fabrications and extraneous elaborations were not counted. Kindergarten children averaged only 1.9 ideas recalled per story, second-graders 4.4, and fourth-graders 9.3.

In order to determine the relationship between initial comprehension and free recall, we computed a stepwise multiple regression analysis to determine which category of questions best predicted free-recall performance. The results of this analysis are shown in Table 4. The right-hand margin indicates that over all grades and stories, grade accounted for 66%

TABLE 4
Stepwise Multiple Regression Analysis:
Percentage of Variance Accounted for by Each
Predictor Variable over and above Preceding Variables[a]

	Grade			
	K	2	4	Total grade −65.8
Rank order of predictors	CTX − 33.2	CTX − 46.2	CTX − 67.2	CTX − 10.3
	VAP − 12.7	LEX − 10.3	VNV − 2.9	VAP − 0.3
	LEX − 2.6	VAP − 3.5	LEX − 1.5	LEX − 0.2
	VNV − 0.4	VNV − 0.9	VAP − 0.0	VNV − 0.2

[a] CTX—contextual inferences; LEX—lexical inferences; VAP— verbatim adjectives and prepositions; VNV—verbatim nouns and verbs.

of the variance ($p < .01$). Correctly responding to contextual inference questions was the next best predictor, and it accounted for a significant portion of the remaining variance ($p < .01$). It should be noted that this analysis means that contextual inferences were significantly related to free-recall performance after subtracting the effects of age-related improvement. In other words, this is not a simple correlation reflecting the fact that older children answered contextual inference questions correctly more often than younger subjects and also recalled more ideas per story. We regard this as tentative evidence that children's abilities to infer elaborate relationships such as presuppositions and consequences may be critical for the abstraction and retention of meaning from prose.

Within grade levels, the best predictor of free-recall performance was always the child's success with contextual inferences, a result that again indicates the predictive value of contextual inferences independent of the age-related improvement. As Table 4 reveals, the percentage of variance accounted for by contextual inferences increased across grades: 33, 46, and 67%. Each of these correlations was significantly better than the preceding grade ($p < .05$) which indicates a stronger predictive power with increasing age. This is congruent with our previous analyses of covariance which showed significant developmental improvement on contextual inference questions.

These studies demonstrate that children's understanding and retention of implicit and explicit information from prose increases with age. However, this trend may not indicate a growth in simple memory capacity; the operations involved in understanding inferential relations appear to improve with age over and above improvements in the retention of explicit nouns, verbs, adjectives, and prepositions. In addition to demonstrating the developmental improvement in inferential abilities, these studies show that such operations of "going beyond the information given" may be necessary for adequate abstraction and retention of the ideas conveyed by sentences.

DISCUSSION

Collectively, these studies indicate that children construct inferential relationships in their effort to comprehend and remember information. The constructive process was observed when children operated upon related sentences or pictures, and it seriously questions the theoretical sufficiency of competence models based only on the storage and retrieval of explicit associations, syntactic features, or images. Formal models of language and memory must incorporate the constructive performance characteristics of the individual in order to integrate the pragmatic, contextual, and connotative processes of knowing with the structural representation of knowledge. Such an approach does not render cognition an idiosyncratic process that prohibits general statements. It simply argues for a broader theoretical framework that recognizes that language and imagery are polysemous and flexible cues employed by individuals to create and express cognitive and perceptual environmental relations.

We have focused on the inferential and integrative aspects of children's comprehension. The act of inferring is an information expansion operation, going beyond the given information and providing elaborative context and relational embellishments. It is a component of assimilation, in the Piagetian sense, which serves to incorporate the new information into schemata that are perceptually salient and conceptually relevant to the individual. In this manner, the elaborative activity assures understanding (according to the individual's generated meaning) and promotes accessibility of the information. Although the constructive nature of comprehension expands upon the explicit information, the consequent memory representation often involves information reduction. Redundant and extraneous information among sentences can be collapsed, by virtue of inferred and conjoined relationships, to yield a semantically integrated memory representation of the context described by the sentences (Bransford & Franks, 1971; Bransford et al., 1972; Evans, 1967; Kintsch & Monk, 1972; Paris & Mahoney, 1974; Potts, Chapter 12). Integration is a parsimonious and efficient manner of storage or, in a different metaphor, it is an assimilative and accommodative process for knowing the importance of the information presented to the individual.

Integration does not always follow from inferring just as memory is not always the automatic consequence of understanding (cf. Jenkins, 1971), yet they are related. The kinds of activities performed during comprehension allow processing at "deeper levels" (Craik & Lockhart, 1972) and the generated relationships provide access cues for memory. Cues that are consistent with the subjects's mental representation of sentences are valuable retrieval aids, even when the cues are not part of the explicit stimuli (Anderson & Ortony, 1973; Paris, Sorkin, & Pisoni, 1974; Paris & Upton, 1974). This is similar to the processes of encoding specificity (Tulving & Thomson, 1973), and emphasizes the functional nature of the constructive operations. Indeed, inference may often be necessary for reconstruction and recall. In the last study discussed in this paper (Paris & Upton, 1974), it was observed that total recall of a story was best when subjects constructed the inferred antecedent and consequent conditions of the paragraph. Inference is not an extraneous by-product of comprehension; it is central to assimilation and retrieval of the achieved significance of the information.

IMPLICATIONS FOR DEVELOPMENTAL THEORY AND RESEARCH

Inference and integration are generic terms for information expansion and reduction operations. They are not language specific or esoteric strategies, but are basic mechanisms of understanding, which can readily be observed in manipulations such as imagery, chunking, clustering, and elaboration. Children infer and integrate when remembering sentences, pictures, and discourse, and their processes are qualitatively similar to adults' constructive comprehension processes. The ability to understand and remember inferred relationships improves with increasing age. In our studies, children between the ages of 6 and 11, roughly the concrete operational period, exhibited striking improvement in understanding and remembering inferences, especially contextual inferences which required subjects to infer plausible presuppositions and consequences of stories. These kinds of inferences require a great deal of elaborative processing, are contingent upon subjects' appreciation of temporal orderings, and also depend on the child's experience and knowledge of environmental relations. The abilities to make inferences and to integrate ideas allows the subject to know the information more completely and in a different manner than a child who does not apply these processes of comprehension.

Our tasks have measured children's spontaneous use of inference and integration. We do not intend to imply that young children cannot infer and integrate; they probably can do so when instructed and given appropriate stimulus materials. What we want to emphasize is the involuntary (cf. Smirnov & Zinchenko, 1969) and spontaneous use of such strategies. These tasks are similar to children's everyday experience in school where they are required to apprehend and remember meaning from movies, stories, and teachers' instructions. Understanding and retaining the meaning of these various contextual events are the goals of the child's processing, and it is not too surprising that the particular means of expression (i.e., particular words or sentences) are forgotten. But why is there developmental improvement in comprehending implicit and explicit information? Our data suggest that the operations underlying inferential abilities change with age in a manner different than a simple increase in memory capacity. There are several possible explanations. Perhaps older children in these studies approached the tasks with metamemorial plans to remember the information and the younger subjects did not. Or perhaps the young children did not apply inferential comprehension processes even though they were capable of doing so. These are both hypotheses of production deficiency (Flavell, 1970), where children do not spontaneously provide effective plans and operations to process information. But even when an inferential strategy is applied, one might expect older children to be more proficient at "deeper" processing by virtue of their practice with the strategy, their better understanding of sequential, temporal orders, entailment, and instrumental relationships, and their increased ability to retain the premise information from which the inferences are made. The efficiency of the strategy may also change as a function of the child's dominant perceptual and conceptual structuring of the material. Perhaps the inferential operation changes little with age, but the particular information to which the child attends may change. For instance, older children may realize that information such as prenominal adjectives is often relatively unimportant for the meaning of the passage and they therefore do not attend to specific details, but devote more processing energy to implicit information. Although these are viable alternatives that need to be investigated, they do not diminish the importance of the present studies, which reveal the developmental improvement in comprehension of inferential relationships and the necessity of such constructive processes for memory.

These studies provide a framework for evaluating comprehension and development changes in knowledge. From the constructivist point of view, people do not file and retrieve information from an entity labeled "memory" and diagrammatic boxes do not multiply or grow in children's heads. As Piaget and Inhelder (1973) have noted, it is the individual's operational intelligence which determines how one acts upon new information, what significance it achieves, and how it is incorporated within one's extant schemata. The processes of knowing and the structure of what is known interact. Brown (1975) has characterized the problem in terms of active versus passive strategies and semantic versus episodic events. Developmental changes in memory or problem-solving are only observed on tasks which require active strategies (Brown, 1974). Furthermore, one can expect more developmental change on tasks that require semantic processing than less "meaningful" episodic events, presumably because semantic processing is dependent upon the child's level of sophistication in his representation of environmental relationships. Developmental differences due to the production of a relevant strategy would reflect quantitative changes with age, whereas differences in schematic organization of the world would result in qualitatively different levels of understanding. In the present context, changes in the probability of producing spontaneously an available inferential and integrative strategy would be a quantitative developmental change whereas the different levels of understanding achieved by children by virtue of inferencing would be a qualitative change.

In order to understand developmental changes in comprehension and memory, we need to investigate both the general metamemorial strategies of planfulness and the particular operations that children employ. An appreciation of the process–structure interaction will allow us to assess cognitive changes in children more adequately by measuring the operations themselves rather than manifest content alone. For example, a test that measures children's ability to understand inferential relations in prose might be a valuable tool for assessing reading proficiency. Knowing how comprehension processes of children interface with their conceptual representations of knowledge would also permit the construction of educational materials which "fit the material to the head" (Jenkins, 1971). In fact, quite a bit of research on children's comprehension of prepositions, connectives, comparative adjectives, and syntax has been concerned with the "head-fitting" (cf. Brown, 1975) relationship between the child's cognitive organization and his interpretation of language. Expanding the inquiry to the developmental course of inferential and integrative strategies of comprehension for prose and discourse and children's construction of meaning appears to have a great deal of theoretical and pragmatic utility.

ACKNOWLEDGMENTS

Much of the research reported in this paper was supported by an NIE Grant NE-G-00-3-0089. I wish to express my appreciation to Frank Restle, Henry Roediger, Barbara Lindauer, Jerry Mahoney, David Snuttjer, and Joe Buckhalt for their comments on earlier drafts of this manuscript.

REFERENCES

Anderson, J. R., & Bower, G. H. *Human associative memory.* Washington, D.C.: Winston, 1973

Anderson, R. C., & Ortony, A. On putting applies into bottles—A problem of polysemy. Unpublished manuscript, University of Illinois, 1973.

Austin, J. L. *How to do things with words.* London and New York: Oxford Univ. Press, 1970.

Barclay, J. R. The role of comprehension in remembering sentences. *Cognitive Psychology,* 1973, **4,** 229–254.

Barclay, J. R., & Reid, M. Semantic integration in children's recall of discourse. *Developmental Psychology,* 1974, **10,** 277–281.

Bartlett, F. C. *Remembering.* Cambridge, England: Cambridge Univ. Press, 1932.

Bransford, J. D., Barclay, J. R., & Franks, J. J. Sentence memory: A constructive versus interpretive approach. *Cognitive Psychology,* 1972, **3,** 193–209.

Bransford, J. D., & Franks, J. J. The abstraction of linguistic ideas. *Cognitive Psychology,* 1971, **2,** 331–350.

Bransford, J. D., & Franks, J. J. The abstraction of linguistic ideas: A review. *Cognition: An International Journal of Cognitive Psychology,* 1972, **2,** 211–249.

Bransford, J. D., & McCarrell, N. S. A sketch of a cognitive approach to comprehension: Some thoughts about what it means to comprehend. In W. B. Weimer & D. S. Palermo (Eds.), *Cognition and symbolic processes.* Hillsdale, New Jersey: Lawrence Erlbaum Assoc., 1975.

Brown, A. L. The role of strategic behavior in retardate memory. In N. R. Ellis (Ed.), *International review of research in mental retardation,* Vol. 7. New York: Academic Press, 1974.

Brown, A. L. The development of memory: Knowing, knowing you don't know, and knowing how to know. In H. W. Reese (Ed.), *Advances in child development and behavior.* Vol. 10. New York: Academic Press, 1975.

Brown, R. *Words and things.* New York: Free Press, 1958.

Bruner, J. S. Beyond the information given. In J. M. Anglin (Ed.), *Studies in the psychology of knowing.* New York: Morton, 1973.

Bryant, P. E., & Trabasso, T. Transitive inferences and memory in young children. *Nature,* 1971, **232,** 456–458.

Carroll, J. B., & Freedle, R. O. *Language comprehension and the acquisition of knowledge.* Washington: Winston, 1972.

Chomsky, N. *Syntactic structures.* The Hague: Mouton, 1957.

Chomsky, N. *Aspects of the theory of syntax.* Cambridge, Massachusetts: M.I.T. Press, 1965.

Cofer, C. Constructive processes in memory. *American Scientist,* 1973, **61,** 537–543.

Collins, A. M., & Quillian, M. R. How to make a language user. In E. Tulving & W. Donaldson (Eds.), *Organization of memory.* New York: Academic Press, 1972.

Craik, F. I. M., & Lockhart, R. S. Levels of processing: A framework for memory research. *Journal of Verbal Learning & Verbal Behavior,* 1972, **11,** 671–684.

Evans, S. H. A brief statement of schema theory. *Psychonomic Science,* 1967, **8,** 87–88.

Fillenbaum, S. Memory for gist: Some relevant variables. *Language & Speech,* 1966, **9,** 217–227.

Flavell, J. H. Developmental studies of mediated memory. In H. W. Reese & L. P. Lipsitt (Eds.), *Advances in child development and behavior*, Vol. 5. New York: Academic Press, 1970. Pp. 181–211.

Garner, W. R. To perceive is to know. *American Psychologist*, 1966, **21**, 11–19.

Glick, J., & Wapner, S. Development of transitivity: Some findings and problems of analysis. *Child Development*, 1968, **39**, 621–638.

Jenkins, J. J. The head remembers what it does. Paper presented at the Eastern Psychological Association, 1971.

Johnson, M. K., Bransford, J. D., & Solomon, S. K. Memory for tacit implications of sentences. *Journal of Experimental Psychology*, 1973, **98**, 203–205.

Katz, J. J., & Fodor, J. A. The structure of semantic theory. *Language*, 1963, **39**, 170–210.

Kintsch, W., & Monk, D. Storage of complex information in memory: Some implications of the speed with which inferences can be made. *Journal of Experimental Psychology*, 1972, **94**, 25–32.

Liberman, A. M. Some characteristics of perception in the speech mode. In D. A. Hamburg (Ed.), *Perception and its disorders: Proceedings of A. R. N. M. D.* Baltimore: Williams & Wilkins, 1970. Pp. 238–254.

McCawley, J. D. The role of semantics in a grammar. In E. Bach & R. T. Harms (Eds.), *Universals in linguistic theory*. New York: Holt, 1968. Pp. 124–169.

Neisser, U. *Cognitive psychology*. New York: Appleton, 1967.

Olson, D. R. Language and thought: Aspects of a cognitive theory of semantics. *Psychological Review*, 1970, **77**, 257–273.

Paris, S. G., & Carter, A. Y. Semantic and constructive aspects of sentence memory in children. *Developmental Psychology*, 1973, **9**, 109–113.

Paris, S. G., & Mahoney, G. J. Cognitive integration in children's memory for sentences and pictures. *Child Development*, 1974, **45**, 633–642.

Paris, S. G., Mahoney, G. J., & Buckhalt, J. A. Facilitation of semantic integration in sentence memory of retarded children. *American Journal of Mental Deficiency*, 1974, **78**, 714–720.

Paris, S. G., Sorkin, J. R., & Pisoni, D. B. The role of implied instruments in sentence memory. Paper presented at the Midwestern Psychological Association meeting, Chicago, May, 1974.

Paris, S. G., & Upton, L. R. The construction and retention of linguistic inferences by children. Paper presented at the Western Psychological Association meeting, San Francisco, April 1974.

Perfetti, C. A. Psychosomantics: Some cognitive aspects of structural meaning. *Psychological Bulletin*, 1972, **78**, 241–259.

Piaget, J., & Inhelder, B. *Memory and intelligence*. New York: Basic Books, 1973.

Pisoni, D. B. Auditory and phonetic memory codes in the discrimination of consonants and vowels. *Perception & Psychophysics*, 1973, **13**, 253–260.

Potts, G. R. Information processing strategies used in the encoding of linear orderings. *Journal of Verbal Learning & Verbal Behavior*, 1972, **11**, 727–740.

Reese, H. W. Imagery and contextual meaning. *Psychological Bulletin*, 1970, **73**, 404–414.

Rumelhart, D. E., Lindsay, P. H., & Norman, D. A. A process model for long-term memory. In E. Tulving & W. Donaldson (Eds.), *Organization of memory*. New York: Academic Press, 1972. Pp. 198–246.

Sachs, J. S. Recognition memory for syntactic and semantic aspects of connected discourse. *Perception & Psyhophysics*, 1967, **2**, 437–442.

Schank, R. Conceptual dependency: A theory of natural language understanding. *Cognitive Psychology,* 1972, **3**, 552–631.

Schlesinger, I. M. Production of utterances and language acquisition. In D. I. Slobin (Ed.), *The ontogenesis of grammar.* New York: Academic Press, 1971. Pp. 63–102.

Searle, J. R. *Speech acts: An essay in the philosophy of language.* Cambridge: Cambridge Univ. Press, 1969.

Smirnov, A. A., & Zinchenko, P. I. Problems in the psychology of memory. In M. Cole & I. Maltzman (Eds.), *A Handbook of contemporary Soviet psychology.* New York: Basic Books, 1969. Pp. 452–502.

Tulving, E., & Thomson, D. M. Encoding specificity and retrieval processes in episodic memory. *Psychological Review,* 1973, **80**, 352–373.

Weimer, W. B. Psycholinguistics and Plato's paradoxes of the *Meno. American Psychologist,* 1973, **28**, 15–33.

Winograd, T. Understanding natural language. *Cognitive Psychology,* 1972, **3**, 1–191.

12

BRINGING ORDER TO COGNITIVE STRUCTURES

George R. Potts
Dartmouth College

If cognitive psychology has any one basic rallying point, it would have to be its view of humans as active processors of information. People do not passively input and store sensory experiences. In their attempt to satisfy various task demands, people actively transform incoming information. This is certainly not a new point of view, but it lay dormant for quite some time because of the failure of its proponents to specify in any satisfactory fashion the nature of these transformations. Hence, although Bartlett was on the right track when, in 1932, he argued that new information was actively incorporated into a set of organized cognitive structures called schemata, his arguments received little attention among experimental psychologists. His conceptions of the nature of these schemata and of the processes involved in incorporating new information into these schemata were simply too sketchy to allow for an adequate test of his views. For a long time, attempts to clarify the conception of a cognitive structure met with only limited success. In recent years, however, we have finally begun to see some real advances in this regard. Two such advances are especially relevant to the present chapter. The first of these is the detailed linguistic analysis of the processes involved in the comprehension of individual sentences; the second is the analysis of the structure of semantic memory.

It is reasonable to suppose that one of the first steps in comprehending text is the linguistic processing of the individual sentences in the text. It has been shown that a relatively few basic linguistic principles can account for comprehension latencies in a variety of tasks (e.g., Chase & Clark,

1972; Clark, 1969; Trabasso, 1972). There was a time in the mid-1960s when it was argued that a linguistic analysis of the transformations performed while comprehending a sentence might prove to be all that was necessary to account for the processing of textual material. According to this view, individual sentences are transformed into their abstract linguistic deep structures (Chomsky, 1957, 1965). When trying to remember text, people store these deep structures (Mehler, 1963; Miller, 1962). Since deep structures are unobservable, abstract, and drastically different in structure from the original sentences, they provided a prime candidate for filling the role of Bartlett's schemata. Hence, it is not surprising that this linguistic theory of individual sentence memory received considerable attention at the time, and served to generate a substantial body of empirical work (e.g., Mehler, 1963; Mehler & Miller, 1964; Sachs, 1967; Savin & Perchonock, 1965).

It has become clear, however, that although linguistic transformations of individual sentences play an important role in the initial stages of comprehension, the final representation of textual material does not correspond to a simple catalog of the representations of the individual sentences in the text. People's information processing strategies extend far beyond merely altering the form of each incoming sentence and storing that altered form. This has been demonstrated in a series of studies by Bransford and Franks (1971) and Bransford, Barclay, and Franks (1972). During the acquisition phase of these experiments, subjects were presented with a series of sentences, and were told to read each for comprehension. After the whole set of acquisition sentences had been presented, subjects were shown another series of sentences, some of which were identical to the acquisition sentences and some of which were not. Their task was to indicate whether each test sentence was or was not identical to any of the acquisition sentences. It was found that if a test sentence contradicted any information that had been presented during acquisition, subjects were very accurate in recognizing that the sentence had not been presented. As long as the test sentence was not inconsistent with any of the acquisition sentences, however, subjects were unable to make the desired discrimination. Specifically, subjects were unable to distinguish between information which had actually been presented and information which they themselves had deduced from the presented information. Assume, for example, that subjects are first presented with the sentences *The robins sat on their nest* and *A hawk flew over the robins.* When later asked if they had seen the sentence *A hawk flew over the nest,* subjects will tend erroneously to indicate that they had indeed seen the sentence before. In Chapter 11, Paris demonstrates that this is the case even for relatively young children.

These results contradict the linguistic theory of individual sentence memory, for they show that subjects do not store individual sentences at all. Instead, the individual sentences in the text are combined both with each other and with subjects' generalized knowledge of the world to form an abstract representation of the general idea underlying the passage. As important as this work is, however, it should be clear that this is only a first step. We are still lacking an adequate formal description of the nature of these abstract representations.

While linguistic theorists were examining the nature of the transformations which people perform on incoming sentences, the semantic-memory theorists began attacking the question of internal representation by attempting to describe the nature of a person's existing knowledge of the world (e.g., Anderson & Bower, 1973; Kintsch, 1972; Quillian, 1969; Rumelhart, Lindsay, & Norman, 1972). In what has been referred to as a return to introspectionism (Collins & Quillian, 1972), these theorists used their intuitions regarding their own knowledge of the world to construct formal descriptions of the abstract structure of such knowledge. Whereas these theories represent major theoretical endeavors, empirical verifications of the theories have been limited. The present research represents an attempt to examine empirically the nature of the abstract representation of certain forms of ordered relationships. The research began as an attempt to clarify one of the points of contention between existing models of semantic memory.

STORING AND RETRIEVING INFORMATION
ABOUT LINEAR ORDERINGS

Some researchers have argued that, when faced with a piece of deducible information, people do not store it (e.g., Quillian, 1969). Instead, they rely on the seemingly efficient strategy of storing only the necessary information and deducing the remaining information whenever required to do so. Other researchers (e.g., Rumelhart, Lindsay, & Norman, 1972; Anderson & Bower, 1973) have argued that this is not reasonable and that people may indeed store deducible information. The present research began as an attempt to determine which of these positions was correct.

The Experimental Paradigm

To test whether people do indeed store deducible information, 10 Dartmouth undergraduates learned 20 paragraphs and answered questions about them. Each paragraph described a single linear ordering of four terms. The terms were chosen and arranged in such a way that no "natural" ordering of the terms was apparent. Such an ordering (which will be characterized as $A > B > C > D$)[1] can be described in terms of six pairwise relationships. Three of these pairs ($A > B$, $B > C$, and $C > D$) describe the relations between adjacent elements in the ordering and will be referred to as *adjacent pairs*. These adjacent pairs are necessary to the establishment of the ordering. The remaining three pairs ($A > C$, $B > D$, and $A > D$) describe the relations between nonadjacent elements in the ordering, and will be referred to as *remote pairs*. Since the relations employed were transitive, these remote pairs could be deduced from some subset of the adjacent pairs. Each paragraph presented only the three adjacent pairs necessary to establish a single ordering. The order of presentation of these pairs was varied across paragraphs. A sample paragraph describing a four-term linear ordering is presented here:

> Jane, a bored housewife, decided to bake some pastries to help pass the time away. When Jane's husband returned home, she ordered him to taste a sample of each batch. He said that her bread was better than her cake, her cake was better than her rolls, and her rolls were better than her pie. From that day, Jane never complained about being bored.

A set of 12 test sentences (6 true and 6 false) was used to assess subjects' knowledge of the information contained in each of the paragraphs. The six true sentences consisted of a statement of the six pairwise relations comprising the ordering. For each true sentence (e.g., $A > B$?), there was a corresponding false sentence consisting of the same two terms in reverse order (e.g., $B > A$?).

A subject was allowed to study each paragraph until he was confident he could remember it. Paper and pencil were provided, and the subject was told he could take notes if he desired. When the subject indicated he was ready, the paragraph and notes were taken away, and the 12 test sentences were presented one at a time in random order. We measured the amount of time required for the subject to respond "true" or "false" to each of these sentences. The importance of not making any errors was stressed. After responding to the set of 12 test sentences for the first paragraph, the subject was given the second paragraph to study. This procedure was repeated until the subject had responded to all 20 paragraphs. Each subject responded to 10 of the paragraphs during one session and the re-

---

[1] It should be noted that the designation of one end-term of the ordering as A and one as D is not arbitrary. Paragraphs employed only the linguistically unmarked form of comparative adjectives. In line with the observations of DeSoto, London, and Handel (1965), we observed that when taking notes, subjects are consistent in arranging the terms of the ordering in such a way that the best, tallest, largest, etc., is on the top or left. This term is designated as A. The worst, shortest, smallest, etc., is consistently placed on the bottom or right. This term is designated as D.

maining 10 during a second session. The first paragraph of each session was treated as a warm-up and was not scored.

The Results:
Answering Questions about Ordered Relationships

Overall proportion correct was .95. Averaged over paragraphs and subjects, reaction times to the adjacent pairs, which were actually presented, were noticeably longer (1.79 sec) than reaction times to the remote pairs, which had to be deduced (1.45 sec). This superiority on the remote pairs turns out to be an unusually powerful effect. Averaging over paragraphs, this effect was demonstrated by all 10 subjects ($p = .002$)[2]; averaging over subjects, the effect was observed on each of the 18 scored paragraphs.[3]

Retrieving Information from Long-Term Memory

When performing in the preceding task, one has the compelling impression of continually rehearsing the ordering of the four terms while proceeding through the set of test questions. In view of this, we must consider the possibility that the short reaction times to remote pairs represents a short-term memory phenomenon. It is important to determine whether the same results are obtained when subjects are forced to retrieve the information from long-term memory.

One way to force subjects to use long-term memory would be to insert a delay between the time they studied the paragraph and the time they responded to the test questions. Although this would indeed force subjects to store the information in long-term memory, it would not solve the problem. Subjects could merely retrieve the appropriate ordering just prior to answering the set of questions about it. This ordering could then by cycled through short-term memory while the subject proceeded through the set

---

[2] Most of the effects described herein are highly consistent over both subjects and paragraphs. Wherever feasible, I have reported the number of subjects and paragraphs showing each particular effect described. In the case of subjects, whose scores may be viewed as independent, this number can be evaluated statistically using a sign test. This was done, and the exact two-tailed probability of that result, or one more extreme, is presented in parentheses after each statement.

[3] Proportion correct is very high for all the experiments described in this chapter. This is necessary in order to make possible a meaningful analysis of the reaction time scores. A separate series of studies has been performed to examine subjects' accuracy on this type of material. In these experiments, subjects were given a large number of paragraphs to remember prior to answering any questions. After studying all the paragraphs, subjects are given paper and pencil tests on the information. The accuracy scores complement the present reaction time results in that proportion correct was found to be significantly higher on the remote pairs than on the adjacent pairs.

of test sentences. Hence, the reaction time scores would again be measuring the time required to retrieve information stored in short-term memory. To circumvent this problem, the preceding experiment was replicated with one major modification. The materials were identical to those employed previously, but subjects (13 Dartmouth College undergraduates) were required to study a set of three paragraphs before answering any questions. They were given as much time as they needed to study each set of three paragraphs. After studying a set of paragraphs, subjects responded to a set of 36 test questions (12 from each of the three paragraphs). The test questions were randomly permuted with the restriction that no two consecutive test questions were ever taken from the same paragraph.

Performance was surprisingly good on this very difficult task. Overall proportion correct was .95. Once again, average reaction time was longer on the adjacent pairs (2.22 sec) than on the remote pairs (2.02 sec). Averaging over paragraphs, this superiority on the remote pairs was shown by 12 of the 13 subjects ($p = .004$); averaging over subjects, it was found for 17 of the 18 scored paragraphs. Hence, even when subjects were forced to retrieve information from long-term memory, the superiority of the remote pairs was still readily apparent.

How Subjects Do Not Store Ordered Relationships

The fact that reaction time to the remote pairs was shorter than reaction time to the adjacent pairs contradicts any theory which argues that, rather than storing deducible information, subjects infer this information when tested. If subjects deduced the remote pairs when tested, then, in order to respond to such a pair, they would first have to retrieve all the relevant adjacent pairs and then draw the inference. Hence, reaction time to a remote pair would have to be longer than reaction time to any adjacent pair necessary to deduce it. Hence, it appears that subjects in this experiment deduced and stored information about the remote pairs along with the information that was actually presented.

At first glance, then, the obtained superiority on the remote pairs would appear to support any model that proposes that subjects do indeed store deducible information. This is not the case, however. Models such as those proposed by Rumelhart, Lindsay, and Norman (1972) or Anderson and Bower (1973) argue that subjects may occasionally infer and store deducible information while studying the material. This is not sufficient. The weakness of such a position can be seen by examining one of these theories in detail. The model of human associative memory proposed by Anderson and Bower is more explicit than most, and will be singled out for closer examination. This model proposes a network of associations to account for the encoding of linear orderings. Although the adjacent relations, being necessary to the establishment of the ordering, are the most readily accessible relations, Anderson and Bower argue that subjects may occasionally form more remote associations as well. Such a model is similar to the one proposed by Ebbinghaus (1885), who also argued that subjects learned serial lists by establishing a set of interitem associations. Although Ebbinghaus acknowledged that remote associations may be formed while learning such a list, he contended that these remote associations were weaker than the adjacent associations. According to such a model, subjects can respond correctly to a remote pair either by remembering that pair (i.e., retrieving the remote association) or by correctly deducing it from some subset of the other pairs. When subjects remember the remote pairs, reaction time to that pair would be at best equal to reaction time to an adjacent pair, since both need only to be retrieved from memory in order to answer the question (it should be remembered that Anderson and Bower make an even stronger prediction by contending that the adjacent pairs are actually more readily accessible than the remote pairs). When subjects must deduce a remote pair, on the other hand, reaction time will be unusually long. Hence, such a model would have considerable difficulty accounting for the fact that overall reaction time to the remote pairs was found to be shorter than overall reaction time to the adjacent pairs.

THE COGNITIVE STRUCTURE OF A LINEAR ORDERING

Although the obtained short reaction-times to remote pairs contradicts several alternative explanations regarding the form in which linear orderings are represented, it does little to specify the true nature of that representation. The characteristics of this representation and of the retrieval processes operating on it are the factors that will determine which pairs will be responded to quickly and which will be more difficult. Hence, one reasonable way to begin to specify the nature of the abstract representation of a linear ordering is by examining the actual reaction time profile of the 12 test sentences.

The reaction time profiles for the two experiments described so far are presented in Fig. 1. The top frame of Fig. 1 presents the reaction time profile for the original experiment; the bottom frame presents the reaction time profile for the replication in which subjects were forced to retrieve the information from long-term memory.

Spatial Distance

In observing subjects take notes on the paragraphs used in the present experiments, it was clear that most subjects adopted a strategy of listing the ordered array of terms. This corresponds closely to Huttenlocher's

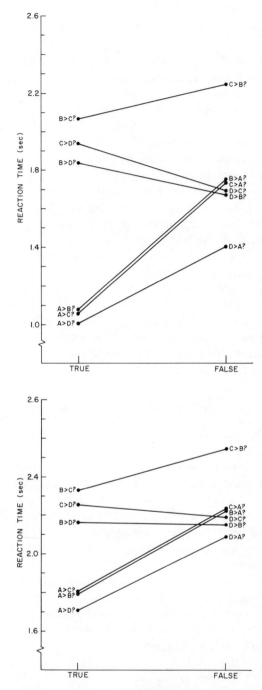

FIG. 1. Reaction time profiles for the 12 test sentences used to test the time required to retrieve information about a four-term ordering: (top) the reaction times from the standard paradigm; (bottom) reaction times from the replication study in which subjects were forced to retrieve the information from long-term memory.

(1968) suggestion that in attempting to solve three-term series problems, subjects order the terms along some imaginary spatial continuum. A natural question to ask is whether reaction time might be a simple inverse monotonic function of spatial distance; the larger the distance, the shorter the reaction time. For a four-term ordering, such a distance hypothesis makes a total of nine ordinal predictions for true sentences and nine for false. Specifically, reaction time to the pair $A > D$ should be shorter than reaction time to any of the other five pairs; reaction time to the pair $A > C$ should be shorter than reaction time to either $A > B$ or $B > C$; and reaction time to the pair $B > D$ should be shorter than reaction time to either $B > C$ or $C > D$.

Examination of Fig. 1 reveals that for the original experiment, all ordinal predictions of the distance model were satisfied for both true and false sentences. In the replication experiment, all but two of the 18 ordinal predictions were satisfied. The reversals were between the pairs $A > B$ and $A > C$ for both true and false sentences.

If spatial distance were the only factor operating, however, then one would predict that the relative ease or difficulty of the six pairs should be the same for both true and false sentences. This was clearly not the case. Examination of Fig. 1 reveals a strong interaction between the specific pair tested and the truth value of the test sentence. Reaction time to true test sentences beginning with the first term (A) in the ordering (e.g., $A > B$?) is short relative to reaction time to false sentences ending with the first term in the ordering (e.g., $B > A$?). Conversely, reaction time to true sentences ending with the last term (D) in the ordering (e.g., $C > D$?) is long relative to reaction time to false sentences beginning with the last term in the ordering (e.g., $D > C$?). When tested using a repeated measures analysis of variance, this interaction proved to be significant for both the original and replication experiments [$F(5, 45) = 23.78, p < .001$ and $F(5, 60) = 6.04, p < .001$, respectively].

Such an interaction poses a problem not only for the distance model, but for any model that attempts to explain the reaction-time profile solely in terms of the form in which the information is stored. To account for such an interaction, one must postulate a specific strategy for retrieving the stored information.

An End-Term Processing Strategy

Several experimenters have argued that the first and last terms in a serial list share a special status in serving as "anchors" for the other terms in the list (e.g., DeSoto & Bosley, 1962; Feigenbaum & Simon, 1962; Wishner, Shipley, & Hurvich, 1957). Much of the present data can be acounted for by arguing that, in addition to the linear arrangement of the four terms, subjects also store the fact that A is the first term and that D is the last. In responding to a test sentence, they first check to see if either of the terms in the test sentence is an end term. If it is, they can respond immediately. A flow chart describing one such strategy is presented in Fig. 2. According to this strategy, subjects examine the first term in the test sentence and ask themselves if it is the first term (A) in the ordering. If it is, they can respond immediately, indicating that the sentence is true. If not, they ask themselves if it is the last term (D) in the ordering. If it is, they can respond immediately, indicating that the sentence is false. Only if neither of these checks is successful do subjects go on to process the second term in the test sentence.

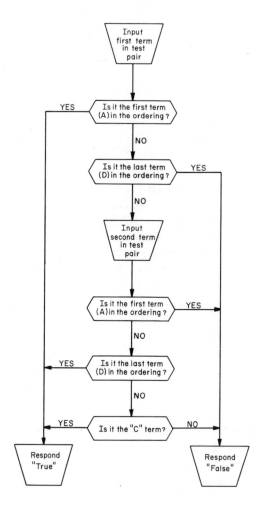

FIG. 2.   Flow chart describing an end-term-processing strategy for answering questions about a linear ordering. (From Potts, 1972.)

Such a strategy would lead to the obtained interaction between specific pair tested and truth value of the test sentence because according to this strategy, an end term must appear as the first term in the ordering in order to facilitate reaction time. If the second term is an end term, subjects must retrieve information about both terms and much of the benefit of having an end term is lost. Hence, reaction times to true sentences containing the term A are shorter than reaction times to false sentences containing the term A because only in a true sentence does the A appear as the first term (e.g., $A > B$?). Similarly, reaction times to false sentences containing the term D are shorter than reaction times to true sentences containing the term D because only in a false sentence does the D appear as the first term (e.g., $D > C$?).

If a subject has successfully stored the fact that A is the first term in the ordering, then reaction times to all test sentences having an A as their first term should not only be short, but also identical. This follows from the fact that if a subject realizes that the first term in the test sentence is the first term in the ordering, he will respond "true" immediately, without bothering to process the second term. Examination of Fig. 1 reveals that this prediction is upheld for both experiments in that reaction times to the three test sentences beginning with A are uniformly short.

If a subject has successfully stored the fact that D is the last term in the ordering, then reaction times to all three test sentences beginning with D should also be uniformly short. For the original experiment, this was clearly not the case. Although the three sentences beginning with D are indeed next shortest, they are not all equal. Reaction time to the pair $D > A$? was noticeably shorter than reaction time to $D > B$? or $D > C$?. Averaging over paragraphs, this effect was found for all 10 subjects ($p < .01$); averaging over subjects, it was found on all 18 scored paragraphs. For the replication experiment (in which subjects were forced to retrieve the information from long-term memory), the differences among the three pairs beginning with D are less pronounced and not significant.

The lack of uniformity among pairs beginning with D in the original study could be accounted for by arguing that although virtually all subjects store the information that A is the first term in the ordering, only some of the subjects code the fact that D is last. Those who do store this information will have uniformly short reaction times to sentences beginning with D. To test the viability of such an explanation, we must examine the reaction time profiles of individual subjects. This is, of course, an interesting thing to examine in its own right, for without such an analysis, one can never be sure whether or not the average reaction time profile accurately reflects the profile of individual subjects.

INDIVIDUAL SUBJECT DATA

In order to get enough observations on each subject to allow us to examine the individual subjects' reaction time profiles, four subjects were given three trials on each of the 20 paragraphs employed previously. Successive trials on a single paragraph were separated by a 2-day lag.

Overall proportions correct for subjects MB, RL, PG, and XZ were .98, .91, 1.00, and .97, respectively. For all four subjects, overall reaction time to the remote pairs was shorter than overall reaction time to the adjacent pairs. Figure 3 presents the reaction time profile for each of the four subjects.

It is clear that the reaction time profile for individual subjects matches closely the average profile obtained for a group of subjects. For all four subjects, reaction times were shortest to sentences beginning with the term *A*. Two subjects (MB and RL) demonstrated uniformly short reaction

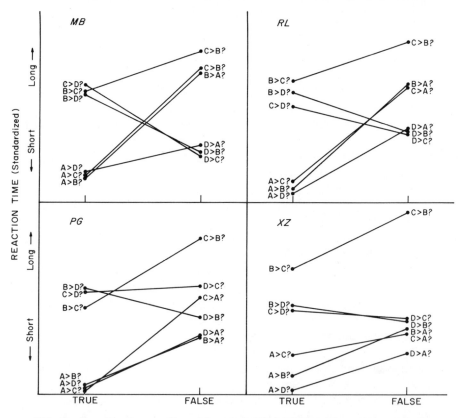

FIG. 3.   Reaction-time profiles of four individual subjects. The reaction times for each subject were normalized by dividing by the standard deviation of that subject's scores. (From Potts, 1974.)

times to sentences beginning with the term *D*. The remaining two subjects did not show this effect. Hence, these data give some credence to the contention that although all subjects store the fact that *A* is first, only some store the fact that D is last. Only those who do store this information will have uniformly short reaction times to sentences beginning with the term *D*.

Reaction Time Profile
for a Six-Term Ordering

The end-term processing strategy described in Fig. 2 accounts nicely for the data from a four-term linear ordering. One is therefore led to question whether the spatial distance hypothesis has any validity at all. Since, on the average, the remote pairs of a four-term ordering contain more end terms than do the adjacent pairs, it is clear that with such an ordering, the effects of spatial distance are confounded with the number of end terms. One can examine the effects of spatial distance independent of number and of end terms by examining the reaction time profile for the four inner terms $(B > C > D > E)$ of a six-term ordering $(A > B > C > D > E > F)$.

Each of 24 Dartmouth College undergraduates learned and responded to a set of 12 paragraphs. Each paragraph described a single six-term linear ordering which was established by presenting the five adjacent pairs in the chained order: $A > B, B > C, C > D, D > E, E > F$. Two sessions were again required, and the first paragraph in each session was not scored. The test materials for each paragraph consisted of 30 sentences (15 true and 15 false) describing all possible pairwise relations between the terms of the ordering.

Overall proportion correct was .97. Averaged over subjects and paragraphs, mean reaction times to the adjacent and remote pairs were 2.39 and 1.97 sec, respectively. Averaging over paragraphs, this superiority on the remote pairs was demonstrated by all 24 subjects ($p > .001$); averaging over subjects, it was found on all 10 scored paragraphs. The reaction time profile is presented in Fig. 4.

The importance of the end terms is readily apparent when one examines the reaction time profile for the nine pairs that contained an end term. These pairs are designated by the solid lines in Fig. 4. Reaction times were again uniform and shortest to the five test sentences beginning with the first term (A) in the ordering and relatively short to the five sentences beginning with the last term (F). Once again, reaction times to true test sentences beginning with the term *A* were substantially shorter than reaction times to false test sentences ending with the term *A*. Reaction times to true test sentences ending with *F*, on the other hand, were longer than reaction times to false test sentences beginning with *F*. This interaction

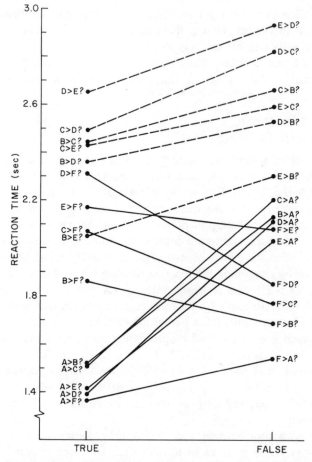

FIG. 4. Reaction time profile for the 30 test sentences used to test the time required to retrieve information about a six-term ordering. Those sentences containing an end term are designated by solid lines; dashed lines are used to designate sentences containing only inner terms. (From Potts, 1974.)

between specific pair and truth value of the test sentence was highly significant [$F(8, 184) = 21.06, p < .001$] and accounted for 52% of the within-subject variance. These results are all in agreement with the predictions of the end-term processing model.

Examination of the reaction time profile for the inner pairs (designated by the dashed lines in Fig. 4) reveals that the observed superiority on the remote pairs cannot be accounted for solely in terms of the presence or absence of end terms, however. Even among these inner pairs, there was a clear inverse relationship between reaction time and inferential distance; the more remote the pair, the shorter the reaction time. All 18 ordinal predictions (9 for true sentences, 9 for false) of a distance model were satisfied by these inner pairs. Average reaction times to the adjacent and remote inner pairs were 2.67 and 2.38 sec, respectively. Averaging over paragraphs, this superiority of the remote pairs was shown by all but one of the 24 subjects ($p < .001$); averaging over subjects, this effect was found for all 10 scored paragraphs.

Hence, it is clear that reaction times to the remote pairs are still consistently shorter than reaction times to the adjacent pairs, even when end-term effects are eliminated. One could account for this by arguing that subjects do indeed process a six-term ordering in the manner described by the end-term processing hypothesis, but that if a test sentence contains neither end term (A or F), subjects begin to search for the presence of one of the two terms adjacent to these end terms (B and D). If this were the case, however, then one would predict that the reaction time profile for the four inner terms of a six-term ordering should be essentially the same as the profile for a four-term ordering. Specifically, the interaction between type of pair tested and truth value of the test sentence should still be observed. This was clearly not the case. This interaction, which was highly significant and accounted for 52% of the within-subject variance for pairs containing an end term, accounted for virtually no variance among these inner pairs and did not approach significance [$F(5, 115) = .26$, $p = .93$]. Thus, far from eliminating the distance effect, removal of the end terms served to clean up the data and accentuate the effect.

A Two-Process Model

These results indicate that neither a distance model nor an end-term processing model is sufficient in and of itself to account for the way subjects store and retrieve information about linear orderings. Scholz and Potts (1974) came to a similar conclusion upon analyzing the number of errors made in a similar task. The data seem to indicate that subjects store two types of information about an item.

One type of item information consists of some measure of the magnitude or position of the item with respect to the other items in the ordering. Typically, in responding to a test sentence, a subject will retrieve the information he stored about the two items and perform some comparison operation to determine the relationship between those two items. The time required to complete the comparison operation is presumed to be inversely related to the inferential distance separating the two terms; the larger the distance, the shorter the reaction time.

If an item is an end term, subjects may also store a second type of information about that item; they may (but need not) also store the fact that the term is first or last. If a subject does store that information, then when that term appears as the first term in the test sentence, he can respond immediately and thus bypass both the retrieval of information about the second term and the comparison stage.

The Nature of the Distance Effect

A key problem that remains is to specify the nature of the comparison process which leads to the obtained inverse relationship between inferential distance and reaction time among the inner pairs. There are several possibilities.

Moyer (1973) has shown that reaction time for determining which of two animals is larger is a monotonic decreasing function of the difference in size between the animals; the larger the difference, the shorter the reaction time. In an attempt to explain this finding, Moyer hypothesized the existence of an "internal psychophysics." He argued that subjects stored in memory actual perceptual representations of the size of various animals and responded to the questions by performing actual perceptual comparisons. The more just noticeable differences (jnd's) of size separating the two animals being compared, the more discriminable the difference and the faster the response.

An experiment by Trabasso and Riley (1973) lends credence to the suggestion that a similar perceptual process may be operating in the present experiments. His stimulus materials consisted of a set of six colored sticks of different lengths. Hence, his stimuli were actual perceptual objects. After subjects had learned the color of each of the sticks, he presented all 15 possible pairs of color names one at a time and measured the amount of time it took subjects to indicate which color had been associated with the longer (or shorter) stick. He obtained a distance function similar to the one obtained in the present experiments.

Although this perceptual argument seems plausible, there is an interesting alternative explanation of the distance effect. Some subjects report that they learned each six-term ordering in two distinct halves, and that they could respond faster to a test sentence if the two terms in that sentence belonged to different halves of the ordering. Such a model could be formalized in terms similar to Clark's (1969) notion of the primacy of functional relations. For items in the first half of the ordering, along with information as to the exact magnitude of position of each item subjects might also store the information that the item was good (tall, fast, etc.). For items in the second half of the ordering, subjects might store the information that the item was bad (short, slow, etc.). If the two items in a test sentence were from different halves of the ordering, subjects would not need to compare actual magnitudes or positions; they could respond by merely noting that one was good and one was bad. Consequently, reaction times in these cases would be shorter than when the two terms belonged to the same half of the ordering. Since a remote pair is more likely to span the break in the ordering than is an adjacent pair, this model would predict that mean reaction times to the remote pairs should be shorter than mean reaction times to the adjacent pairs.

Although this model would predict shorter reaction times to the remote pairs than to the adjacent pairs, it would not predict the inverse monotonic relationship between reaction time and inferential distance that was obtained in the present studies. It predicts, instead, a step function for reaction times. If a pair spans the break in the ordering, then reaction time will be short; if a pair does not span the break, then reaction time will be long. The obtained relation between reaction time and distance could be accounted for in the the context of this model, however, if one were willing to argue that the place at which the ordering was broken varied as a function if idiosyncratic characteristics of individual subjects and/or paragraphs. We are currently engaged in research designed to evaluate the viability of this type of model as an explanation of the distance effect.

STORING INFORMATION OTHER THAN LINEAR ORDERINGS

There is a body of semantic memory data that indicates that when retrieving information from one's preexisting knowledge of the world in an attempt to verify a true sentence such as *A collie is a dog,* reaction time is shorter than when trying to verify a more remote relation such as *A collie is an animal.* Collins and Quillian (1969) have cited this result as evidence in favor of their notion that rather than storing deducible information, subjects infer this information when they are tested. Reaction time will be longer, they argue, the larger the number of inferential steps required to verify the relationship. This result and the conclusion based on it are diametrically opposed to the results and conclusions drawn on the basis of the present results with linear orderings.

In evaluating this apparent contradiction, it must be noted that, whereas the semantic memory research has received a considerable amount of attention, this research has also been severely criticized on methodological grounds. When examining the amount of time required to retrieve preexisting knowledge, serious confounding can occur because the variables of interest covary with a large number of other variables (e.g., Conrad, 1972; Landauer & Meyer, 1972; Rips, Shoben, & Smith, 1973). It can be argued, for example, that the short reaction time to the sentence *A collie is a dog* results not from the small number of inferential steps between the concepts "collie" and "dog," but from the fact that the concept "collie" has been more frequently associated with the concept "dog" than with the concept "animal." This type of confounding is extremely difficult, if not impossible, to remove when dealing with the retrieval of preexisting relationships. Nevertheless, we must at least consider the possibility that the results obtained in the present studies are unique to linear orderings and are not obtained when dealing with set-inclusion relations such as *A collie is a dog*. If we were to replicate the present results using a novel set-inclusion relationship established during the experimental session, we would have provided evidence that when confounding effects such as frequency of association are eliminated, the relationship between inferential distance and reaction time may be opposite that hypothesized by Collins and Quillian.

To examine this question, 16 Dartmouth undergraduates received four trials on each of four paragraphs. Each paragraph described a four-term set-inclusion relation by presenting the three adjacent pairwise relationships comprising the ordering. These pairs were presented in chained order (i.e., *All A are B, All B are C, All C are D*). A sample paragraph is presented here:

> The plain of Central Ugala is the homeland of some primitive people. All Fundalas are outcasts from other tribes in Central Ugala. All the outcasts of Central Ugala are hill people. All the hill people of Central Ugala are farmers. There are about 15 different tribes in this area[modified from Frase, 1972, p. 341].

Subjects were told to study each paragraph until they knew the information contained in it. They were tested using a set of six true and six false sentences similar to the ones employed for linear orderings. The six true sentences again consisted of a statement of the three adjacent and three remote pairs. For each true sentence, there was a corresponding false sentence having the same terms in reverse order. The importance of not making any errors was again stressed.

Overall proportion correct was .91. Mean reaction times to the adjacent and remote pairs were 2.76 and 2.49 sec, respectively. This superiority on the remote pairs was demonstrated by 14 of the 16 subjects ($p = .004$). Hence, the superiority on the remote pairs is obtained with set-inclusion relations as well as with linear orderings.

The set-inclusion relations in this experiment were extremely simple in that they described a simple linear hierarchy. It would be interesting to know if these effects can be replicated using more complex relations. Karl Scholz (personal communication) has performed some preliminary work designed to examine this question. A sample paragraph from his study describing a complex heirarchic relation is presented here:

The country of Sembia, which lies just south of Morita, consists of two provinces. Britta, which was colonized by the English, includes the coastal area. Provisk, colonized by Russia, includes Sembia's mountainous terrain. Sembia's largest city, Pedopolis, is also Britta's only seaport. The country's capital, Plainfield, is also located in Britta. The capitol building is located on Plainfield's main street, Broadway, just west of the Midland highway, which leads from downtown Plainfield south to Pedopolis on the coast.

The associative structure of the information in this paragraph is diagrammed in Fig. 5. Information on which the subjects were tested is circled in this diagram. The test materials for each paragraph consisted of a set of 18 sentences. The six true sentences consisted of a statement of the three adjacent and three remote hierarchical relations (e.g., *Plainfield is located in Britta*). Six of the false sentences consisted of a simple reversal of the terms in each of the true sentences (e.g., *Britta is located in Plainfield*). The remaining false sentences traverse the hierarchy in the correct direction but describe the subset term as being a member of the wrong superset (e.g., *Plainfield is located in Provisk*). Once again, reaction time was found to be significantly shorter on the remote relationships than on the adjacent ones. This was true for all three question types.

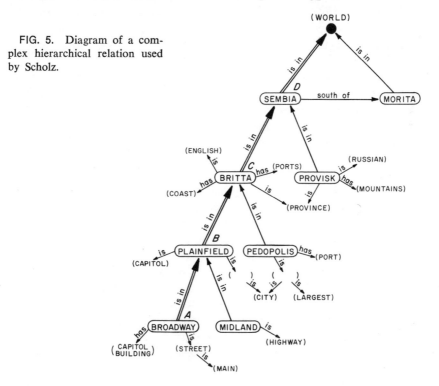

FIG. 5. Diagram of a complex hierarchical relation used by Scholz.

This work on other types of ordered relationships is just beginning, and many questions remain. Preliminary results are encouraging, however, and seem to indicate that there are a variety of experimental situations that lead to an unusually short reaction time to deducible remote pairs.

INCORPORATING NEW INFORMATION
INTO AN EXISTING COGNITIVE STRUCTURE

To date, experiments attempting to examine the nature of various cognitive structures have fallen into one of two classes. One type has examined the processes involved in the storage and subsequent retrieval of an artificial body of knowledge presented during an experimental session. The present research falls into this category, as does the linguistic work described in the introduction. Another type, represented by the semantic memory literature, has examined the amount of time required to retrieve information from one's preexisting knowledge of the world. Whereas this approach has generated some provocative data, there are serious methodological problems inherent in it.

It should be recognized that the key to comprehension lies in the successful incorporation of new information into a preexisting cognitive structure. Very little empirical work has been focused in this direction, however. We have recently begun a line of research addressed to this question, and the preliminary results are quite exciting.

It is reasonable to assume that most college students know that horses are heavier than rats. It is also reasonable to assume that most subjects know that dogs are animals. The present experiment examines the way in which new information is integrated with this existing knowledge. During the experimental session, subjects were presented with a set of three sentences that described the relations between a set of three imaginary animals (designated by nonsense syllables) by relating those imaginary animals to real animals (of course, the materials used were not limited to relations between animals). For example, subjects might be told that *BAJ are larger than horses. Rats are larger than SOH. SOH are larger than KAW.* For set-inclusion relations, subjects might be told that *All LOZ are dogs. All animals are CUY. All CUY are ZUL.* Each subject studied and answered questions about a set of 10 such groups of sentences. Five described linear orderings; five described set-inclusion relations. The order of presentation of the three sentences was randomized for each group of sentences and for each subject. Subjects were given as much time as they needed to study each group of sentences. After studying a group of three sentences, subjects responded "true" or "false" to a set of test sentences. Test sentences described many relations involving both real and imaginary animals, but our main interest was in those sentences testing the relations between the imaginary animals. Predictions will be described by referring to the ordering of the terms

BAJ–horses–rats–SOH–KAW

from heaviest to lightest. The fact that *SOH are heavier than KAW* was stated explicitly among the presented sentences. The fact that *BAJ are heavier than SOH* was not stated explicitly and required subjects to draw an inference using not only the presented information that *BAJ are heavier than horses* and that *Rats are heavier than SOH,* but also their preexisting knowledge that horses are heavier than rats. The fact that *BAJ are heavier than KAW* was not stated explicitly, and required subjects to draw an inference using all of the above information, along with the fact that *SOH are heavier than KAW*.

In the example just described, the effects of inferential distance are confounded with end-term effects in that the more remote pair *BAJ are heavier than SOH* contains the first term (*BAJ*) in the ordering, whereas the adjacent (and actually presented) pair *SOH are heavier than KAW* does not. To circumvent this confounding, half of the groups of sentences described orderings of the form

BAJ–horses–rats–SOH–KAW.

The other half described orderings of the form

BAJ–SOH–horses–rats–KAW.

The specific form of each particular ordering was counterbalanced across subjects.

Overall proportion correct for the linear orderings and set-inclusion relations were .95 and .93, respectively. The mean reaction times for the various pair types are presented in Fig. 6. Examination of Fig. 6 reveals that for linear orderings, the predictions of a distance model are satisfied. Reaction time was significantly shorter to the pair representing the large inferential distance than to the adjacent pair that was actually presented. This was the case for both forms of the ordering and, hence, cannot simply reflect the beneficial effect of various end terms. Reaction time to the most remote pair was shortest of all. This is probably a function of both inferential distance and the presence of two end-terms. Interestingly, these effects were not observed for the set-inclusion relations. None of the critical differences were significant for this type of relation.

The present paradigm is a promising one for examining the processes involved in incorporating new information into an existing cognitive structure. The results obtained with linear orderings serve to extend the previous

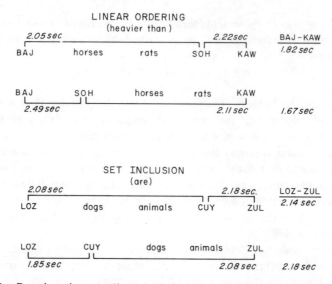

FIG. 6. Reaction times to linear ordering and set-inclusion relations when not all the necessary information is presented in the text.

results using totally novel relationships. For the set-inclusion results, there appears to be an interesting discrepancy between the present results and the results of experiments using totally novel relationships. Further work is necessary to determine the nature of that discrepancy.

An extension of the present paradigm could serve to help answer the question posed earlier regarding the nature of the comparison process leading to the distance effect. If this effect is indeed a perceptual one, then reaction time to the pair *BAJ are heavier than SOH* should be shorter when the relation is *BAJ–elephants–rats–SOH* than when the relation is *BAJ–horses–rats–SOH*. We are currently performing experiments to test this prediction.

SUMMARY AND CONCLUSIONS

In an attempt to specify the nature of the cognitive representation of certain types of ordered relationships, the present experiments examined the time required to answer various questions pertaining to such relationships. Reaction time to questions about certain kinds of deducible information was found to be shorter than reaction time to questions about information that was actually presented. This proved to be a very robust effect, which was found for virtually all subjects and paragraphs. On the basis of this result, it was concluded that subjects drew and stored inferences as an integral part of the process of studying the material. This superior performance on deducible information appeared to reflect the operation of two separate factors. First, reaction time was very short to test sentences beginning with one of the end terms of the ordering. Second, with end-term effects eliminated, reaction time was found to be a simple monotonic decreasing function of inferential distance; the more remote, the shorter the reaction time. Two possible explanations of this effect were presented. Finally, some possible directions for further work were described. Preliminary results indicated that superior performance on deducible information can be demonstrated with set-inclusion relations as well as with linear orderings. A second set of preliminary results indicated that in drawing inferences while studying text, subjects use not only the relations described in the text but also relations stored as part of their existing knowledge of the world.

ACKNOWLEDGMENTS

Portions of the research reported herein were performed pursuant to Grant NE-6-00-3-0170 from the National Institute of Education, Department of Health, Education, and Welfare. However, the opinions expressed herein do not necessarily reflect the position or policy of the National Institute of Education, and no official endorsement by the National Institute of Education should be inferred. Portions of this research are described in Potts (1974). I would like to thank Tom Tighe and John Polich for their critical comments on an early draft of this paper.

REFERENCES

Anderson, J. R., & Bower, G. H. *Human associative memory*. New York: Wiley, 1973.
Bartlett, F. C. *Remembering*. Cambridge, England: Cambridge Univ. Press, 1932.
Bransford, J. D., Barclay, J. R., & Franks, J. J. Sentence memory: A constructive versus interpretive approach. *Cognitive Psychology,* 1972, **3**, 193–209.
Bransford, J. D., & Franks, J. J. The abstraction of linguistic ideas. *Cognitive Psychology,* 1971, **2**, 331–350.
Chase, W. G., & Clark, H. H. Mental operations in the comparison of sentences and pictures. In L. W. Gregg (Ed.), *Cognition in learning and memory*. New York: Wiley, 1972.
Chomsky, N. *Syntactic structures*. The Hague: Mouton, 1957.
Chomsky, N. *Aspects of the theory of syntax*. Cambridge, Massachusetts: M.I.T. Press, 1965.
Clark, H. H. Linguistic processes in deductive reasoning. *Psychological Review,* 1969, **76**, 387–404.
Collins, A. M., & Quillian, M. R. Retrieval time from semantic memory. *Journal of Verbal Learning & Verbal Behavior,* 1969, **8**, 240–247.
Collins, A. M., & Quillian, M. R. Experiments on semantic memory and language comprehension. In L. W. Gregg (Ed.), *Cognition in learning and memory*. New York: Wiley, 1972.
Conrad, C. Cognitive economy in semantic memory. *Journal of Experimental Psychology,* 1972, **92**, 149–154.
DeSoto, C. B., & Bosley, J. J. The cognitive structure of a social structure. *Journal of Abnormal & Social Psychology,* 1962, **64**, 303–307.

DeSoto, C. B., London, M., & Handel, S. Social reasoning and spatial paralogic. *Journal of Personality & Social Psychology*, 1965, **2**, 513–521.

Ebbinghaus, H. *Memory: A contribution to experimental psychology*. New York: Teachers' College, Columbia Univ., 1885.

Feigenbaum, E. A., & Simon, H. A. A theory of the serial position effect. *British Journal of Psychology*, 1962, **53**, 307–320.

Frase, L. T. Maintenance and control in the acquisition of knowledge from written materials. In J. B. Carroll & R. O. Freedle (Eds.), *Language comprehension and the acquisition of knowledge*. New York: Wiley, 1972.

Huttenlocher, J. Constructing spatial images: A strategy in reasoning. *Psychological Review*, 1968, **75**, 550–560.

Kintsch, W. Notes on the structure of semantic memory. In E. Tulving & W. Donaldson (Eds.), *Organization of memory*. New York: Academic Press, 1972.

Landauer, T. K., & Meyer, D. E. Category size and semantic memory retrieval. *Journal of Verbal Learning & Verbal Behavior*, 1972, **11**, 539–549.

Mehler, J. Some effects of grammatical transformations on the recall of English sentences. *Journal of Verbal Learning & Verbal Behavior*, 1963, **2**, 346–351.

Mehler, J., & Miller, G. A. Retroactive interference in the recall of simple sentences. *British Journal of Psychology*, 1964, **55**, 295–301.

Miller, G. A. Some psychological studies of grammar. *American Psychologist*, 1962, **17**, 748–762.

Moyer, R. S. Comparing objects in memory: Evidence suggesting an internal psychophysics. *Perception & Psychophysics*, 1973, **13**, 180–184.

Potts, G. R. Information processing strategies used in the encoding of linear orderings. *Journal of Verbal Learning & Verbal Behavior*, 1972, **11**, 727–740.

Potts, G. R. Storing and retrieving information about ordered relationships. *Journal of Experimental Psychology*, 1974, **103**, 431–439.

Quillian, M. R. The teachable language comprehender: A simulation program and theory of language. *Communications of the ACM*, 1969, **12**, 459–476.

Rips, L. J., Shoben, E. J., & Smith, E. E. Semantic distance and the verification of semantic relations. *Journal of Verbal Learning & Verbal Behavior*, 1973, **12**, 1–20.

Rumelhart, D. E., Lindsay, P. H., & Norman, D. A. A process model for long-term memory. In E. Tulving & W. Donaldson (Eds.), *Organization of memory*. New York: Academic Press, 1972.

Sachs, J. S. Recognition memory for syntactic and semantic aspects of connected discourse. *Perception & Psychophysics*, 1967, 437–442.

Savin, H. B., & Perchonock, E. Grammatical structure and the immediate recall of English sentences. *Journal of Verbal Learning & Verbal Behavior*, 1965, **4**, 348–353.

Scholz, K. W., & Potts, G. R. Cognitive processing of linear orderings. *Journal of Experimental Psychology*, 1974, **102**, 323–326.

Trabasso, T. Mental operations in language comprehension. In J. B. Carroll & R. O. Freedle (Eds.), *Language comprehension and the acquisition of knowledge*. New York: Wiley, 1972.

Trabasso, T., & Riley, C. A. An information processing analysis of transitive inferences. Paper presented at the meeting of the Eastern Psychological Association, Washington, D.C., May 1973.

Wishner, J., Shipley, T. E., & Hurvich, M. S. The serial-position curve as a function of organization. *American Journal of Psychology*, 1957, **70**, 258–262.

13

ANSWERING QUESTIONS FROM COGNITIVE STRUCTURES

Frank Restle
Cognitive Institute, Indiana University

When a person comprehends, he extracts meaning from the paragraph. But what is this meaning? The question of the nature of meaning is an ancient and fundamental one in philosophy, and yet no matter how difficult it is, we must have some answer to it in the psychological laboratory if our work on comprehension is to have any validity. Fortunately, we do not need a comprehensive answer, nor do we require a formal method that yields the exact meaning of any arbitrary paragraph. All we need are some examples of paragraphs and knowledge of the meaning of each.

In the experiments described in this chapter, subjects are allowed to read paragraphs and then answer detailed factual questions. We assume that their answers depend upon comprehension rather than rote memory, partly because the subjects can answer questions on the basis of elementary inferences, and partly on the basis of the work of Bransford and Franks (1971), Paris (1972, and Chapter 11), and Potts (1972, and Chapter 12).

The meaning of the particular paragraphs used in our experiments can be represented in several ways. First, each paragraph names a set of entities and a relation between them, and the meaning can be summarized as that of set and relation. However, the paragraph usually does not state all possible ordered pairs in the relationship, but leaves some for the reader to infer. This process of inference is based upon general properties of the relation. In Potts' experiments, such relations as "is smarter than" are expressed in the comparative form, and imply an ordering. That is, this relation is irreflexive, antisymmetric, and transitive. These *axioms* on the relation constitute an essential part of the meaning. When the paragraph is

271

read by ordinary college freshmen and sophomores, they may not form sets and relationships or educe appropriate axioms. Instead, it seems more plausible that the data in the paragraph are related to a "model," that is, a familiar cognitive system that the subject can easily manipulate. Faced with a system that satisfies the axioms of a group, the subject might use the addition group on numbers as a model, or given a linear ordering he might use a spatial ordering.

This means that the meaning as extracted by the subject may differ in some respects from the objective logical structure of the paragraph. We shall give a name to the meaning as the subject understands it: cognitive structure.

Our theoretical framework is quite simple, at the present stage of exploratory experimentation. It is represented in Fig. 1. We conceive of three stages in an experiment of our type. In the first stage, the subject reads and comprehends the paragraph. Presumably the text is subjected to a syntactic analysis or parsing, and we believe it quite possible that the propositions may be reorganized according to a case grammar (Anderson & Bower, 1973; Fillmore, 1968). Actually, none of our observations bears on any particulars of these processes. However, we are sure that our subjects extract the relevant information from the paragraph, since they later can answer questions.

In the second stage, the subject somehow stores the information extracted as a cognitive structure, possibly including an axiom (rule) system and possibly using a model or image.

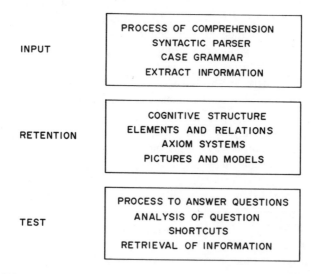

FIG. 1.   Three stages in answering questions about a paragraph.

In the third stage, the subject answers questions. Our first naïve idea was that the answers to questions would directly reveal properties of the underlying structure, but we are now more inclined to look closely into the process by which the subject selects his answer. First, of course, he must analyze the question and extract certain information from the stated question. Given that information, our subjects usually try to "shortcut" the process of answering, using general information or information in the question rather than specific information from the paragraph. If the question cannot be answered on the basis of a shortcut, then the subject retrieves whatever information he needs to answer the specific question asked.

BALANCE THEORY

A number of experimenters have shown that Heider's concept of "structural balance" has a significant relationship to learning and memory. A study by Picek, Sherman, and Shiffrin (in press) strongly suggested that cognitive balance is a cognitive property that subjects attribute to social structures of certain types, rather than an inescapable axiomatic property of human cognition. Our study set out to answer two questions about cognitive balance.

Figure 2 shows three basic triads, two of which are "balanced" and the other of which is unbalanced. In Fig. 2, each node represents a person, and the relation between any two persons is either positive (and reciprocal) or negative. In the first triad, all three people are friends. In the second, two are friends and have a common enemy. In the third triad, no such representation can be made, and the structure is described as unbalanced. A fourth triad, in which all three relationships are negative, is known not to behave like the other unbalanced triad, for reasons to be seen later. Heider's original statement of the theory (Heider, 1946) builds upon triads, which are the simplest structures that can show the balance or imbalance properties.

A general theorem about balance, derived by methods of graph theory, is the following: Consider any set of N people, all interrelated with positive or negative lines. This structure is *completely balanced* if every triad that can be made from the N people is a balanced triad. The theorem is that

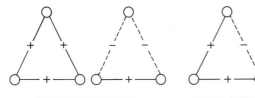

BALANCED TRIADS   UNBALANCED

FIG. 2.   Basic social triads.

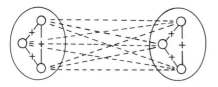

FIG. 3. A completely balanced relational system.

PROPERTY OF A COMPLETELY BALANCED GRAPH

this set of N can be divided into subsets such that all relationships within a subset are positive, and all relationships between members of two different subsets are negative (Flament, 1963). An example of a completely balanced structure is shown in Fig. 3. If the triad with all three negative relationships is classified as unbalanced, then every completely balanced structure can be divided into exactly two subsets. If the all-negative triad is accepted as balanced, then every completely balanced structure can be divided into some number of subsets, possibly more than two.

This theorem suggested two possibilities. First, since a completely balanced structure can be divided into natural subcategories, it is possible that cognitive balance is a property of a relation that classifies a set into homogeneous subsets. If so, then the relation has nothing much to do with friendship, but has a great deal to do with categories. To test this hypothesis, we made up paragraphs saying things like *Hanson is friends with Jones,* forming a traditionally social context for balance, and other paragraphs based on *Hanson is similar to Jones,* suggesting merely a basis for classification. If structural balance is mainly a basis for classification, then the two structures should show similar degrees of balance. If the traditional interpretation of cognitive balance as an aspect of social perception is right, then there should be no cognitive distortion of the unemotional relation, "is similar to."

Another hypothesis arises from the general theorem. If subjects show a tendency to make memory errors in the direction of balance, is this tendency shown only within unbalanced triads, or is it a tendency to balance the given structure as a whole? Since triads are the logical building blocks of larger structures, it appeared at first that this question could not be answered. However, by judicious choice of a five-person structure, a clear experimental test can be displayed.

Figure 4 shows the two experimental structures used. The structure on the left is balanceable, in that if the relation between A and X is filled in as negative, and that between X and Z is filled in as positive, the whole structure becomes balanced. In terms of the theorem, A and B form one subset, and $X, Y,$ and Z are the other. We should, therefore, expect subjects to fill in the AX relation, not presented in the paragraph, as negative, and the XZ relation, also not presented in the paragraph, as positive.

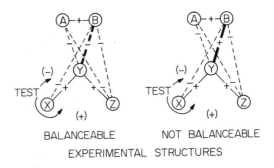

FIG. 4. Systems used in the experiment.

BALANCEABLE   NOT BALANCEABLE

EXPERIMENTAL STRUCTURES

The structure on the right is identical to the structure on the left, except that the relation between B and Y is now positive. Because of this change, the entire structure now cannot be perfectly balanced; there already are some unbalanced triads such as ABY or BYZ. However, let us see what would happen if the subject filled in the AX relation as negative, and the XZ relation as positive. The whole structure still would not balance, but all the triads involving AX and XZ would balance. The triads involving AX are $AXB, AXY,$ and $AXZ,$ and inspection shows that all are balanced if AX is negative and XZ is positive. The triads involving XZ are $AXZ,$ $BXZ,$ and $YXZ,$ and all of these are balanced when AX is negative and XZ is positive.

In summary, if the subject fills in the right-hand structure with AX negative and XZ positive, he will balance all the triads involved with those two relations. If he is trying to balance *triads,* then this is a satisfactory outcome. On the other hand, if his tendency toward balance is an attempt to regularize the whole structure, then filling in AX negative and XZ positive will not be satisfactory if the whole structure is unbalanceable. If balance is a matter of triads, both structures should be filled in the same, but if balance is a property of the total structure the balanceable structure should be consistently filled in and balanced, but the unbalanceable structure should result in less consistent responses.

The experiment was realized by having subjects read a paragraph, either of the structure of the left- or right-hand panel of Fig. 4, then answer questions about all pairs of names.

The results, expressed in terms of the frequency of appropriate responses to AX and to XZ, give a clear answer to both questions (Table 1). First, notice that when the paragraph used the property "is similar to," subjects made slightly *more* balance-type inferences than when the relation was "is friends with." This seems clearly to indicate that the phenomenon of cognitive balance is not purely social or emotional, but may be a relationship of classification.

TABLE 1
Frequency of Responses That Balance Triads
Test Items Only

| Relationship | Nature of total structure | | |
	Balanceable	Unbalanceable	Difference
"Is friends with"	.845	.735	.110
"Is similar to"	.854	.715	.139

Second, notice that when the structure is balanceable, about 85% of all filled-in responses to AX and XZ are balanced, whereas when the total structure is unbalanceable, only less than 75% of the responses are balanced. If balance depended only on triads these percentages would be equal, so it follows that cognitive balance is a property of the structure as a whole, not merely of the specific triads.

In addition, we attempted to determine what cognitive structure arises when subjects are given the unbalanced structure. For a rough indication, we did a proximity analysis (Shepard, 1962) on the five points. The more frequently subjects said two people are friends (or similar), the closer together we would plot the two points, choosing a metric that would preserve the rank order of these proximity measures. The results are shown in Fig. 5. In the case of the balanceable structure, it is good enough to place the points within each cluster close together, and separate the clusters. In the case of the unbalanceable structure, element B, who is friends with both A and Y, is placed somewhat between them, with X and Z more distant.

As a last remark about the results of the experiment, subjects' responses to the "inference" items AX and XZ fit the pattern of the structure as a whole. Subjects evidently answer the question from their cognitive structure, rather than from the list of sentences in the original paragraph.

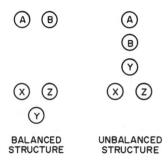

FIG. 5. Structures derived from balanceable and unbalanceable systems.

BALANCED STRUCTURE

UNBALANCED STRUCTURE

NARRATIVES

The next experiments attempt to determine how the mind stores information about narratives. My son has recently taken to reading science fiction novels, and from time to time, will ask me if I have read a certain book. In that genre, titles are notoriously confusable and the garish covers on paperbound volumes are also not easy to remember. Therefore, to identify the story, he will tell me a few sentences about main characters and the events of the story, and I sometimes then recognize the narrative he is recounting, and can fill in many of the events myself. At the time of recall, how is the information arranged? Are the events arranged in the order they were stated in the story, or in the order they were supposed to have occurred? These would be different orders if the story contained flashbacks. Is the temporal order in the story coded as temporal order in memory, so I remember the events sequentially but compressed in time, or is the time dimension of the story coded as some other dimension in memory? Finally, when a story contains plots and sublots or the interweaving of narrative threads, how are these complications arranged in the cognitive structure in memory?

The first experiment to be reported, done by Charles W. Arnold III as a first-year graduate project in our laboratory, approached the question of the order of presentation of events. Arnold's subjects would read a paragraph recounting five events, symbolized here as A, B, C, D, and E. When the paragraph was arranged in "forward" order, the events were mentioned in the order A, B, C, D, E. The paragraph could also be arranged in "backward" order, with the events being mentioned in the order E, D, C, B, A, in the form "E before D before C before B before A." Arnold also used a "scrambled" order, "B before A, then C, then E before D," which just interchanged A, B and D, E.

Arnold wrote his paragraphs so that each event centered around a unique concrete verb. For example,

> *A big Ford emerged from a side street while John was driving on Tenth Avenue. He swerved into the other lane. Then his head cracked into the windshield when he jammed on the brakes.*

This example is "scrambled" and in the order B, A, C, E, D. The five verbs are

(*A*) *was driving*
(*B*) *emerged*
(*C*) *swerved*
(*D*) *jammed*
(*E*) *cracked*

and in his first experiment, Arnold took advantage of this fact. He asked his subjects, not the order of events, but the order of the verbs in the paragraph, by asking such questions as *Did "emerged" appear before "swerved"?* Subjects clearly understood from both the instructions and the form of the questions that they were to respond with respect to the order of presentation of words, not the imputed order of events. A subject on this task need not even understand the paragraph, but need only identify the verbs and memorize a simple ordering of them. Nevertheless, subjects found it easier to perform this task when the verb order agreed with the order of events (forward presentation) and much more difficult when events were mentioned backward. The scrambled order was between, as shown in Table 2.

In a second experiment, Arnold presented the same paragraphs but now asked meaningful factual questions like, *Did John's head crack into the windshield before he swerved into the other lane?* Although these questions involve comprehension, they resulted in fewer errors than the questions about order of verbs in the first experiment. Since the questions presented to the subjects in this second experiment were much longer and required full syntactic analysis, it is not surprising that response times were longer than in the first experiment. In our procedure, response time is measured from the instant the question is exposed on the screen until a response button is chosen, and therefore the time measured includes time taken to read and analyze the question. However, in the second experiment as in the first, subjects make more errors and are slower when the paragraph is presented in backward order than in forward order (see Table 2).

These two studies together indicate that in ordinary reading or narratives, the reader is aware of the order of words and phrases, and is also

TABLE 2
Errors of Memory of Order of Events in Narrative

Question asked		Presentation order		
Question asked		Forward (A,B,C,D,E)	Scrambled (B,A,C,E,D)	Backward (E,D,C,B,A)
Order of verbs	$P(E)$	.08	.13	.22
	RT	3.8	4.1	4.6
Order of events	$P(E)$	.04	.06	.15
	RT	4.6	4.8	5.1

aware of the supposed order of events. Our language has a "canonical" order of presentation of narratives, and a reader will suppose that events occurred in the order they are mentioned unless specific connectives, such as "before that," or "while," are employed. When order of events does not correspond to order of phrases, our subjects seem to be unable to keep the two orderings entirely separate.

A review of popular literature reveals that narratives are not usually so simple as in Arnold's experiment. Instead, most stories involve an element of suspense. A standard device for generating suspense is the use of what I shall call a "dual narrative," consisting of two narrative threads involving two characters that occur overlapping in time, and often are presented in alternate segments. An example of a dual narrative passage is this:

> *The spy ran across the garden and up to the window.*
> *The butler put out the lights in the library just as*
> *The spy pried open the window.*
> *The butler spoke to the maid just as*
> *The spy searched for the papers.*
> *Then the butler went to his apartment.*

Such a story can be diagrammed by indicating that the events belong to two narrative threads, and then specifying the overall order of events. Such a schematic diagram is shown in Fig. 6. In our experiments, the subjects were asked (and knew they were going to be asked) about the order of events. The appropriate cognitive structure to answer such questions is indicated as the temporal structure in Fig. 6. An alternative cognitive structure, that would seem to be cognitively coherent, would be to form two orderings of events, each constituting one of the narrative threads. This is sketched in Fig. 6 as organized by threads.

DUAL NARRATIVE· MODELS OF STRUCTURE

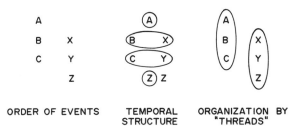

FIG. 6. Arrangement of events in dual narrative, first study.

If organization is temporal, it means that the subject uses two different relationships. One is a relation of comtemporaneity, which is used to place certain sets of events into equivalence classes with respect to time. This relation forms the classes including events B and X, and the events C and Y, as shown in Fig. 6. A second relation is one of temporal precedence or ordering, the "before" relation, which orders these equivalence classes. As a consequence, the subject using such an organization would see no difference in saying that B is before C and B is before Y, since C and Y are members of the same equivalence class.

If the organization is by threads, on the other hand, the subject's primary classification is according to the two threads or characters, into the (A, B, C) set and the (X, Y, Z) set. Temporal orderings would exist between elements of one set, so that A, B, and C would be ordered and X, Y, and Z would also be ordered. However, the temporal relationship between the two sets would be more complex. If the subject organized the information by threads, he would perform easily on comparisons within a thread, comparing B with C, and would have a more complex task to make comparisons between threads, comparing B with Y.

To decide between these two hypotheses, Richard Griggs and I had subjects read paragraphs like the preceding one, and then asked all possible questions about whether one event occurred before the other. These questions were then separated into subcategories. First are questions within a thread, such as *Did the spy open the window before he ran across the garden?* For the purpose of this analysis we selected eight such questions, all the true and false items relating two events adjacent in time, as shown in Fig. 7. We also selected questions in which the two events were in different threads, but also were adjacent in time; AX, BY, and CZ. Such a question might be, *Did the spy open the window before the butler went to his apartment?*

As can be seen from the data in Fig. 7, our subjects made only about .13 errors when the two events were within the same thread, and almost twice as many errors, .25, when the two events were in separate threads.

DUAL NARRATIVE: WITHIN vs. BETWEEN

FIG. 7. Performance on questions of precedence within threads and between threads of dual narrative.

P(Error)= .13   P(E)= .25   P(E)= .36

This clearly seems to suggest that the predominant cognitive structure was to organize the threads separately. But then how does the subject answer questions involving events in the two threads? The results on a final type of question are suggestive. The subject might notice that in the story, the actions of the spy tend to occur earlier in time than the actions of the butler. A shortcut way to answer questions would then be to notice the characters mentioned in the two parts of the question *did (M) occur before (N)?* If M belongs to the thread (A, B, C) and N belongs to the thread (X, Y, Z), then the subject may respond "yes" and be right three-fourths of the time, being wrong only on the C before X question. As is shown in Fig. 7, subjects made a very high proportion of errors on the (C, X) question.

From these results we may draw the conclusion that in this experiment, the main organization of the cognitive structure is not temporal, but is by narrative threads. Furthermore, when asked to compare an event in one thread with an event in the other, subjects often responded on the assumption that one thread occurred before the other, as shown in Fig. 8.

The results of the preceding experiment are so clear, that we asked whether the organization by narrative threads occurs universally, or whether it was an artifact of the experimental conditions. The most prominent candidate for an artifact was the fact that the two threads were offset in time, so that subjects could answer almost all the questions by (*a*) knowing the order of events within each thread, and (*b*) assuming that one thread is before the other. To test for this possibility we repeated essentially the same experiment except to change the underlying structure of events so that A was simultaneous with X, B, with Y, and C with Z, as illustrated in Fig. 9.

When the subject studies a paragraph, after perhaps reading it through in order rapidly, he is free to scan its sentences in any order. One would assume that such scanning is an important, perhaps essential, stage in reorganizing the information. Therefore, in a second condition, *successive* presentation, when we gave the same dual-narrative information to half

CONCLUSION

FIG. 8. Cognitive structure induced from question answering.

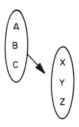

DUAL NARRATIVE: WITHIN vs. BETWEEN
(ADVERSE CONDITIONS)

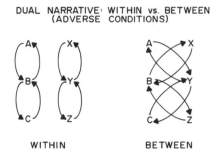

FIG. 9. Arrangement of events in dual narrative, second study.

WITHIN   BETWEEN

the subjects we presented one pair of events at a time. The procedure was that the subject could study a given sentence as long as he wanted to. Then he would push a button and get the next sentence, but could not return to earlier sentences. In this procedure, the subject has no opportunity to form a within-thread structure by reviewing the events within a thread, and would be forced to use memory capacity to rehearse and arrange information. Our expectation was that this form of presentation (rather like oral and unlike written presentation) would force subjects into a temporal order.

The results, as shown in Fig. 10, are clear-cut. First, subjects used an organization by threads even when the two threads were contemporaneous. The error frequencies for the two types of questions, which were .13 and .28 (averaging both types of between-thread questions) in the first experiment, in this second experiment were .12 and .20, under the conditions of simultaneous presentation. These two results are roughly similar, and support the idea that the subjects' tendency to organize dual narratives by threads does not depend entirely on an artifactual advantage of having one thread occur before the other. However, when presentation was successive, sentence by sentence, there was almost no advantage to within-thread questions, and subjects may have depended almost solely on a temporal organization. Notice that in this condition error frequencies are quite high.

	WITHIN	BETWEEN	DIFFERENCE
P(ERROR) (N=48)			
SIMULTANEOUS	.12	.20	.08
SUCCESSIVE	.22	.24	.02
RESPONSE TIME (SEC)			
SIMULTANEOUS	5.2	6.1	0.9
SUCCESSIVE	5.0	5.6	0.6

FIG. 10. Performance on questions of precedence within threads and between threads of second dual narrative.

From these results, our tentative conclusion is that subjects, when reading a dual narrative, have good memory for the order of events within each thread, and much less memory for the relative order of events in the two threads. It is apparently necessary for subjects to have the whole paragraph available during study to bring about this change in structure.

EFFECT OF QUESTIONS ON STRUCTURE

In the experiments first discussed, we studied the subject's cognitive structure as a function of (a) the structure of the information in his paragraph, as in the balance study and the dual-narrative study, along with (b) details of the order of presentation of material within a paragraph, as in the Arnold study of order of presentation within a narrative, and the second dual, narrative study with its study of successive versus simultaneous presentation. However, experience as a teacher leads me to the hypothesis that subjects may form different cognitive structures from given material, depending on the questions they expect to have to answer. In the classroom, one may notice the different modes of organization used by students expecting a recall (essay) examination as contrasted with a recognition–discrimination test (multiple-choice or true–false).

The experiment to be reported last in this chapter was performed by Michael Swaine for his second-year project. The hypothesis is that subjects may form quite different cognitive structures from exactly the same paragraph simply because of differences in what questions they expect. Three groups of subjects all read the same paragraphs. One group was asked questions that demanded only a simple structure, for paragraph after paragraph, with the hope that they would form this simplified structure when finally shown the last, test paragraph. A second group of subjects were given the same paragraph but asked questions that required a different simplified cognitive structure, and they too finally received a last test paragraph. A third group of subjects saw the same sequence of paragraphs but were asked a mixed bag of questions which, all in all, require the complex structure. Then these subjects, too, were tested on the final test paragraph. The three groups should, in such an experiment, develop different general expectancies as to what questions will be asked, and, if the hypothesis is correct, would form different cognitive structures. If different cognitive structures do form, the process of building cognitive structures must be an active one of preparing for certain questions. If this procedure does not result in different cognitive structures, then for the present we can retain the hypothesis that the cognitive structure educed by the subject depends on the structure of information in the paragraph and the method used to present that information, but not the expected test questions.

The first problem in carrying out such an experiment is to devise a complex enough structure that subjects can "simplify" it in two different ways. For this purpose, an organization tree (as in an Army, business, or other hierarchical structure) is appropriate. In such a tree, every individual has a *level,* how high or low he is in the organization, and a *branch,* indicating which chain of command he is in. The experiment can be performed if it is possible to get one group of subjects to learn merely the levels of people in an organization, another group to learn merely which branch people are in, and a third group to learn both level and branch, that is, the complete tree. Furthermore, for the purposes of this experiment, subjects must be induced to build one of the three structures merely on the basis of the questions asked, not by varying instructions or the content of the paragraph in any way.

In an organization tree, if it is true that X can give orders to $Y,$ then X is at a higher level than Y in the tree and both are in the same branch. Asking subjects to verify true statements cannot selectively direct him toward one or the other structure. However, there are different kinds of false statements describing situations in which X cannot, according to the paragraph, give orders to $Y.$ Some such statements are false strictly on the basis of level, that is, they describe a lower-ranking person giving orders to a higher-ranking person in the same chain. Other false statements are false strictly on the basis of branch. They have a high-ranking person in one branch giving orders to a lower-ranking person in another branch. A sample tree, true statements, and the two types of false statements are shown in Fig. 11.

The first group of subjects read a paragraph and was asked to verify a series of true statements, interspersed with false statements that are false strictly on the basis of level. All of these questions could be answered correctly merely by learning the appropriate level of each person in the tree. If X is above $Y,$ the answer is true, and if Y is above $X,$ the answer is false. Any other information the subject might collect is unnecessary. A subject who was exposed and tested with such batteries of questions over several paragraphs was expected to build a cognitive structure of mere levels.

A second group of subjects read the same series of paragraphs and received the same true sentences in test, but received as false items sentences that were false strictly on the basis of branch. If X and Y were in the same branch, the answer was true, whereas if X and Y were in different branches, the answer was false. All such questions can be answered solely by learning the branches of various people in the structure. Information about levels is not necessary.

A third group of subjects read exactly the same series of paragraphs and received exactly the same true statements in the test, but as false items

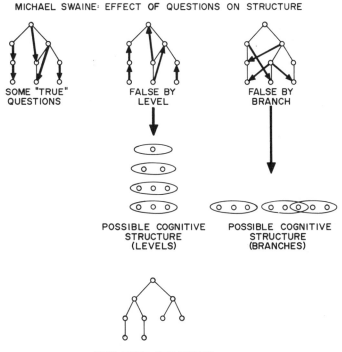

MICHAEL SWAINE: EFFECT OF QUESTIONS ON STRUCTURE

SOME "TRUE" QUESTIONS

FALSE BY LEVEL

FALSE BY BRANCH

POSSIBLE COGNITIVE STRUCTURE (LEVELS)

POSSIBLE COGNITIVE STRUCTURE (BRANCHES)

NEW TEST STRUCTURE

FIG. 11.   Sample tree, some true statements, and two kinds of false statements.

had some questions that were false on the basis of level, others that were false on the basis of branch. Subjects given these questions must learn the full tree structure to answer the questions given them.

Swaine devised five paragraphs involving different groups (National Security Council, a city boy's gang, a beanbag factory, etc.) and also devised five different tree structures, each with eight or nine individuals in a four-level structure with at least three branches. In the experiment the subject read a paragraph and then answered 12 test items, 6 true and 6 false. He then read a second paragraph with different detailed structure and a different subject matter, and again answered 12 items, 6 true and 6 false. After the fifth paragraph the subject received a more comprehensive examination.

The result of the experiment was clear-cut. If the test items on the first four paragraphs merely required level information, then on the final paragraph the subject did better on level than on branch information. If the first four paragraphs led him to a branch structure, the subject would do better in the final test on level information. A schematic presentation of part of the results, based on response times, is shown in Fig. 12.

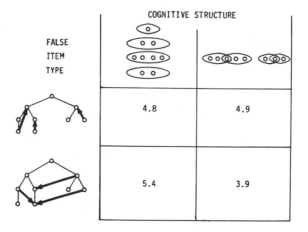

FIG. 12.   Part of response-time data for study of organizational tree.

The results given in Fig. 12 are, however, subject to two slightly different interpretations. Our hypothesis was that changes in the process of questioning, on early paragraphs, would change the *cognitive structures* developed by the subjects. However, all we have shown is that the groups differ with respect to their speed and accuracy in answering questions. Is this difference to be attributed to differences in cognitive structure, as we intended, or does it merely reflect that subjects, asked to verify different classes of statements, will adopt different strategies or shortcuts for answering? A close analysis of Swaine's data reveals that the several levels of structure constitute a linear ordering, and responses analyzed by level were found to resemble the findings from Potts' experiments. It is evident that subjects are developing particular strategies for verifying sentences.

Is it possible to show that the subjects in the several groups are also developing different cognitive structures? Differences in time to verify statements cannot discriminate between two possibilities; the subjects might have different cognitive structures, or they might have adopted different strategies for verifying sentences.

If the differences lie entirely in strategy for answering items, and not at all in the cognitive structures formed, then we should expect all three groups to take equally long to read and study the paragraph. Remember that subjects were free to read and study the paragraph just as long as they wished. Swaine found that those subjects who had to form a tree structure to verify sentences took an average of 87.0 sec to study the final paragraph. Those who had to form only the levels structure studied for only an average of 63.8 sec, and those required to form only the branch structure studied for an average of 74.3 sec. These differences in study time seem to reflect differences in complexity of the cognitive structure employed, and the natural conclusion is that the subjects actually were forming different cognitive structures in anticipation of different task demands.

CONCLUSIONS

Building on Potts' studies of the linear ordering, we have extended his concepts and methods to several other relational systems. Potts concluded that the separate relationships presented to the subject are not separately stored, but instead form a single ordering or list in the subject's cognitive structure. Our experiment on "balance" established that structural balance is a property of the whole system of relationships, and not just of triads. Potts had shown that a subject may establish an elaborate system for answering and minimizing his dependence on rote memory. A new example of such a shortcut was found in our first experiment on dual narratives. When one thread of narrative occurred somewhat earlier than the other, subjects overgeneralized on the basis of that fact and were thereby able to make fairly quick, but inaccurate, responses to items bridging between the two narrative threads.

In addition to generalizing earlier findings, these experiments have added new facts. We found that structural balance is more a matter of forming a consistent classification of elements than it is a result of emotional or social forces. The following results support this conclusion:

1. The relation "is similar to" shows an even stronger tendency toward balance than "is friends with," and similarity is neither emotional nor social but can serve as the basis for classification.

2. Balance is apparently a property of the whole structure, as a classification would be, rather than depending on triads as emotional or social structures would.

3. When a system is unbalanceable, subjects still respond in accord with a simple proximity system, which is related to processes of classification.

Our studies of narratives showed, first, the power of the order of mention of events, and thereby suggested that any storyteller who uses the method of flashbacks should take account of errors of memory his reader may later suffer. Second, we showed that there is a strong tendency, when remembering a dual narrative, to remember the succession of events within a single thread more readily than across threads. A possible reason for this may be that such narratives are assimilated to "normal courses of events," tied into casual sequences. Subjects may use general rules in addition to memories in answering questions, or it is possible that a sequence of events occurring to the same character can more readily be imagined as a single interactive scene.

The subject's expectancy for questions can control the cognitive structure he educes from a paragraph. Recall that in Swaine's experiment, subjects in all groups read the same set of paragraphs. Organizational trees are well known to most college students, whereas memorizing the information merely by level or merely by branch would be relatively unnatural. The only experimental variable manipulated was the structure of the negative test items, since positive items are always the same. If one inspects the list of questions given each group of subjects, it is by no means obvious what principle might distinguish them. Nonetheless, a difference appeared in subjects' ability to answer specific types of questions on the final test, depending on the questions they had earlier been asked. Since subjects who could use simpler structures took less time to read the paragraphs, we concluded that these subjects were forming simplified cognitive structures, not full trees.

From the Swaine study, one might conclude that subjects select from a passage that information they expect to be asked. However, in dual narrative experiments the subjects were quite aware that they would be asked not only the order of events within a thread but, equally often, the order of events across threads. Nevertheless, in the narrative experiments, subjects were much more efficient at within- than between-thread questions. From this we may conclude that expectation of questions exerts a significant force on the selection of a cognitive structure, but the meaning of the paragraph is probably an even more important determiner of the structure developed. The experiments reported here are not sufficient to compare the relative importance of internal meaning and external expectation.

The practical significance of these studies lies in their relation to skilled reading and learning, as by a college student. The ability to learn by reading is an essential skill in the modern world, and an important variable in reading and comprehension is the logical structure of the information given. The experimental passages used in these experiments are considerably longer and more complex than the usual materials of research in learning and memory. On the other hand, these passages are much simpler in structure than would be found in a college textbook or other serious written communication. Further research must push on until it can explain the process of comprehension of real materials, and thereby aid both instructor and student, writer and reader, in the successful consummation of this fundamental cognitive act, communicating through the written word.

REFERENCES

Anderson, J. R., & Bower, G. H. *Human associative memory.* Washington: Winston, 1973.

Bransford, J. D., & Franks, J. J. The abstraction of linguistic ideas. *Cognitive Psychology,* 1971, **2,** 331–350.

Fillmore, C. J. The case for case. In E. Bach & R. T. Harms (Eds.), *Universals in linguistic theory.* New York: Holt, 1968.

Flament, C. *Applications of graph theory to group structure.* Englewood Cliffs, New Jersey: Prentice-Hall, 1963.

Heider, F. Attitudes and cognitive organization. *Journal of Psychology,* 1946, **21,** 107–112.

Paris, S. G. Proposition logical thinking and comprehension of language connectives: A developmental analysis. Unpublished doctoral dissertation, Indiana University, 1972.

Picek, J. S., Sherman, S. J., & Shiffrin, R. M. Cognitive organization and coding of social structures. *Journal of Personality & Social Psychology* (in press).

Potts, G. R. Information processing strategies in the encoding of linear orderings. *Journal of Verbal Learning & Verbal Behavior,* 1972, **11,** 727–740.

Shepard, R. N. The analysis of proximities: Multidimensional scaling with an unknown distance function. *Psychometrika,* 1962, **27,** 125–140, 219–246.

AUTHOR INDEX

Numbers in *italics* refer to the pages on which the full references are listed.

A

Abercrombie, D., 24, 28, *51*

Ades, A. E., 30, 34, 39, 40, 42, *51*, 56, *75*

Abramson, A. S., 16, *21*, 25, 31, 33, 34, 35, 36, 44, 45, *53*

Allmeyer, D. H., 199, *217*

Ambler, S., 28, 33, *52*

Anderson, C. M. B., 182, *190*

Anderson, J. R., 175, *190*, 223, *244*, 249, 252, *269*, 272, *289*

Anderson, N. H., 107, 108, 110, *117*, 135, *147*

Anderson, R. C., 178, 180, *192*, 241, *244*

Annis, R. C., 16, *19*

Anstis, S. M., 35, *53*

Appley, M. H., 29, *51*

Arnold, J. B., 5, *20*

Atkinson, R. C., 151, 156, *169*, 175, 181, *190*, 197, 200, 207, *215*, *216*

Austin, J. L., 223, *244*

B

Baddeley, A. D., 13, *20*, 173, 180, 187, *190*

Bailey, P., 24, 29, 39, 43, *51*, 56, *75*

Barclay, J. R., 225, 228, 229, 232, 240, *244*, 248, *269*

Barlow, H. B., 23, *51*

Baron, J., 49, *51*

Bartlett, F. C., 224, 225, *244*, 247, *269*

Bartoshuk, L. M., 23, *53*

Bartz, W. A., 157, *170*

Bartz, W. H., 79, *99*

Bayes, T., 131, *147*

Beach, L. R., 134, 137, *147*

Beaton, R., 16, *21*

Becker, G. M., 138, *147*

Bekker, J. A. M., 62, *77*

Bell-Berti, F., 17, *19*

Benson, P., 80, *99*

Berlin, C. I., 82, 98, *99*

Bieber, S. L., 180, *191*

Biederman, I., 61, 63, 65, 72, *75*

Birnbaum, M. H., 107, 108, 110, 113, 114, 115, 116, *117*

Bjork, E. L., 156, *169*

Bjork, R. A., 157, 158, 159, 160, 161, 162, 168, *170*, *171*, 173, 181, 183, *191*, *192*, 211, *216*

Blakemore, C., 16, *19*

291

SUBJECT INDEX

A

Acoustic code, 180
Acoustic features, *see* Features, auditory
Active memory, 164, *see also* Primary
   memory; Short-term memory;
   Short-term store; Working memory
Adaptation-level theory, 104
Adaptation, selective, *see* Selective adaptation
Additivity, linear models, 122
Analyzers, *see* Sensory processing
Associative structure, 206
Attention, 153, 163, 166–67, 180,
   182–183, 187, 197, 200, 202–203,
   211–212
  control processes, 197, 200
  filter(s)(ing), 180, 197
  locus of, 198
  scanning, 176–178, 180, 183–184, 196,
    200–201
  selectivity, 167, 182, 195, 199, 211–212
    attenuating, 195
    filtering, 197, 211
    gating, 211
  sensory memory, 182
  short-term retrieval, 153, 182, 212

Attention (*contd.*)
  see also Capacity; Control processes;
    Sensory processing
Attenuating, *see* Attention, selectivity
Auditory features, *see* Features, auditory
Auditory levels of analysis, 198
Auditory processing, 55–57, 81, 87, 96,
   194
  feature detectors, 28, 33, 96
  and lag effect, 87
  memory, *see* Memory, auditory
Auditory signal detection task, 204
Auditory system, 197
Automatic processing, 153, 175, 195
Automaticity, *see* Sensory processing

B

Backward mask, 198
Balance theory, 273, 287
Bayes' theorem, 131–132, 141, 147
  as descriptive model of judgment, 132
  external use of, 133
  internal use of, 135
Binary decision tasks, 142
Bootstrapping, 121